Given

by the

Lincoln Christian College

Alumni Association

As Part

of a

$100,000 Gift,

1968-1971

The Age of George III

Frontispiece: 'The Age of Youth' from a portrait
of George III by Liotard *(copyright reserved)*

The Age of
George III

by

R. J. White

WALKER AND COMPANY
New York

First published in the United States of America in 1968 by Walker and
Company, a division of the Walker Publishing Company, Inc.

Library of Congress Catalog Card Number: 68-22243.

Printed in the United States of America from type set in Great Britain.

Acknowledgments

Frontispiece: 'The Age of Youth': Reproduced by gracious permission of Her Majesty the Queen.

George III in the first and sixtieth years of his reign, Lord North, Ickworth House, Adam Smith, Caricature of Pitt the Younger, the Gordon Riots: the Radio Times Hulton Picture Library, London.

Joseph Wright's 'Dovedale' by kind permission of Colonel Sir John Crompton-Inglefield.

'The Mill in the Dale': The Courtauld Institute of Art.

Richard Arkwright, Jeremy Bentham, Edward Gibbon, John Wilkes, Samuel Johnson, Pitt the Younger, Pitt the Elder: National Portrait Gallery, London.

Heveningham Hall: the Heveningham Hall Estate, London.

The Cognoscenti: Collection of Mr. and Mrs. Paul Mellon.

Conversation piece by Zoffany: Glasgow Art Gallery and Museum.

The Wedgwood Family by Stubbs: Josiah Wedgwood & Sons Ltd. (the Wedgwood Museum Trust).

A great deal of the material used in chapter 13 first appeared in *Silver Renaissance, Essays in 18th Century English History,* edited by Alex Natan, published by Macmillan & Co. Ltd. in London, and by St. Martin's Press, Inc., in New York, by whose courtesy it is reproduced.

I would also like to record my gratitude to my wife for the preparation of the index and for her help with chapter 14.

List of Illustrations

Contents

What good is it to me though innumerable Smolletts and Belshams keep dinning in my ears that a man named George the Third was born and bred up, and a man named George the Second died; that Walpole and the Pelhams, and Chatham and Rockingham, and Shelburne and North, with their Coalition or their Separation Ministries, all ousted one another; and vehemently scrambled for 'the thing they called the Rudder of Government, but which was in reality the Spigot of Taxation'? To the thirsty and hungry mind all this avails next to nothing . . . The thing I want to see is not Redbook Lists, and Court Calendars, and Parliamentary Registers, but the LIFE OF MAN *in England: what men did, thought, suffered, enjoyed: the form, especially the spirit, of their terrestrial existence . . .*

Carlyle

Preface

This book proceeds from politics to civilization. Politics come first, partly because they really were of unusual importance in the early years of George III's reign, and partly because recent historians have made them so, men being prone, as Giambattista Vico observed, to 'glorious opinions' about the periods they are particularly interested in. Scholarly circles have recently begun to call this 'empire-building'; a large and industrious school of historians having magnified out of all proportion the importance of politics in the field where Sir Lewis Namier set on foot extensive schemes of research about thirty years ago.

Some highly intelligent men who lived in the early part of the reign of George III were inclined to think that politics and civilization might be inimical to each other, even mutually exclusive. 'Politics are too much attended to in England to allow a due respect to be paid to anything else,' Arthur Young protested in 1787, and predicted that the cultivated people of France would fall to the level of the English, especially in the matter of the respect paid to learned men, if they ever came to establish 'Freer government' and to suffer from 'orators who hold forth liberty and property in a free parliament'; whereas, of course, as everyone knew, the most important thing in the world was agriculture. David Hume, some few years earlier, had found the English so obsessed with politics that they were in danger of falling ever more rapidly into 'superstition, Christianity, and Ignorance'. I have tried to avoid this fate, although the early chapters do, of necessity, contain a good deal of political history.

The other peril I have sought to avoid is that of what might be called 'contentious historiography', or substituting the history of history for history itself. This illness takes control the moment the historian begins to concern himself overmuch with the game of destroying myths. The history of the early years of George III's reign was for long darkened more than most by the smoke-trails of the myth-makers and the acrid fumes of their hunters. The fantasies, for the most part fabricated by Horace Walpole and Edmund Burke, were never difficult to detect and to dispose of. Unfortunately the process has often been mistaken for the writing of history. It is so much easier.

1968   R. J. W.

The Age of George III

CHAPTER I

Good King George

The English people were pleased to see in him a crowning
specimen of themselves—a royal John Bull.

Leigh Hunt

HE WAS the son of Poor Fred, the People's Prince, properly
known as Frederick Louis, Prince of Wales (1707–1751). Poor
Fred had married the Princess Augusta of Saxe-Gotha.
Augusta opened her career as a mother somewhat unpromis-
ingly by producing what her mother-in-law, the clever Queen
Caroline, called 'a poor little ugly she-mouse', later to be known
as 'the Lady Augusta' in order to distinguish her from her
mother. In the month of May 1738 she presented Poor Fred
with a son, and when Poor Fred died in 1751 little George
became heir-apparent at the age of thirteen. When his grandfather, George II, died in October 1760, this young man became King of England at the age of twenty-two. He was to
reign over the British dominions for sixty years, a period longer
than any British sovereign, with the exception of the one
who resembled him most closely, his grand-daughter, Queen
Victoria.

No other principle than that of hereditary succession could
have brought so small a person to preside over so great a
dominion. Physically he was well built and of personable
appearance. Mentally he was commonplace to a degree that
was remarkable in a century of Enlightened Despots, the
century of such 'Greats' as Peter and Catherine of Russia and
Frederick of Prussia. There was nothing great about George III
unless it was his obduracy, his devotion to duty, a certain mulish
courage. That his name should be affixed to an age is purely the
consequence of his own longevity and the galactic brilliance of

his great subjects. He ruled over Pitt and Fox, Johnson and Burke, Wordsworth and Coleridge, Gainsborough and Constable, Sir Walter Scott and Jane Austen, Arkwright and Wedgwood, and James Watt and (for a time) George Washington. His reign was as bright with stars as a tropic night. It witnessed revolutions in America and France and Lancashire. It opened with Brindley's canals and Arkwright's cotton-mills. Within a decade of its ending, Mr Pickwick and Sam Weller were travelling in the last of the mail-coaches and the President of the Board of Trade was run over by a train. When that notable wit, W. S. Gilbert, set a Noble Lord to sing an anthem in praise of 'Good King George's glorious days', he concentrated on the time when Wellington thrashed Bonaparte. No great poet out of all the host who lived under his sway ever sang the glories of the King, though the people's bards praised him McGonagall fashion, and Byron let him slip into Heaven while no-one was looking.[1] When twentieth-century historians like Sir Lewis Namier have spoken up for him one suspects that they have done so rather out of dislike for his servants. Namier obviously preferred King George to King Rockingham much as Hilaire Belloc preferred George the Fifth to Lloyd George the First, which must have been the sole example of these two historians sharing common ground. A slightly later historian[2] went so far as to describe the King as 'one of the most energetic though not the most discriminating highbrows of his day', largely it would seem on the strength of his somewhat disrespectful remarks about Shakespeare's lesser plays.[3] In fact, however, the King preferred the plays of Frederick Reynolds author of *Cheap Living* and *Laugh While you Can*, the latter being a piece which made the King laugh enormously and incidentally made the playwright's fortune. 'The accession of George the Third to the throne of these kingdoms', James Boswell was to assert, some twenty-five years after the event, 'opened a new and brighter prospect to men of literary merit . . .' It was during the brief ascendancy of Lord Bute, the hated Scottish favourite, that the King provided Samuel Johnson, *malleus*

[1] See *The Vision of Judgement*, concluding stanzas.
[2] Richard Pares, see *George III and the Politicians*, p. 66.
[3] Ibid.

scottorum, with a pension. A little later he gave Gibbon a place worth £800 a year to prevent him (it was unkindly said) from writing *The Decline and Fall of the British Empire*.

As for painting, the King liked sitting for his portrait, and few kings have left so many square feet of canvas dedicated to the cause of self-perpetuation. In the year of his accession he accorded his patronage to the newly founded Royal Academy of Arts, and his reign gave birth to some of the greatest glories of English portraiture, as the age of Hogarth was succeeded by that of Gainsborough and Reynolds and Raeburn. Here again, however, the King revealed a passion for the second-rate. He greatly favoured the enormous neo-classical works of Benjamin West, sometimes known as 'The American Raphael', and when Richard Wilson asked sixty guineas for his fine view of Sion House at the Academy show of 1776, he let it be known that he jibbed at the figure, so that Wilson offered to receive payment in instalments if the King could not afford the lump sum. In the fine arts, the best things accomplished under royal patronage owed more to the taste of Queen Charlotte than to the King, notably the matchless rococo furniture supplied to Buckingham House from the workshops of William Vile. In most matters, the King's taste ran to the conventional and the safe. He preferred the substantial to the elegant, the practical to the theoretical, sentimentality to sentiment, humour to wit. His reading included *The Sorrows of Werther*, *The Paston Letters* and the novels of Miss Burney. In science he took an interest in exploration and astronomy. Gibbon, the happy placeman, found room in a footnote to his third volume for praise of the Royal Master's patronage of Captain Cook's five great voyages as evidence of his 'pure and generous love of science and mankind', bracketing the King's encouragement of the culture of pigs and potatoes at the Antipodes with his enlightened patronage of the Royal Academy. Perhaps the royal desire to study comets through a roof-telescope amounted to little more than the traditional concern of kings with auguries and omens, and he derived much pleasure from furtively hanging his hat over the lens when other people were looking through it. At the theatre he was liable to forget the play while quizzing the celebrated visitor, Jean-Jacques Rousseau, from the royal box.

Indeed, he took an intense interest in Rousseau's quarrelsome career in England, and was notably prompt in agreeing to offer him a pension. He was an inveterate gossip.

'Servants talk about People,' a Victorian proverb was to run; 'Gentlefolk discuss Things.' George III, as Dr Johnson declared after meeting him, was as fine a gentleman as Louis XIV or Charles II, but the fact remains that he always talked about people. If an idea came up, he disposed of it rapidly by a staccato resort to one or other of his habitual specimens of clap-trap about the royal independence and his high-minded devotion to the cause of virtue and religion. His independence was to him what her virginity was to Pamela Andrews, and he somehow became persuaded at an early age that God had set him on the throne to inaugurate the reign of virtue, in a country too long debauched by 'the dirty arts' of politicians. He certainly possessed the outward aspect of a virtuous and brave John Bull, or an English country gentleman. He still looks true to his own idea of himself where he rides in equestrian bronze at the junction of Pall Mall and Cockspur Street, a pop-eyed, sturdy, powerfully shouldered man with a bullet head, sitting well to his horse and mistakable for William Cobbett setting out for a rural ride. The mistake would not wholly displease him, for there was nothing he liked more than to be known as Farmer George.

Of course, the King's image was no single thing, but changed over the course of his long reign. At first it was the image of the good young man, wishful to put 'those proud Dukes' in their place and to slay the dragon of corruption. Then, with the American War, it was the King who was right to thrash the rebels but wrong to persist long after it was worthwhile. Then it was the distressed father of the wicked Prince of Wales, driven out of his mind by domestic strife and rebellious Americans. After that, when the King was well again, everyone rejoiced at the recovery of the father-figure, and, when he stood beside Pitt to defy the malice of Bonaparte, the King was the Patriot King in a sense different from and superior to the image created by Lord Bolingbroke. In his last ten or fifteen years, 'the Good Old King' was the object of universal love and compassion. From beginning to end, however, certain characteristics remain constant, characteristics which by some mysterious alchemy serve to compose the lasting image of long-lived monarchs. The best of these is undoubtedly his devotion to duty in performing the role to which Almighty God and the Matchless Constitution of his country had called him. Secondly, though primary in the eyes of the great middling multitude of his people, was his cult of domestic virtue, a cult in which he was not to be surpassed even by his grand-daughter. The notion that years of fidelity to the *belle-laide* Charlotte was responsible for his mental sufferings (incorrectly described as Madness) is a faddish fancy of a later age which assumes too readily that fidelity = frustration = neurosis = lunacy. The King at home toasting muffins while the Queen fried sprats was only one version of the frugal family-man offered by the cartoonists. The King taking tea with his ugly daughters, the King hobnobbing with the Windsor tradesmen or mingling with the shopkeepers and their wives while the band played on the castle terrace on Sunday afternoons, were others. The King leaving his watch with a shopkeeper when he found himself without ready money is not necessarily a symptom of a bourgeois mind and habits, but rather of the decent feelings of ordinary humanity.

The worst of the King's characteristics were the offspring of an inveterate obstinacy which he mistook for firmness, along with his capacity for convincing himself that he alone was a paragon of rectitude in an age of corrupt politicians. In an age replete with brilliant men and vexed by some of the most contentious issues of modern history, his self-righteousness, combined with the commonplace nature of his intellect, produced in him intolerable tensions and eccentric mannerisms. His habit of staccato questioning, usually on matters of a trivial nature, generally ending with the celebrated 'What? What?' or 'Hey? Hey?' are typical of the means taken by nervous persons to fill up awkward silences. To his humbler subjects the King's mannerisms were acceptable as symptoms of his kindly nature, more especially when, as often happened, his fussy questions were directed at whatever Tom, Dick or Harry happened to come within his line of vision. For he was a most approachable monarch, loving to ride about his lands like a gentleman-farmer, or to drive down to Weymouth like an ordinary gentleman going on holiday with his family, stopping at inns unexpectedly on the way and talking to anyone he happened to meet. Thomas Hardy, born in the west country only twenty years after the King's death, heard much of him from old people who remembered him in the flesh. He introduced a typical glimpse of him in familiar style into the famous chapter of *The Trumpet Major* where Anne Garland meets the King in a lane above Weymouth after watching the *Victory* passing down-channel *en route* for Trafalgar. The King questioned her kindly about her sweetheart, Bob Loveday, who was one of the ship's company, and she went home rejoicing to envisage Bob 'promoted to the rank of admiral, or something equally wonderful, by the King's special command', for the King had wanted to know his name and had promised to remember it. Others laughed at his eccentric manner, including Charles Dickens, who was also born one of his subjects. He introduces Lady Tippins (in *Our Mutual Friend*) as a lady whose husband the King had knighted in mistake for someone else. This was the celebrated occasion when the King had been graciously pleased to inquire: 'What, what what? Who, who who? Why, why, why?' The laughter only became unpleasant when his graceless son gave private performances of his father's odd behaviour for the entertainment of his friends.

CHAPTER 2

The King's Dominion

THE KING of England had become the King of Great Britain after the Act of Union with Scotland in 1707. Until 1801 he bore also the title of King of France.[1] As Elector of Hanover, the King of England headed the personal union of England and Hanover until the accession of Queen Victoria, though George III liked to pretend that he could not find Hanover on the map. The home-base was always the island, from the Channel to the Hebrides, with its population of something under six million. Another three million of the King's subjects (many of them black) lived on the eastern seaboard of North America and in a number of settlements in the Indies, east and west. Had he been given the choice, George III would no doubt have preferred to be known, like King Harold, as 'King of the English'. His celebrated boast that he gloried in the name of Briton, delivered at the opening of his reign in his speech from the throne, appears to have been an amendment proposed by his friend and counsellor, John, Earl of Bute. The substantial basis of his power and glory in 1760 was a territory considerably less than half the size of France and considerably less than a third in population. Within a few months of his accession, however, the decisive battles had been won which were to bring under his dominion Canada and the greater part of India, sundry West Indian islands, and valuable outposts in Africa, in fact the basic territories of 'The First British Empire'.

What his realm lacked in area and in numbers was more than made up in material resources and the enterprising vigour with which they were exploited. It was still in some respects the little rustic England of Queen Anne, but it held within itself

[1] Assumed by Edward III at the opening of the Hundred Years' War in 1340 and dropped by the terms of the Peace of Amiens in 1801.

the swelling seed of the revolutions in agriculture and industry, in science and technology, in poetry and religion which have made the modern world. When George III came to the throne, Viscount Townshend of Rainham had already set on foot the agricultural improvements that were to turn the sandy soils of eastern England into gold, and to fatten the pastures of the midland shires for Robert Bakewell's pedigree sheep. The temper and outlook of these great lords and country gentlemen were strongly akin to the temper and outlook of their frankly commercial cousins of the counting-house and the Exchange. They saw their lands, quite literally, as fields of investment, every bit as susceptible of speculative skill and scientific management as the distant markets favoured by their mercantile kinsmen; fields, moreover, that were conveniently situated at the doorsteps and under the windows of the great houses which sérved as the centres of social life in the countryside. The English aristocracy, great and small, lived on their estates. The dull Court of the Hanoverian kings, the long political monopoly of Robert Walpole, the passion for all forms of country sport and pastime, made these men the truly 'residing aristocracy' that Cobbett was later to contrast so forcibly with the 'now-and-then residing gentry' who came to the countryside in increasing numbers at the close of the century. While the *grands seigneurs* of France, as Arthur Young observed, only improved their estates when they were compulsorily exiled from Versailles, the resident aristocracy of England shared to the full in the inveterate business outlook which characterized every section of English society. Thus Robert Bakewell defined a sheep as 'a machine for turning grass into mutton'; Viscount Townshend wrote the Norfolk crop-rotation into the leases of his tenant-farmers, and insisted on the letter of the bond; Thomas Coke turned the Palladian splendours of Holkham Hall into an enormously profitable agricultural show. Nothing less than aristocratic patronage and resources could have achieved the transformation of agricultural organization and technique within the intensely conservative society of rural England at that time. Business activity on the parts of lords and gentlemen among the fields and heaths was to make good farming a fashion. It was also to make England a land of large

farms, enclosed fields, and landless labourers at the very time
when the peasant proprietorship of France was being born.
While the ancient enemy became the land of *le petit propriétaire*,
England was becoming a land that could support the large
urban populations which made the machines and the goods of
the industrial revolution. Not that the large farm or the improved technique waited upon the increased demands of urban
England for their incentive. For several generations before
1760, the 'big fish', as Cobbett called them, were swallowing up
the little fish. Land was not only a rich alternative to trade and
commerce. It was also the emblem of social prestige and political authority. The two went together, and the newcomers who,
during the reign of Queen Anne and the first Hanoverians,
were buying out the lower gentry and small squires 'were not
so much investing their money in land as buying up the pre-
requisites of a social class, the undisturbed control of the life
of a neighbourhood'. Before long, agricultural enlightenment
was to flourish under the patronage of the wearer of the crown,
who rejoiced in no prouder title than 'Farmer George'.

The latest wonder of the world at the opening of the new
King's reign, however, was not a model farm, but a hanging
river. It was in 1759, 'The Year of Victories', that James
Brindley undertook to cut the Worsley Canal for the Duke of
Bridgwater, to carry the coal from the underground galleries
of the Worsley collieries to the Mersey. Brindley carried his
canal over the river Irwell by means of an aqueduct forty feet
high, and all the world wondered at the spectacle of water
carried over water, of barges sailing high in air while others
sailed along the river below. 'The greatest artificial curiosity in
the world,' it was called by a Manchester correspondent of the
St James's Chronicle. Again aristocratic patronage stood in the
forefront of progress, although 'The Canal Duke' came nearer
to beggaring himself before he reaped 'The Bridgwater
Millions'. His engineer, a rough Peakland millwright, acquired
the reputation of a magician. The ingenious Mr Brindley, it
was said, was 'one of those great geniuses which nature sometimes rears by her own force, and brings to maturity without
the necessity of cultivation'. The man could handle rocks 'as
easily as you and I handle plum-pies, and makes the four

elements subservient to his will . . .' The practical effect of
James Brindley's magic was to halve the cost of coal at Manchester, and to lay the foundations of the industrial revolution
in Lancashire.

The intimate connexion between industrial and agricultural
development and improved communications is evident at every
stage of our history during the last three centuries. By the
accession of George III, road communications were no better,
and probably worse, than they had been at any time since
the Roman occupation. Since 1748, however, small bodies of
private investors, with parliamentary sanction, had been form-
ing 'Turnpike Trusts' for the improvement and maintenance
of the highways in their own districts, recouping themselves by
the levying of tolls. Such private adventure in the cause of
improvement was widespread in many spheres of social life in
the eighteenth century, when the country lacked almost every
modern organ of public administration in local government.
And the Turnpike Trusts possessed both the virtues and the
vices of their kind. Like Gibbon's tutor, they remembered that
they had a fee to receive, but too often they overlooked the
fact that they had a duty to perform. Nonetheless, by 1760,
there were scores of these agencies up and down England, and
in the absence of a nationally planned or locally financed
system of road-works, they were serving a useful purpose. By
1776, it was possible for Dr Johnson to declare, as he went
along the Stratford road in a post-chaise with James Boswell:
'Life has not many things better than this.'[1] It was not until
the 1780s that the 'Canal Mania' set in, and when it did the
canal companies shared some of the disadvantages of private
endeavour which characterized the work of the Turnpike
Trusts. A foreign visitor regarded it as typical of English
individualism that there was no uniformity in the system of
locks, so that it was often impossible to get from one of these
inland waterways to another.[2]

---

[1] It was not until the following year that he expressed his famous wish to
spend the rest of his life in 'driving briskly in a post-chaise with a pretty
woman'.

[2] 'The English have never thought of arranging the two systems (of locks)
into one uniform and perfect whole. The very nature of English institutions

Arthur Young was never tired of marvelling at the emptiness of the fine roads and waterways of France. 'Circulation is stagnant in France,' he was to write. In England, however, the amount of traffic that made use of the improving communications by land and water was swelled not only by the increasing harvests of farm and field, but by the steadily advancing output of the raw materials of industry and of manufactured products. England was already the land of coal-pits and coke-ovens, though not yet of the dark satanic mills. Indeed, coal-mining had undergone a revolution in output during the preceding century, and the metallurgical trades which depended upon the output of coal were already in full swing. Abraham Darby, the Quaker ironmaster of Coalbrookdale in Shropshire, had made the application of coke fuel to iron-smelting a commercial proposition as early as 1709, although it was not widely adopted for another half-century. By 1742 another Quaker, Benjamin Huntsman of Sheffield, had discovered the crucible and sand-mould method of making cast steel. The crucial link between the coal-fields and the metallurgical industries had been forged by the casting of iron cylinders for stationary steam-engines of the Newcomen variety by the Darby dynasty, long before the days of James Watt. By 1779, the third Abraham Darby had thrown an iron bridge over the Severn, the first of its kind in the world. The Carron Ironworks were founded in 1759, and the Dowlais works started the large-scale exploitation of Welsh mineral resources in the year of the new King's accession. As for the cotton-trade which, with its gaunt mills and smoking chimney-stacks, was to stand for so long in the public mind—somewhat misleadingly—as the symbol of 'The Industrial Revolution', the process of invention was going on apace with Paul and Wyatt's schemes for mechanical spinning and Kay's flying-shuttle for a broader loom. But the work of Hargreaves and Arkwright, Crompton and Cartwright, Watt and Strutt, was still to be accomplished; and the fully fledged factory system, based on power-driven machinery, was not to show itself, save in isolated instances, until Richard Arkwright set up his spinning-mills at Cromford in the 1770s. The silk-mill

is in opposition to such a harmony.' Baron Dupin, *The Commercial Power of Great Britain*, 1825.

which the brothers Lombe had built on an island in the Derwent at Derby, with its six floors, its three hundred employees and its single enormous plant of water-driven belts and wheels, had been one of the wonders of the world since the early years of the reign of George I. In 1760, the English textile-workers still sat at their wheels and looms in thousands of cottages up and down the English countryside. They laboured at piecework, generally on machines hired from a small capitalist, and upon material supplied by him, and they depended upon him for the marketing of their product. This 'outwork', or semi-capitalized system of industry, still allowed the labourer to take a holiday when the nausea of monotonous toil overpowered him, unregimented by the overseer and the factory bell.

Indeed, the vast majority of the King's subjects still lived and worked in rural conditions, whether as farmers or farm-labourers, as village blacksmiths and craftsmen, or as domestic workers in the 'outwork' system of the textile trades. Even the colliers and foundrymen were within easy reach of the woods and fields. Most coal-pits were in small mining villages, scattered across the lovely land that was still England. The first factories sprang up in the remote and beautiful gorges where the swift streams ran from the flanks of the Pennines. The inhabitant of Birmingham, or Liverpool, or London itself, had little reason yet to complain of being 'long in city pent', when the countryside was still within a short walk of the shop, the wharf or the workbench. People had complained of London's smoke since Stuart times, or earlier. There were always some to complain, like the Hon. John Byng,[1] that England's green and pleasant land was in danger of being overrun by the ugly minions of industry, even in the midst of the Derbyshire dales. But there was little that was idyllic behind the thatch and plaster of the cottages which appear so charming in the paintings and woodcuts of eighteenth-century England. Rural slums could be no less evil than the courts and alleys of a town. Indeed, the country-dwellers who went off in increasing numbers to seek employment in the towns rightly believed that they were on their way to better material conditions of life.

And yet, taking it by and large, England was at that time a

[1] *Torrington Diaries*, p. 251.

fairer place than she was ever to be again, whether in the works
of nature or of man. The towns were still small by any later
standard of measurement. The vast and shapeless agglomera-
tions of the nineteenth century were still mercifully hidden in
the womb of time. In the eighteenth century, England was
evolving for the first time a style of urban living. What it promised was already visible in such towns as Bath and Buxton,
Blandford and Tunbridge Wells. By 1760, the work of Kent and
Burlington was already done, and the formal classical style of
building was spreading to the towns. At Bath, the North and
South Parades were already completed; the designs for the
Circus and the Royal Crescent were already in being, and
the work of building was to be completed during the 'sixties.
Occasionally, when some of the old huddle of medieval chaos
was burnt down, as Blandford was burnt down in 1731, the
architects and builders of the Augustan age had an opportunity
to show what they could do with a cleared site—the kind of
opportunity which had been presented to London after the
Great Fire, and which had been so shamefully squandered by
the City of London. North of the border, ancient Edinburgh
was to transform itself into one of the most beautiful cities in
Europe by the building of the New Town across the Nor' Loch
in the 1770s, where the Augustan amenities of George Street
and Queen Street and the Squares were to rival anything at
Bath or at London itself. The great misfortune of England in
the evolution of an urban style was the fact that the problem of
housing a rapidly growing population in the industrial areas
overtook her before anyone had conceived it to be either possible or desirable for central or local government to assume
authority in the matter. The first appearance of an authentic
urban architecture in England since the Romans was to be
overwhelmed by the rush of an industrial revolution and the
financial exigencies of a twenty-years' war.

Even so, the flower of the urban genius of George III's
England has survived at least in part unwithered in the remains
of John Nash's London, and in the splendid terraces and
crescents at Bath and Brighton and a dozen inland towns
where wealth and fashion forgathered for health and con-
viviality. At the time of the accession of George III, indeed,

London could show both the best and the worst of the urban world. By far the biggest urban conglomeration in England, it had then some 700,000 inhabitants, which means that about one person out of every ten in England and Wales lived there. By the middle of the eighteenth century it was growing far more rapidly in bricks and mortar than in people. Movement away from the ancient crowded City into the out-parishes beyond the Walls had been going on more or less rapidly since the sixteenth century. By the middle of the eighteenth, improvement and development in road-works—for example, the New Road from Paddington to Islington,[1] and others leading south from Westminster and Blackfriars bridges—were opening up such important areas of future development as Marylebone, St Pancras, St George's Fields and Lambeth. This spread-out brought acute problems of poverty, sanitation and police into areas possessed only of the rudimentary, rural, and often medieval authorities of the parish and the ancient manorial courts. Yet after 1750 the death-rate in London as a whole was beginning to fall, a process that was to be accelerated most noticeably after 1780. Indeed, London after the mid-century was becoming an altogether healthier, cleaner, safer and more sober place than it had even been before. Crimes of violence were on the decline. The brutality of the lower orders was far less noticeable. Legislation on the subject of spirituous liquors, after a good deal of trial and error, not to mention contest with vested interests, had culminated in the Gin Act of 1751, which has been called 'a turning-point in the social history of London.'[2] There was nothing of the temperance mentality about such intervention. It was part of an heroic effort to prevent the national suicide that had been threatened by the incredible orgy of gin-drinking during the past thirty years. Beer and porter were still consumed in enormous quantities, and this was held to be thoroughly healthy, British and commendable. Hogarth's *Beer Street* was happily presented as Heaven contrasted with the Hell of *Gin Lane*.

The improvement that was taking place in London life after

[1] Now Marylebone, Euston and Pentonville Roads.
[2] M. Dorothy George, *London Life in the XVIIIth Century*, 2nd edn, 1930, p. 36.

about 1750 is to be accounted to a large number of inter-
related factors. Not only was a lethal current of disease and
premature death cut off at its source by legislative action over
spirituous liquors. The sick and infirm, young and old, were
being kept alive in increasing numbers. Thomas Coram had
got his Foundling Hospital chartered in 1739, although indis-
criminate reception tended to increase rather than decrease
mortality from infectious diseases among children until Parliament stepped in to regulate its organization in 1760. Jonas
Hanway, a Governor of Coram's foundation, and one of the
most indefatigable philanthropic workers of the age, considered
a death rate of 50 per cent to be an improvement over the
years 1742–56, but after 1760 the figure fell to 25 per cent,
and went on falling. At the same time, scientific midwifery
was being practised (and taught) at a number of newly founded
lying-in hospitals. There were at least half a dozen such centres
in London by 1760, and midwifery service was being extended
from the hospitals to thousands of women in their own homes.
In the ten years from 1749, one in forty-two mothers and one
in fifteen children died in childbed. By the end of the century
the figures were 1 in 913 and 1 in 115. General hospitals were
being founded, too, in these years: Westminster in 1719, Guy's
in 1723, St George's in 1734, the London in 1740, the Middlesex
in 1745. But it was long before they contributed much to life-
saving, owing to their deficiencies in ventilation and general
hygiene. Sometimes infectious disease swept through these
crowded and unclean hospitals with even greater virulence
than elsewhere. Cheap cotton nightgowns, cheap soap, and
the principles of aseptic surgery were to make all the difference,
but not yet.

The most noticeable improvement in London life—that
which makes such a distinction between the London of the
first and the second halves of the century—was undoubtedly
the decline in violence and brutality. One of the most important factors in bringing about this change was the improvement
in quality and status of magistrates and police officers. The
old 'trading-justice', who lived and profited by the frequency
of crime, and whose court was often little more than a shop for
traffic in fines and commitments, was beginning to give place

to the paid court-justice, the immediate predecessor of our
police-magistrates. The watershed between the old justice and
the new is marked by the appointment of Henry Fielding to
the Bow Street office in 1749 as chief magistrate for Westminster. Fielding 'set himself to composing instead of inflaming
"the quarrels of beggars and porters". He realized the terrible
state of the poor and the perversities of the laws with the
imaginative sympathy of a great novelist who was also a
trained lawyer.'[1] It was Fielding who said: 'We sacrifice the
lives of men, not for the reformation but for the diversion of the
populace.' His appointment, like the passing of the Gin Act
two years later, must ever stand as one of the great turning-
points in the social history of London. He was succeeded at
Bow Street in 1754 by his brother John, who ruled there for
more than a quarter of a century. Between them, the Fieldings
made the police-court an organ of social reform. Henry Fielding's *Covent Garden Journal* publicized, as only the author of
Jonathan Wild and *Amelia* could, the nature and causes of the
social evils that had come in his way as a justice. John Fielding
not only treated juvenile offenders as cases to be cured rather
than as criminals to be hanged; he also laid the foundations
of a paid and permanent police to replace the swarm of petty
informers and bullies who profited by fomenting crime in order
to reveal it. And, as an accompaniment to the faithful labours
of these, and other enlightened men who were coming to the
charge of London's underworld, there was a growing sense of
'social compunction' on the part of the ordinary citizen with the
spread of education and the civilizing influence of evangelical
religion.

It is true that London, and indeed England in general, still
accepted a good deal of violence, disorder and brutality as the
normal accompaniment of human life. Tyburn, the pillory,
public flogging, the press-gang and the footpad, all were to
afford both 'moral instruction' and public entertainment for
a long time yet. Only six months before the first public appearance of George III in his State, all London had turned out to
see the last public appearance of Lord Ferrers, hanged at
Tyburn for the murder of his steward. His Lordship elected to

[1] M. Dorothy George, *London Life in the XVIII Century*, 2nd edn, 1930, p. 6.

be hanged in his wedding garments, since it was well known that all his troubles dated from his bridal day. People did not know whether to admire more the testimony to the equality of the laws or the propriety of his Lordship's performance of his role. Even Dr Johnson thought that the people had an indefeasible right to see the penalty prescribed by their own laws enacted on the criminal. And yet, when George III became King of England, his capital city was not only the richest, but the most progressive and improving capital in the Western world. It was, no doubt, a place of crude and often tragic contrasts. It still stank more than sufficiently,[1] and it was still the delight of young blades, like James Boswell, to model themselves on Captain Macheath. What it could produce in the way of criminal savagery and carnage when the surviving underworld of the *Beggar's Opera* poured into the streets was to be made horribly evident in the Gordon riots of 1780. But the London of 1760 was not faithfully represented by the stinking bedlam portrayed by William Hogarth. Indeed, Hogarth himself has left us the other side of the picture in his lovely paintings of Ranelagh and the Green Park. It is as well to remember also that Canaletto, who was accustomed to painting the most magnificent cities in Europe, was inspired by London to settle there for some years in order to paint his pictures of Whitehall and the Thames from Richmond House. Even if every one of the five senses of the traveller were horridly afflicted at Seven Dials and Clerkenwell Green, few cities in the world could present so fair a picture as the London of Wren's skyline, of Leicester Fields, the Horse Guards' Parade, and Covent Garden Piazza.

All this rich activity in field and city, this conglomeration of style and squalor, was guarded by His Majesty's fleets and armies at an annual cost of some fifteen million pounds. The land forces of the Crown alone were costing something over six million to maintain in 1760. A naval personnel of 70,000 cost a further three million and a quarter. The Prussian subsidy, and various sums paid to our other German allies, accounted for nearly two and a half million more. These sums, vast indeed

---

[1] As late as the 1830s, the Thames at Westminster stank so vilely that the House of Commons had to keep the windows closed in warm weather.

for that time, were chiefly raised by means of a land tax of four shillings in the pound and by a huge array of duties levied upon our rich importations of sugar, cotton, rum, coffee, tobacco, spices, and other valuable products of the Indies, east and west. This extensive national expenditure really amounted to a highly profitable national investment in the trade and commerce of the five continents and the seven seas. Its handsome dividends were attested in the English scene by the dense forests of masts in the ports of London, Liverpool and Bristol; in the commodious houses of a class of rich merchants in town and country; in the esteem in which the man of business was everywhere held in a none-the-less aristocratic society. 'Who will laugh at sugar, now?' William Pitt demanded of a cowed House of Commons in 1759, and was met by a respectful silence. Alderman Beckford, the Sugar King of the West Indian trade, 'had done more to support Government than any minister in England', the Great Commoner went on to avow. Pitt, indeed, once declared that he would be prouder to be an Alderman than a Peer. For England lived by her trade. No longer did trade follow the flag; rather, the flag followed trade. The Seven Years' War was, as far as England was concerned, a gigantic mercantile project under arms. When, nearly two centuries later, Oswald Spengler likened the people of the island to a race of 'maritime leopards', or a nest of Norsemen sallying forth from their inviolable base to enslave the world in their vast net of piracy and plunder, he spoke nearer to the truth about the England of the age of William Pitt than the natives would have cared to admit.

At the time, however, it all looked rather different, at least to the islanders themselves. There were, of course, some to raise an equivocally satirical eyebrow. 'You shall hear from me again if we take Mexico or China before Christmas,' Horace Walpole wrote to a friend by way of a postscript in the Year of Victories. And again, with his sharp little tongue stuck into his nicely rouged cheek: 'It really looks as if we intended to finish the conquest of the world next campaign.' But the ordinary Englishman of 1760 simply thought himself to be the chosen of God, very much as he had thought in the days of John Milton, and thereby entitled to the special patronage of Divine

Providence in his labours by land and sea. 'Rule Britannia!'[1]
belongs to this time, and Dr Arne had given the nation its
Anthem as early as 1745. The one was merely the celebration
of an accomplished fact, and the other a confident prayer for
the continuance of not unmerited favours:

> Counfound their politicks,
> Frustrate their knavish tricks,
> And—make—them—fall!

By 1760, it certainly seemed that God was an Englishman.

Thus the amazing victories of the war, which in 1759 had
threatened to wear the church-bells threadbare, had already
taken their place in the comfortable perspective of a people
whose Constitution in Church and State had been perfected
in 1688, and whose energies, under the aegis of that divinely
inspired instrument, were now rightly rewarded. George III
was not alone in believing the Constitution of his country
to be 'the most beautiful combination that ever was framed'.
The supposedly perfected model of 1688-9 had acquired the
reverential prestige of Holy Writ, despite the fact that it was
largely unwritten. 'Our blessed Constitution, in Church and
State', stood enshrined in the minds and imaginations of
Englishmen in that age as the Constitution of the United States
was soon to stand in the minds and imaginations of His
Majesty's rebellious subjects across the Atlantic. The knee was
bent, the hand went involuntarily to the hat, at the mention
of its name. Only when Sir William Blackstone had exposed
the sacred corpus to the indignity of analysis in his *Commentaries
on the Laws of England* did irreverent young men like Jeremy
Bentham begin to question the justification for this idolatry.
Blackstone, in submitting the Constitution to a process of
reverential scrutiny, did what King James I did for the king-
worship of the Tudors when he undertook a pedantic exposition
of the Divine Hereditary Right of Kings. To expose a mystique
of government, however reverentially, to intellectual analysis
is the surest way of dissolving it, as Edmund Burke well knew.
'To split and atomise the doctrine of a free government,' Burke

---

[1] A party ballad, to advocate sea-power and sea-warfare as England's
proper concern, rather than continental adventures.

warned his countrymen, during the quarrel over the taxation of the American colonies, was the quickest way to break up the Empire. But it was too late. The mind of man is never still, and it is of the nature of freedom to inquire regularly into its own premises. It was not long before reformers like Major Cartwright were denouncing 'Burkism'—or 'never speaking on the Constitution . . . but in trope or figure, in simile, metaphor, or mysterious allusion'.

But this time was not yet come. In 1760, Blackstone held the field, and in the years 1765-9 he published the four volumes of the *Commentaries* which were to give the *cachet* of a weighty learning and a graceful style to the ordinary educated Englishman's notions about his glorious Constitution. The work was based on the lectures which he had been delivering at Oxford since 1758 as the first Vinerian Professor of English Law. Transcripts of his lectures had been passed from hand to hand for some years before he published the book, and it is said that they were used in the education of George III himself. It was appropriate that a man like Blackstone should have served as the high-priest of the mysteries of English law and government on the eve of the new reign. The son of a London silk-merchant, and a Fellow of All Souls', Blackstone was a comfortable, old-fashioned Whig, a man of obese body and sedentary habits, who liked to compose with a bottle of port at his elbow. 'Of a Constitution so wisely contrived, so strongly raised, and so highly finished,' he wrote, 'it is hard to speak with that praise which is justly and severely its due.' Nevertheless, Blackstone accomplished the task with remarkable ease. The beautiful perfection of the Constitution, he maintained, consisted in its being a harmonious whole composed of delicately balanced parts. It was a 'mixed' constitution, in which the principles of monarchy, aristocracy and democracy interlocked in Kings, Lords and Commons. It also enshrined the principle of the separation of powers between executive, legislative and judiciary, in which the immortal Montesquieu had detected the principal guarantee of the people's liberties. Under this balanced and harmonious distribution of power, and under the Common Law of England, 'all of us have it in our choice to do everything that a good man would desire to do, and are restrained from

1. George III
in the first
year of his
reign

2. George III
in the sixtieth
year of his
reign

3. 'Dovedale', painting by Wright of Derby

4. 'The Mill in the Dale', a contemporary drawing

nothing but what would be pernicious either to ourselves or
our fellow-citizens'.

By a singularly appropriate separation of ideas, Blackstone
was able to combine this general description of a system of
separate yet harmonious powers and orders in state and society
with a full-blown doctrine of sovereignty. 'There is and must
be,' he insisted, 'in all forms of government a supreme, irresistible, absolute, uncontrolled authority, in which the *jus summi
imperii*, or the rights of sovereignty reside.' And the repository
of this authority Blackstone found to be Parliament. He managed at the same time to hold the fashionable eighteenth-
century doctrine of the sovereign 'Laws of Nature' or 'the
eternal immutable laws . . . which the Creator has enabled
human reason to discover'. He was content to pass over this
possible conflict of jurisdiction without undue distress of mind.
'I know it is generally laid down that Acts of Parliament contrary to reason are void,' he confessed, but he could find no
example of judicial rejection of a Statute on the ground of its
being contrary to reason or nature. Nor did Blackstone allow
himself to be unduly troubled by the juxtaposition of an
absolute prerogative in the King and an absolute sovereignty
in Parliament. His work, indeed, is full of the typical confusion
of mind of an age which loved its Constitution because it
worked, and because under it the nation had flourished in
peace and proved victorious in war, but had not hitherto given
over-much thought to the questions 'How?' and 'Why?' The
future was to be sufficiently vexed by attempts to 'split and
atomise' doctrines of sovereignty and of free government. Meanwhile, everyone could find in Blackstone what he wanted to
find. George III could find that 'the law ascribes to the king
the attribute of sovereignty', and that 'in the exertion of lawful
prerogative the king is and ought to be absolute'. Parliament
could find, *vis-à-vis* rebellious colonists, that it alone was
the repository of 'supreme, irresistible, absolute, uncontrolled
authority'. Rebellious colonists could find (and did find, for
the *Commentaries* sold nearly as many copies in America as in
England) that the Laws of Nature stood above all princes and
parliaments. The subjects of the King in general could find
that they possessed at law a whole catalogue of 'Absolute

Rights' (the opening chapter of the first book of the *Commentaries* bears the title: 'Of the Absolute Rights of Individuals'),
including a final civic 'right of resistance'—as was appropriate to a people whose Constitution had been preserved by a
Glorious Revolution. Thus this flourishing and victorious people
found in their Constitution the best guarantees of further progress in all the arts of war and peace. For a long time yet, they
were to ascribe to 'the blessed constitution' those blessings
which a Righteous Providence saw fit to withhold from less
happy lands. Why, asked the Younger Pitt, in defending his
free-trade treaty with France, in the House of Commons in
1787—why should England fear the superiority of France in
natural resources? Britain might not be so blessed by nature:
'but, on the contrary, it possessed, through the happy freedom
of its constitution and the equal security of its laws, an energy
in its enterprise and a stability in its exertions, which gradually
had raised it to a state of commercial grandeur . . .' The commercial value of such a constitution could not be overlooked
by a commercial people. A year later Daniel Hailes, Secretary
to the British Legation in Paris, reported that the French were
becoming 'convinced that it is vain to attempt to struggle . . .
against a power that possesses an innate and constitutional
superiority'. Was it surprising that King George III was prepared, as Lord North avowed, 'to live on bread and water for
the Constitution'?

CHAPTER 3

Politics

'The word politics, sir,' said Mr Pickwick, 'comprises in itself a difficult subject of no inconsiderable magnitude.'

'Ah!' said the Count, drawing out his tablets again, 'ver' good—fine words to begin a chapter . . .'

Pickwick Papers

THE SOLEMNITY of Count Smorltork on this perennial subject assumes an air of levity beside that of modern historians when writing of the politics of the early years of King George III's reign. Ever since the publication of Sir Lewis Namier's classic work, *The Structure of Politics at the Accession of George III* in 1929, their output has gone on with the remorseless energy of a major industry. In 1957 a disrespectful contributor to *The New Statesman* clinched the industrial image with what purported to be an annual report of L. B. Namier Ltd, containing an account of the year's work on the deposits of raw namierite up and down the country, a survey of the activities of the subsidiary companies within the group, and some disparaging references to the activities of such rival concerns as Herbert Butterfield's skeleton light industry and J. H. Plumb's imaginative or narrative-firing alloy at the Chatham Laboratory. The Chairman, as the discoverer and patentee of namierite, wound up his Address to the meeting with subdued rejoicing at the collective achievement of his great Magnitogorsk and the declaration of an interim dividend of 20 per cent on all graduate theses submitted within the group.

The solemnity of the Namier school (the school which has so largely subdued narrative history to structural analysis) about the politics of the years 1760–80, and the inordinate amount of time and space it has devoted to what might be called 'the politics of manœuvre', seem often to be little more than an elaborate

extrapolation from a famous passage in Chapter XII of Charles
Dickens's novel, *Bleak House*. This is the point where Lord
Boodle raises the question—'What are you to do with Noodle?'

> He perceives with astonishment, that, supposing the present
> Government is to be overthrown, the limited choice of the Crown,
> in the formation of a new Ministry, would lie between Lord
> Goodle and Sir Thomas Doodle—supposing it to be impossible
> for the Duke of Foodle to act with Goodle, which may be assumed
> to be the case in consequence of the breach arising out of that
> affair with Hoodle. Then, giving the Home Department and the
> Leadership of the House of Commons to Joodle, the Exchequer
> to Koodle, the Colonies to Loodle, and the Foreign Office to
> Moodle, what are you to do with Noodle? You can't offer him the
> Presidency of the Council: that is reserved for Poodle. You can't
> put him in the Woods and Forests; that is hardly good enough
> for Quoodle. What follows? That the country is shipwrecked, lost
> and gone to pieces . . . because you can't provide for Noodle!

These are the great actors for whom the stage is reserved,
although a People doubtless exists off-stage, supernumeraries
who are to be occasionally addressed, and relied upon for
shouts and choruses. But Boodle and Noodle, their followers and
families, their heirs, executors, administrators and assigns, are
the born first-actors, managers and leaders, and no others can
appear on the scene for ever and ever.

It is perfectly true that when George III came to the tasks of
government the stage was very much reserved for these actors.
These years present a tedious kaleidoscope of shifting alliances,
petty intrigue, and trivial incident. Only two men in English
politics spoke and acted as if they were informed by anything
remotely resembling an idea, a principle, or a political doctrine.
William Pitt was one, Edmund Burke the other, and both were
outsiders, deeply distrusted by the Boodles and Noodles, and—
it is important to note—by the King himself. Pitt was man-
œuvred out of power in 1761, and Burke never attained it.
After all, ideas, doctrine, what the twentieth century calls by
the ugly name of 'ideology', had gone out of politics when the
swords were put away after the Great Civil War. Between
1660 and 1760 there had intervened a 'tired lull', a state of
things pleasing to the heart of Sir Lewis Namier.

Some political philosophers complain of a 'tired lull' [he wrote in 1955], and the absence at present of argument on general politics in this country; practical solutions are sought for concrete problems, while programmes and ideals are forgotten by both parties. But to me, this attitude seems to betoken a greater national maturity, and I can only wish that it may long continue undisturbed by the workings of political philosophy.

Only one issue really divided English politicians in the middle of the eighteenth century. This was 'The German Question', or the question of isolation versus intervention in the affairs of Europe *vis-à-vis* the King's Electorate of Hanover. 'When this controversy slept,' the late Richard Pares wrote, 'as it often did, there was nothing to think about in the middle of the eighteenth century, but the control and composition of the executive government itself . . .' Which means the question 'What to do about Noodle?'

Not that it mattered very much, for the sum of public obligation on the part of any British government at that time was conceived in exceedingly limited terms: the maintenance of law and order at home, the maintenance of sufficient armed forces to meet commitments abroad and in the colonies, and the provision of financial supply sufficient to these purposes. Government undertook no welfare concerns or social services. Indeed, its functions were as yet hardly conceived as legislative at all, but rather as judicial and executive, so that David Hume could declare without complete absurdity that 'we are . . . to look upon all the vast apparatus of our Government as having ultimately no other object or purpose but the distribution of justice, or, in other words, the support of the twelve judges'. It required a combination of factors—the demagogy of John Wilkes, the prophetic propaganda of Edmund Burke, the vitality of a multitude of purse-proud Americans—to bring forth anything resembling a clash of principles.

The role of most men in politics at that time, as for most men in most ages, was spectatorial. Public life, and a fair proportion of private life also, was a performance to be watched and enjoyed, hissed or applauded. Everything from an election to a hanging took place on an open stage, for all to see, and everyone from the King on his throne to the Bishop in his lawn, the Judge in his ermine, the soldier in his scarlet and pipe-clay, down to the labourer in his smock-frock, dressed his part and acted in character. The matron, the widow, the maiden, each wore distinctive clothing, as did the cobbler, the weaver, the City Man. Life was lived 'in costume', and everyone, including the audience, was part of the play, down to the 'mob' which acted the part of Chorus. People looked for 'a good show', whether from the King riding in his glass coach to the opening of Parliament or the cutpurse riding in his tumbril to Tyburn. Parliament, which sat for about six months in the year, was the central stage of the national drama, where any man who hoped to cut a figure in society had to compete. Only a minute fraction of the male population possessed the franchise, but everyone belonged to some form of 'Supporters' Club'.

This spectatorial society was inveterately political, bringing to politics all the passionate contentiousness they brought to money-making, litigation, and sport. Everything, from music and the theatre and the writing of history, down to a man's choice of wine or a school for his son, had affiliation with faction-fighting in the political arena. The High Whigs drank port and sent their sons to Eton. The High Tories generally drank claret and generally preferred to employ private tutors.[1] The Court of St James's went to the King's Theatre in the Haymarket where Handel presided. The 'opposition court' of the Prince of Wales went to John Rich's Theatre in Lincoln's Inn Fields and clapped for Bononcini. Fielding wrote for Walpole and mocked at the 'Italian Warblers'. Gay wrote against Walpole, disguising the great Minister as Captain Macheath, whereby he was to saddle the theatre with the censorship of the Lord Chamberlain for more than two centuries. When David Hume published his *History of England* (1754–61) his London publisher advertised the work as 'neither whig nor tory but truely imparshal', but it succeeded in offending both. Hume never tired of complaining of the absurd way

---

[1] Claret was regarded as the Jacobite tipple. Many gentlemen kept their sons away from the Universities ('those dens of dunces' Cobbett called them), which were at a low ebb intellectually and morally for much of the eighteenth century. Thomas Coke's aunt offered him £400 p.a. to go on the Grand Tour instead, having lost her own son to debauchery at the University.

in which the English made politics out of everything and nothing. They were, he concluded, fast relapsing into 'the deepest Stupidity, Christianity, and Ignorance'. Twenty-five years later, Arthur Young predicted the same decline for the civilized French if they were to imitate the English and establish a freer form of government with its respect for 'orators who hold forth liberty and property . . . Politics are too much attended to in England to allow a due respect to be paid to anything else.'

Political contest was not between Whigs and Tories, but between Whigs in office and Whigs out of office, Courtiers against 'Patriots', Bute against Pitt, one shifting coalition of Whig factions against another combination who wanted their places. The great Tory party of the age of Queen Anne had gone to pieces on the rocks of Jacobitism. Plenty of Tories remained, but scarcely one of ministerial timber. Country gentlemen, elderly dons, Scotchmen on the make coming south, like James Boswell, provincial geniuses on the way up, like Samuel Johnson. It was Johnson who used to say that if England were fairly polled, King George would be packed out of the kingdom by night and his adherents hanged by morning. England was not fairly polled, and most Englishmen, like the great Doctor himself, preferred the devil they knew to the devil they knew not. More than half a century of Whig rule, together with almost unbroken and mounting prosperity, had done its work. There was no particular point in being a Tory by name or profession when Tories could get along well enough with Whiggish notions. There were, after all, enough varieties of Whiggery to satisfy almost any possible or practicable shade of political opinion. So the Tories changed their idol, if not their idolatry, and thought the good young man who wore the crown would do well enough to provide cheap and honest government, and to beat the Duke of Newcastle and the Cavendishes at their own game, if need be. In this situation, with the original Tory party in perpetual hibernation, and Whiggery achieving acceptance as the possession of the nation at large rather than the platform of a party, it is hardly surprising that politics was rather a matter of personalities, prejudices, and local affiliations than of intellectually grounded principles.

Political activity, indeed, was more limited in its range and less ideological in its inspiration at that time than it was ever to be again. It is not a matter of men lacking political convictions, or going into politics simply for what they could get out of it. The fashion of dismissing the whole problem of motivation by a simple reference to self-interest is no less naïve than the older fashion of attributing motives to superior morality. Men held political convictions even in the age of the Duke of Newcastle.

Party names and party principles, then, were but tenuously related to political realities in 1760. Not a single seat was won or lost on party grounds at the general election of 1761, and less than half the House of Commons at that time thought or acted in party terms. About one third of the men in Parliament were courtiers, placemen, or the contemporary equivalent of permanent secretaries or under-secretaries of state, who looked to the King for permanence of 'employment'—or, as it was then called, their 'interest'. These men, who together made up Court and Administration, might be described as the permanent 'ins'. They were prepared to support any minister the King might choose to do his business, simply because he was the King's minister, and they ranged from noblemen like Lord Barrington, who served at the War Office under six ministries and was never out of employment from 1746 to 1778, to hardworking Secretaries to the Treasury or Admiralty or to the Board of Trade, like Charles Jenkinson and Soame Jenyns. Such men were rarely or never 'out', and they could generally count on their immunity from the vicissitudes that overtook the great office-holders. It was all very well for Burke[1] to talk of them as 'the Court Party' that turned every administration into a confused and divided 'double-cabinet', but the fact is that they were the men who gave continuity and stability to the King's government amidst the day-to-day tergiversations of party politics. Nor could they see that there was anything

---

[1] Burke's celebrated analysis appears in his *Thoughts on the Causes of the Present Discontents*, 1770. The division and confusion were undoubtedly there: their attribution to a sinister plot on the part of a Court Cabal with the King as its centre (and victim), however, is rather the product of his somewhat disordered imagination.

particularly reprehensible in looking to the King for employment rather than identifying their interest with the fluctuating
fortunes of some group of politicians fighting for their own
hand. Noblemen, royal servants of the administrative type,
hard-working officials, simple parasites: all might be found in
the 'Court' party, and it would be invidious to label them with
any other name.

Sharply contrasted with these men in all else but their
habitual attachment to the Crown, were the country gentlemen, or Knights of the Shire. At the mid-century they made
up about a fifth part of the House of Commons, or about one
hundred members. They may be said to have composed the
permanent 'outs', and this by choice, indeed almost by definition. Their watchword was 'independence'. They entered
Parliament out of a sense of duty to their 'country', which
meant in the first instance their 'county'—the native heath
where they enjoyed primacy and high consideration. To them
the government was the King's government, and it was their
duty to support it as long as they could do so with conscience
and with due regard to their own people among the broad
acres and ancient boroughs of rural England. They thought
of themselves less as legislators than as jurymen, concerned to
come to just and public-spirited views of whatever was put
before them as members of the 'Grand Inquest of the Nation'
that was Parliament. 'If you are in parliament', wrote Governor
Pitt to his son in 1705, 'show yourself on all occasions a good
Englishman, and a faithful servant to your country . . . Avoid
faction, and never enter the house pre-possessed; but attend
diligently to the debate and vote according to your conscience
and not for any sinister end whatever. I had rather see a child
of mine starve than have him get his bread by voting in the
House of Commons.' The country gentlemen sought neither
place nor profit, and wished to be beholden neither to ministers
nor to courtiers. If one of them did seek to make his court to
Lord Bute, as did Nathaniel Curzon, he was at pains to stress
his desire to rest all his hopes on the King's own graciousness
rather than ministerial favour. It was on this basis, having
obtained a peerage as Lord Scarsdale, that Curzon built himself
that splendid palace at Kedleston which Dr Johnson thought

'would do excellently for a town-hall'. And in the process, he
may be said to have been the last of a long line of country
gentlemen called Curzon who had served as Knights of the
Shire for the county of Derbyshire since the reign of Richard II.
Not a few country gentlemen whose fathers had, like Sir
Nathaniel, stood aloof from the contest of court favour out of
'disinclination to Sir Robert . . .' were going the same way in
the middle decades of the century. Many more, however, stood
firm by the view expressed by Sir Roger Newdigate in 1762
that landed men should be 'presented with fools' caps if they
made ladders for tyrant Whigs to mount by'. Sir Roger's
politics were summed up in the words: 'I like the King and
shall be with his Ministers as long as I think an honest man
ought and believe it best not to lose the country gentleman in
the Courtier.' There was also Sir Watkin Williams Wynn,
member for County Denbigh from 1722 to 1749, who declined
a peerage with the remark that 'as long as His Majesty's
Ministers acted for the good of their Country, he was willing
to consent to anything; he thanks His Majesty for the Earldom
he had sent him, but that he was very well content with the
honours he had and was resolved to live and die Sir Watkin'.

The country gentlemen were not a solid phalanx in the sense
of a disciplined party with a leader and a programme. They
might, and did (as was proper to their independent attitude),
vote on opposite sides of the House on almost any question unconcerned with Land Tax. They broke fairly even over General
Warrants in 1764, while they were in the proportion of three
to two against the expulsion of Wilkes from the Commons in
1769. When it came to reducing the Land Tax in 1767, however, they voted 52 to 9 in favour, and they were to show a
fairly uniform approval of Dunning's Resolution in 1780. This
indicates the nature of their politics, in so far as they may be
said to have had a consistent attitude. It was, by and large, the
politics of the Country Party of the previous century and the
reign of Queen Anne,[1] involving the demand for frequent
parliaments, the exclusion of placemen from the House of

---

[1] The country gentlemen in Parliament were little short of 200 strong
in Anne's reign, and the typical programme of the Country Party found
expression in the constitutional clauses of the Act of Settlement of 1701.

Commons, and the imposition of suitable penalties for bribery and corruption. Suspicion and dislike of courtiers and 'politicians' generally; criticism of Court extravagance; opposition to costly continental wars; in fact, strenuous resistance to anyone or anything that debauched the independence of gentlemen or invaded their pockets. Because they did not think of Parliament as providing a government, the country gentlemen declined to equivocate over the dubious, if necessary, means employed by Court and ministers in that age of unorganized and undisciplined parties in order to get a government and keep it in the saddle. This meant that the temper of their politics was rootedly oppositional, as far as ministers were concerned, even when they professed most loyally to support the King. And in so far as there was a single entity that could be called 'public opinion' in the eighteenth century, they were its most typical voice. All governments were obliged to take careful account of their attitude on important questions. When many of them voted with the opposition over General Warrants in February 1764, Grenville knew his government to be in serious danger; and it was the tidings that the country gentlemen were withdrawing their support that told Lord North that the game was up in the spring of 1782.

The fortunes of the country gentlemen, both socially and politically, underwent important changes in the eighteenth century. During the early part of the century, the process which Cobbett was later to describe as 'the big fish swallowing up the little fish', was going on apace in rural England. The weight of a Land Tax of four shillings in the pound, largely to pay for the long and expensive wars against Louis XIV, and the costly spread of a more urban style of living into the countryside, induced many a small landowner to sell his estate at a high price to monied men seeking that 'stake in the country' which was the especial *sine qua non* of political importance in the eighteenth century. Moreover, the politics of the old-style country gentlemen went into eclipse with the House of Stuart, to whose cause a great many of the breed had remained loyal for so long.[1] At the middle of the century, the name 'Country

[1] Lord North's father, the first Lord Guildford, is a case in point: though the family had been in the peerage for two centuries, the Norths had

Gentleman' was still a fairly accurate definition of a Tory. By 1760, however, the drift of the country gentlemen away from Toryism was becoming apparent. Many had gone over unobtrusively to the 'tyrant Whigs' during the long Walpole–Pelham ascendancy. Within twenty years of the new King's accession, country gentleman no longer meant Tory but simply 'independent' or 'unconnected'. More than a hundred Tories were returned to Parliament at the general election of 1761, but thereafter their situation lost any definition it had ever possessed. Some turned courtier to Lord Bute,[1] some joined the Rockinghams, others went with Chatham. Many still remained independent. In 1768, only a half of the 1761 contingent were re-elected. They were steadily ceasing to be a clearly recognizable group, although they still made much of their independence, and no government could afford to disregard them as indicative of prevailing opinion in the country at large. It may be said, indeed, that their very existence, with their deep-rooted sentiments of loyalty and honesty in both Church and State, imposed a certain tributary respect for principles upon the inhabitants of the political landscape in general. Even 'mere politicians'—the men who were in politics for the big prizes—were concerned to clothe their political nakedness in some shreds of decency when they turned in their direction.

Domesticated, the country gentlemen had for long lived in the comfortable fug of the manor houses of old England, with their tapestried walls, their low-beamed ceilings, their immovable diamond-paned windows. Some of them were able to afford the newer fashions in sash-windows, panelling and high-pitched plaster ceilings that came in with the domestic architecture of Dutch William and Queen Anne. But there was always something of rusticity about the country gentleman,

---

remained very typical country gentlemen of the Tory tradition and had been prepared to suffer neglect out of loyalty to the Stuarts. No doubt this accounts for the glib and misleading description of George III's favourite minister as a 'Tory', *tout court*.

[1] The case of Sir Nathaniel Curzon (see pp. 31–2 supra), who thereby acquired the title of first Baron Scarsdale, should not be regarded as typical, since Curzon was seeking the barony of Powis, to which his family had some claim.

even though he might go in for more elegant appointments and wider cultural horizons. Few were bumpkins, some were scholars, but all were vigorous sportsmen, farmers and justices, living very close to the tenantry and tradesmen of village and market-town. They set the standard to which most Englishmen have in most ages wished to conform. It was the standard to which King George III, with his plain tastes, his agricultural interest, and above all his jealousy of his independence and hatred of 'mere politicians', wished to conform. It would be absurd to regard the King as a transcendant version of 'Squire', but he was probably more closely akin in tastes, morals and political outlook to the country gentlemen of his time than to any other class among his subjects. And if there was one feature of the political landscape that both King and country gentleman disliked more than any other, it was the great Whigs who filled the central stage of politics with the clamour of contending factions. These were the men whose elegant racketeering beneath the banners of Bedford and Newcastle, Devonshire and Rockingham, had tended to monopolize the whole horizon of English history in the early years of George III. They were indeed the only characters in the political scene who may truly be said to bear the labels of party politics, and it is largely by reason of their prominence that the history of these years has generally been written in terms of a party 'system' which, in fact, did not exist.

While Court and Administration supplied the permanent staff which did the work and filled the division-lists; and while the country gentlemen supplied something like a detached force representative of general opinion; it was the select pavilions of the Bedfords, the Rockinghams, the Devonshires, and a handful of other great chieftains, that supplied the palladian façade of eighteenth-century politics—a façade none the less substantial for all the kaleidoscopic transformations that went on within the composite structures known as Cabinets or Administrations. Their political importance was the counterpart of their social and material eminence. Great peers of the realm, if not 'proud Dukes', they stood at the centre of an assortment of clan-followings or 'connexions', highly complex alignments of friends and relations, dependent commoners, and mere parasites. They were the indispensable stars of the political firmament. Indeed, in a sense, they were the only real 'politicians' in sight. The King had to have one or more of them, with their attendant followings, in order to do his business in Parliament, for it was always within their power to make government possible or impossible. They could lay claim to his favour alike by virtue of their social authority, their widespread connexions, and (not least) their traditional association with the major principles on which English government had been based since the Glorious Revolution. And if he unwisely thought to deny them, or at any rate some of them, his favour, they were in a position to compel it. It was the threat of this compulsion on a comprehensive scale that filled George III with angry dread of the process which he called 'storming the closet' or 'enslavement'.

These lofty peaks of the political landscape were, on at least one occasion, to be denounced by the young King as 'those proud Dukes'. He meant, of course, the Dukes of Newcastle and Devonshire, and in general the heads of that rather vague association known as 'The Revolution Families'. There was, of course, no question of a royal contest with the peerage as an 'order', or against aristocratic authority in general. George III had lofty ideas about the bestowal of peerages, and was indeed as good a snob as any man in England. His attitude to the heads of the great 'Revolution Families' was personal, moralistic, and jealous. The good young man wanted the wicked old men to know who was master. He wanted the Duke of Devonshire to know it. 'I dismissed him before he could dismiss me,' he said. He wanted the Duke of Newcastle to know it: especially the Duke of Newcastle, with his 'dirty arts'. He set himself up as a judge, and as the moral superior, of the men who comprised the greatest and most inescapable political fact in eighteenth-century England. It was as if a Swiss Calvinist guide had set himself up as a moral critic of the Alps. The notion that he could do anything about it—aside from personal snubs and insults—was ludicrous.

The position in England, *vis-à-vis* King and nobility, was the reverse of that which existed in France. Instead of a splendid Court populated by a *fainéant* nobility, there was a dull Court and a splendid nobility whose lives centred in a dozen or more places like Chatsworth and Woburn, Wentworth Woodhouse and Stowe, scattered across the length and breadth of England. These great lords were not the King's enemies (as distinct from his 'friends'), any more than the medieval baronage had been an alien element intent on frustrating the royal government in the interests of their own order, although it is true that they were sometimes personally offended, and even angry, with George III for his behaviour towards them. The fact is that ordered government was impossible without the active goodwill of these men, and they knew it. What irked George III was that he was compelled to know it too. An infinitely superior statesman to any member of their order, William Pitt, made it clear to the King time and time again that he could not govern without them. Pitt disliked and distrusted them almost as much as the King did, but he possessed the political prescience to realize that it was more important to have them (or some of them) in the government than outside it. Indeed, by reason of their great stake in the real estate of the realm, and by their long and intimate connexion with its government, they bore a greater and more conscious responsibility for the fame and fortune of England than the whole of the rest of the nation. Not that they monopolized political power. The leading statesmen of the age—Walpole, the Grenvilles, and the Pitts—were not drawn from their ranks. Nor did they monopolize electoral influence. It is true that the Duke of Newcastle possessed landed estate in thirteen counties, and could control political influence in proportion, but in 1760 the Duke of Bedford could dispose of only four boroughs, the Duke of Devonshire of three, while several other Dukes had none at their command. The fact is that they ruled the State because they ruled society. They were, and they knew themselves to be, responsible for the way things went. This was the hard fact that George III could not wish away.

Each of these noble lords stood on his family estates like a little king in his kingdom: an inheritance strictly preserved from the ravages of individual whim by ancient laws of entail. His house was a palace, the acme of conspicuous expenditure, affording ostentatious witness to work in progress. For these great lords were always building. Year after year, sometimes

generation after generation, whole armies of masons, plasterers,
and carvers toiled to refashion such perennial masterpieces
as Chatsworth and Eastbury, Woburn and Wotton and Wentworth. The travellers in search of stately homes—already going
the rounds in these years—were generally permitted to inspect
the mounting magnificence on payment of a fee to the house-
keeper or major-domo. Nor can anyone today measure the true
magnificence of mind which went with the English Whigs at
their splendid apogee until he has stood on the bridge before
the grave grey beauty of Chatsworth, or traversed the great
lawn that leads to the imperial golden façade of Stowe. The
wonder of these things is undiminished by the thought that
Palladio planned for the warmer climes of southern Europe,
and that his English disciples had to break his lovely linear
roof-lines with chimneys. Even so, the dwellers beneath must
often have gone cold to bed, and board, and we shall never
know what coughing and sneezing went on behind those
elegant pillared faces and beneath those high ornate ceilings.
Terrace and lawn, parkland and grotto, these were surely meant
for the *fête champêtre* so deliciously portrayed by Watteau, but
such classic revels were hardly a practical success under the
cool rainy skies of Bucks in an English summer, as Horace
Walpole was not surprised to discover when he took part in
them at Stowe in July 1770. 'It made me laugh as we were
descending the great flights of steps from the house to go and
sup in the grotto on the banks of Helicon,' he wrote; 'we were
so cloaked up, for the evening was very cold, and so many of
us were limping and hobbling . . .'

The great lord's palace was not only a social centre. It was
the repository of a tradition, the nursery of a family, the nucleus
of a following, the centre of an intricate complex of hopes, fears
and expectations. Eighteenth-century England might be regarded as a federal republic of country houses where politics
were canvassed, governments made and unmade, alliances and
desertions planned and executed. At Bowood and Stowe the
lords of creation matched their wits with Wilkes and Bentham,
Franklin and Priestley, after a fashion that made Windsor and
Kew look like very dull conventicles indeed. In the more
easterly counties—at Woburn, Euston, Houghton, Rainham

and Holkham[1]—politics and the arts were rivalled, and even outmatched, by the sciences of improved arable and pasture farming. The economic basis of the great house, however, was not uniformly agricultural. Just as the great house itself often resembled a town house set down in the country, so its economic nourishment was drawn from a whole network of channels running from urban land-values, industrial enterprises, and commercial ventures beyond the seas. Many great lords drew a significant proportion of their revenues from urban rents and mineral royalties. The Duke of Bedford is said to have more than doubled his income from these sources between 1732 and 1771: indeed, they accounted for something between a quarter and a half of his receipts. Likewise, the noble lord derived considerable profit from the rewards of public office. After all, he was in politics for the richer prizes, and was often in a position to ensure an ample distribution of loaves and fishes for his dependants, kinsmen or protégés. A Secretaryship of State (there were as yet only two of them) was worth eight or nine thousand a year in 1762. Other emoluments—reversions, pensions, etc.—might be worth several thousand more. Jobs for younger sons were especially sought after: in the customs, excise, tax-office, and above all the Exchequer. As a younger son of the great Sir Robert, Horace Walpole enjoyed £3,400 per annum from his sinecure Tellership of the Exchequer for a great many years. Precisely how much any particular nobleman might be worth at any particular time was not always easy to compute, since it was common for great estates to be encumbered by book-debts and mortgages. Shortage of ready money, however, was nothing to go by. Sir William Pulteney, 1st Earl of Bath, left a million. Thomas Thynne, 3rd Viscount Weymouth, later Marquess of Bath, died owing £130,000. Circumstances, however, were favourable to landed incomes in the eighteenth century in general; rents were rising—particularly rapidly by 1770, and in a spectacular fashion in the war years at the end of the century; taxation was not severe, at least until the younger Pitt instituted the Income Tax. Edmund

[1] Although the great Thomas Coke of Holkham remained Mr Coke, by reason of his own obduracy, until the accession of Queen Victoria, he was ever the type of the Whig magnate *par excellence*.

Burke, protégé of the Marquess of Rockingham, liked to speak of the inner ring of the peerage as 'great oaks which shade a country', and great they were, though hardly ancient. The Devonshire dukedom, for example, went back only to the Revolution of 1688. A high proportion took their rise from the Tudor revolution in property after the dissolution of the monasteries, which saw the phenomenon known as 'the rise of the gentry'. They were, for the most part, gentry who had risen further than most. Their especial spheres of influence were in the north and the midlands where monastic estates had been particularly extensive: Nottinghamshire, Yorkshire, Bedfordshire, notably. Not a few of them lived in converted monastic buildings. The south and the west, on the other hand, were in general the regions of smaller estates and more typical 'gentry'. The great men, however, were not a closed élite or order, after the continental model of nobility. There is no reason to imagine that because blood is not ennobled in England, and the younger sons of peers are commoners, therefore the peerage was constantly dropping its less affluent members into the lower ranks of society. It was rare for the son of a peer to go into a trade. Most went into the army, the church or the lower-placed offices of the public service. In wealth, style of living, social standing and habits of mind, the English nobility were rather a different species than a different genus from the nobility of continental countries. They were certainly never simply 'a wealthier middle class'. There was, in fact, little movement downwards, and very little intermarriage below the ranks of the lower aristocracy. There was, however, a good deal of inbreeding, and more sons of the peerage married actresses than married ladies of the bourgeoisie. And misalliances were still intensely shocking. Something like a seismic wave ran through the ranks when, in 1744, Henry Fox secretly married Lady Caroline Lennox, daughter of the Duke of Richmond. At the opera, the news ran along the front boxes 'exactly like fire in a train of gunpowder'. After all, Lady Caroline was a great-grand-daughter of His Sacred Majesty Charles II. When, exactly twenty years later, Henry Fox's niece, Lady Susan Strangeways, daughter of the first Earl of Ilchester, secretly married the handsome Irish actor, William O'Brien, there may have been some who de-

tected the judgment of an outraged Providence. 'Even a foot-
man were preferable,' wrote Horace Walpole. 'I could not
have believed that Lady Susan would have stooped so low.'
The fact that both marriages were ideally happy, and that the
first produced Charles James Fox, while the second helped to
fertilize the imagination of young Thomas Hardy,[1] should
serve to make amends to the deity who watches over the Whigs.

On the whole, then, this phalanx which presented to King
George III the arrogant and evil face of 'the proud Dukes', was
in reality a closely knit and immensely powerful affair. It was
not yet 'The Grand Whiggery', that wonderful society which
was to flower in the halcyon days of the 'eighties and the youth
of the Prince of Wales, and to survive into the nineteenth
century with the splendours of Holland House, the nimble wit
of Sydney Smith, and the sunset elegance of Lord M., Pam,
and the Duchess of Manchester. Rather it was the Palladian
and rather ornate Whiggery which lived behind the façades
of Vanbrugh, Kent, and Burlington and the brothers Adam.
Widely cultivated, often dissolute, more mightily equipped with
manners and taste than with morals, afflicted with gout as its
occupational disease, and readily indulgent with mistresses as
a diversion from the rigours of *le mariage de convenance*, it was
nevertheless well on the way to becoming that matchless
aristocracy which Matthew Arnold was to regard as 'the
worthiest, as it certainly has been the most successful, aristocracy of which history makes record'.

[1] 'Squire and Lady Susan' of the poem 'Friends Beyond' is only one
example.

CHAPTER 4

New Reign—New World

I was at Court this day, and pleased to see it by many examples
proved how rightly I had ever called a new reign a new world.
Henry Fox

THE YOUNG man who came to the throne in 1760 lacked confidence in everything but the wisdom of his friend and tutor,
Lord Bute, and the rightness of his own intentions. The notion
that this rather dull and backward young man of twenty-two
was casting a machiavellian eye over a political landscape torn
by faction in order to turn its divisions to the augmentation of
his own authority on the principle of *divide et impera* bears no
relation either to his character or to the realities of the situation
in which he found himself. As for the notion that he wanted 'to
change the Constitution', the merest attempt to express it in
words at once strikes a note of fantasy. He could not have done
so, even if he had wanted to, and he did not want to. The
weight and authority of established political and social forces
were perfectly capable at that time, and are perfectly capable at
most times, of baffling the misdirected energies of would-be
revolutionaries—or counter-revolutionaries. George III was
neither. He was a timid and conscientious conservative. He
was above all a product and a part of the existing complex
of his age and country. There was no trace in him of that
enthusiasm for reformed and centralized absolutism which
obsessed the minds of so many European rulers in that 'Age of
Repentant Monarchy'.

The King had his part to play in the Constitution of 'mixed
and balanced powers' which he knew to be the especial glory
of his country. He may not have possessed what Coleridge
called 'the Idea of the Constitution', but then, as the philo-

sopher was the first to admit, 'it is the privilege of few to possess an idea; of the generality of men, it might be more truly affirmed that they are possessed by it'. This is certainly true of that least philosophic of monarchs, George III. He was possessed *by* the idea of the Constitution in Church and State, and he was firmly and dutifully resolved to act the part of a constitutional king within the traditions of behaviour which he had inherited. Predominance within the Constitution had for many centuries lain with the monarchical element. Within another century it was to pass to the parliamentary element. It was unfortunate for the comfort, and the reputation, of George III that he came to the throne when it was precariously balanced between the two. He had to play the part of King in a kind of constitutional limbo, between a world that was well-nigh dead and another world still powerless to be born. It was no longer possible for the King actively to govern by his own initiative, nor could the initiative pass effectively to Parliament and Cabinet until Parliament was organized into a party-system. Nor could that come about until party ways of thinking and acting had developed in the nation at large, free from the inhibitive taint of action and the hangover of historic memory of civil war. At this moment, if the 'mixed' constitution were to work at all, it was important that the monarchical element should play its part boldly and responsibly. The King was still indeed the mainspring of the balance. The royal initiative, exercised with due regard for what was politically possible, was essential for the setting up, the maintenance, and in due course the dismissal of ministries. It was indispensable to coherent government. The royal independence in the choice and dismissal of his servants was indispensable to the King's function as the 'governor' of the machine, and everyone who understood the realities of politics was concerned to avow, and cherish, it.

George III has been blamed for trying to be Charles I. He has also been blamed for not being Queen Victoria. Some have even been disposed to blame him for not possessing the constitutional insight of Sir Lewis Namier. In fact, he was a constitutional king within a mixed, but not yet a parliamentary (because not yet a party), system of government. His duty was to diminish, not to play upon, divisions between his subjects;

to enlist the service of all groups ('parties' would be an improper term, as yet) who could best do his business and that of the country. In his first speech from the throne he professed to detect a recent and gratifying growth of 'union and good harmony' among his people. Nor did he ever cease to deplore the disappointing instability of the political scene. He was always looking for the man who would work with him in his role of an independent force, above the smash and grab of factions, or as he sometimes put it 'the pulverizing of parties'. Bute, Chatham, North, each in his day seemed to hold out the hope of fulfilling his ideal. All failed him. They were bound to fail him, for the future of coherent government lay with party politics. Deep down, below the surface, obscure, perplexed, parliamentary government as we now know it, was shaping its course to the destruction of mixed government. Prophetic minds, like the mind of Burke, were already aware of this, and exerted themselves to hasten the process. Unfortunately, in his passionate advocacy of the future, Burke was less than just to the present, and more especially to the King's intentions in striving to preserve and exercise the royal independency so indispensable to the nature of mixed government. He was able, it seems, to see and to state only the case for the independence of a member of Parliament. For the rest, he took his full share in propagating the celebrated legend of George III as the would-be perverter of the Constitution; the prince whose mother had brought him up on *The Patriot King*; who held up 'the smooth course of our constitutional development' by reducing the Prime Minister to a mere instrument of the royal will and the Cabinet to a group of 'the King's servants' in fact as well as in name; and who succeeded only in losing the American colonies and ultimately his own reason. This is the legend which was propagated, mainly by Whig historians, for more than a century; the legend which was to become part of the package-history that (as the greatest of the Whig historians was fond of saying) 'every schoolboy knows'.

It scarcely required the sledgehammer of a Namierite to pulverize the notion that George III was indoctrinated by the poison of *The Patriot King*. To anyone who reads that excellent essay, as distinct from reading sinister things into its title, or

listening to gossip about its content, it soon becomes apparent
that those who would attribute to it a malign influence over
the mind of George III are as little likely to have studied it as
the young prince. Indeed, there was no need for him to have
read it. Lord Bolingbroke's notions were in the air, an ubiquitous element of the mental climate of the age. To deplore corruption, to equate party with faction, and to wish the King to
stand above all factions like a true Patriot, in the interests of his
people—these were the platitudes of the hour. Everyone made
use of them when out of office, and everyone (including George
III) found it impossible to do very much about them when in
possession of the means of government. More especially were
they the property of those who foregathered at Leicester House,
the home of the Prince of Wales, where the opposition to the
servants of the reigning monarch rather naturally congregated,
since the Prince represented 'the reversionary interest'. The
Leicester House politicians were, indeed, investing in 'futures';
and the older the King, the more valuable became their holdings
in view of the prospective accession of the Prince. It was to their
interest to maintain that the King was 'the prisoner of a faction'
—the ruling ministers—and that they stood for his 'liberation'.
In the event, however, when the Prince succeeded his father,
he always found himself saddled with more or less the same
gang of place-seekers, while the disappointed investors rallied
round the new Heir Apparent, uttering the same battle-cries
that had sounded in the ears of his predecessor.

George III had lived all his life in this atmosphere of the
'reversionary interest'; first of all at the Court of his father,
Frederick, Prince of Wales; and then, on becoming Prince of
Wales himself at his father's premature death in 1751, in the
household of his mother, the Dowager-Princess of Wales,
Augusta. Here he was steadily subjected to a fantastic interpretation of the latter-day glories of the reign of George II, the
ill-tempered old military gentleman who was fond of growling:
'Ministers are Kings in this country,' a remark which—if he
ever made it—he must have known, and his ministers with him,
to bear witness to nothing but a disordered liver. This old
'prisoner of a faction' ended his days in a blaze of glory with
Pitt and Newcastle doing his business for him at home, and

Clive and Wolfe piling up his laurels abroad. Only a very stupid man could have supposed himself to be succeeding to a *damnosa haereditas*. Burke, a few years later, was to offer up a prayer that 'he should live, and should reign, and when Providence ordains it, should die, exactly like his illustrious predecessor'. His tutors, in these early days, had generally to report that His Royal Highness was mentally asleep. All through the first eighteen years of his life he was possessed of an abnormally backward and torpid intelligence. The manner, and the moment, of his awakening seems likely to have done permanent injury to his psychological make-up. It was in June 1756 that he was threatened with removal from the household of his mother and the tutelage of Lord Bute, and at the same time he was told of Court gossip about his mother's relations with his 'd. Friend' and tutor, the gossip that Wilkes was to furbish into an analogy of the story of Roger Mortimer and Queen Isabella, the mother of Edward III.

Neither the Princess-Dowager, nor Lord Bute, were in fact sinister characters. The worst that can be said of Augusta of Saxe-Gotha is that she possessed the typical craft of a mother defending her young against the perils of a wicked world. She had neither the intelligence nor the political prescience to subject her eldest born to a course of ideological indoctrination. If she ever said, 'Be King, George', it was a highly proper thing for the mother of a Prince of Wales to say from time to time. As for Lord Bute, he was a Scottish gentleman of unimpeachable Whig descent, a long neglected and politically disappointed fortune-hunter, who had made himself indispensable to the widowed Princess. It was said that his principal assets were the finest pair of calves in high society and a gift for private theatricals, though in fact he was a gentleman of highly cultivated tastes in art and literature, and possessed no small degree of political sagacity, as events were to prove. With the assistance of this pair of rather unpromising mentors, to both of whom he was neurotically devoted, the Prince had been turned into something of a prig, and a good deal of a dissembler. Caught up in the typical pattern of Leicester House politics, he came to his majority on a note of dramatic, even histrionic, fury, which expressed itself privately in all the symptoms of persecution-mania. In future, his grandfather was an ogre whose death was a consummation devoutly to be wished. The Duke of Newcastle was 'his knave and counsellor'; Pitt was 'the blackest of hearts', who had sold himself to the old King and the Duke of Newcastle, and should in future be made to 'smart' for his 'ingratitude'. In fact, the play was set, complete with Blunderbore, Iago, the Distressed Widow, and the Faithful Friend. It awaited only the Noble Prince.

His traumatic experience of June 1756 played much the same part in the youth of George III as the evil face of the Fronde played in the childhood of Louis XIV. All his apathy and indolence vanished overnight. He had been stung wide awake by the words and actions of men called 'Ministers'. These men had traduced his mother and his dearest friend. On the first day of July, in the year 1756, he swore that he would never forgive them. And he never did. 'Ministers have done everything they can to provoke me', he wrote to Lord Bute. 'They have called me a harmless boy . . . They have also treated my mother in a cruel manner (which I will neither forget nor forgive to the day of my death) . . . My friend is also attacked in the most cruel and horrid manner . . .' And all this because his mother and his tutor had tried to save him from 'the many snares that surround him' and to secure his succession to the throne 'with honour and not with disgrace'. Therefore, he would look upon himself as 'engag'd in honour and justice to defend these two my friends as long as I draw breath'. He swore all this in the presence of Almighty God, and he resolved with equal solemnity to cast aside his indifference and indolence, and 'to take upon me the man in everything'. He concluded: 'I hope, my dear Lord, you will conduct me through this difficult road and will bring me to my gole. I will exactly follow your advice, without which I shall inevitably sink . . . I sign my name with the greatest pleasure to what I have here written, which is my firm and unalterable resolution.'

It requires no more than a simple reference to the inveterate stubbornness of his nature to understand that he would abide by all that he had said, quite literally, as long as he drew breath. Nothing was ever to succeed in shaking George III's resolution, once he had made up his mind that a certain line of action accorded with his personal and quite simple notions of honour and rectitude. He was an Englishman, and 'firmness is the characteristic of an Englishman'. Others might look upon politics as a game: 'I always act from conviction.' Others might doubt of their own rectitude: 'I know I am doing my duty and therefore can never wish to retract.' His was the unyielding obduracy of a strongly emotional and almost completely unintellectual nature, moulded in its earliest years by a preponderantly feminine education, and governed at every turn by a feminine obsession with personalities. His earliest resolve, as expressed in this famous letter to Lord Bute—one of the most coherent he ever wrote—was essentially a personal one. A backward youth, emotionally undeveloped and inclined to neurotic attachments to any good-looking elder person who was kind to him, had been awakened to the life of politics at the age of eighteen by experience of the emotions of hatred and revenge. Not politics, but politicians, had flung him into activity. Politicians, not politics, were finally to drive him mad.

The Princess-Dowager had shielded her son from all unnecessary contact with the typical aristocratic society of the England of his youth. She took the view that the generally profligate young people of quality in Hanoverian England were unfit company for a virtuous prince, and he had grown to manhood in that 'privacy and lifeless solitude' which Horace Walpole later ascribed to the domestic life of his sovereign. It was a mistaken policy. The Prince should have at least been afforded the opportunity to experience familiarity with the kind of men with whom he would have to work at the head of affairs, even if only as a member of the Drones Club, for he was always inclined to overwork. A certain levity would have saved him, and his people, much travail. Perhaps that is what Uncle Timothy Bramble meant when he regretted the King's lack of 'devil'. Squire Bramble applauded the King as 'a very honest kind-hearted gentleman . . . too good for the times'. But he added: 'A king of England should have a spice of the devil in his composition.'

He was dedicated from the beginning to the cause of 'conscious rectitude'. He was Good, and he knew that he was Good, and by 'Good' he meant, quite simply, 'devoted to the ways of

religion and virtue'. He saw himself as God's good man sent to
redeem his country from the grasp of the vicious and the
clever—epithets which, in his mind, as in the minds of all
Philistines, were pseudonyms. One aspect of Goodness, according to his strictly Protestant mode of looking at things, was hard
work. He knew himself to be naturally of a sluggish temperament and he was resolved to seek justification by works. A great
deal of the blame that was to be laid upon him for 'interference',
or even 'usurpation' of ministerial functions, was really the
penalty he paid for a determination to work harder than anyone else in the service of the State. Domesticity, too—the
cult of family virtue[1]—was an obvious aspect of Goodness; and
in this above all else his people could contrast him favourably,
even enthusiastically, with his two predecessors of the House of
Hanover. Altogether George III was a change from George I
and George II. Nobody with half an eye for character could
fail to understand that something really had happened to the
British monarchy in 1760. His preference for morals over mind,
for persons over ideas, for virtue over everything, and in his
assurance that he was himself the virtuous man contending
against clever wickedness on behalf of a nation debauched
for many years of servitude to the 'dirty arts' of politicians,
George III really was a new kind of monarch to wear the
Crown of England, and his accession really does mark a great
change in both the public and private affairs of his people.

In themselves, his personal preferences and peculiar fantasies
would have mattered little had they not been matched by a
rising tide of moralism among his subjects. He was the very
man for the moment; at least it was possible for the multitudes
who watched and applauded his performance from a deceptive
distance to think so. He seemed to respond to something profoundly deep-stirring in the ethos of English society at that
time. It had begun to stir some years before George III came
to the throne. The hard frost of 'The Age of Reason' was breaking up, and a season of warm feeling, of emotionalism, of

---

[1] He treated Nelson with frigid disapproval over the Emma Hamilton
affair, and it is said that the great sailor's only fear as he sailed for Trafalgar
was that he might be driven into Weymouth Bay within range of the royal
telescope.

enthusiasm—that bugbear of the eighteenth-century intelligence—was at hand. Sense was giving place to sensibility, *Tom Jones* to *Evelina*, Walpole to Pitt, Hoadly to Wesley. It is true that England had always worn her 'Age of Reason' with a difference. The hangover of seventeenth-century pietism had never ceased in some sort to moderate the confidence of the English rationalists of the tradition of John Locke. William Law's *Serious Call* (1723) was published thirteen years before Bishop Butler's *Analogy*, and we know from the case of Samuel Johnson how powerful an influence it could exercise over young minds even in the heyday of latitudinarianism. And after all, Locke himself is more comprehensible in terms of the Protestant pietism from which he sprang than in those of his 'interpreters', Bolingbroke and Pope.[1] Indeed, it was never a profitable occupation to search eighteenth-century England for a uniformly prevalent ethos which might be summed up in such adjectives as brilliant, brittle, heartless, sophisticated, or rationalist: the favourite adjectives for that equivocal term 'the eighteenth century'. At no time was there a single and undivided 'eighteenth century' in England, even though the age of Pope and Bolingbroke comes nearest to expressing what is usually meant by the label. George Moore, seeking in these years an affinity with his own most fondly cherished mood, was compelled to admit this when he read *Tristram Shandy*. Here, he found, was a personal jargon which broke all the rules of classic eighteenth-century prose: the free-play of an eccentric spirit every bit as wilfully personal as the style of Carlyle, or Meredith, or Stevenson. And *Tristram Shandy* was published in the first year of the reign of George III, and dedicated most fittingly to one of the greatest exponents of individual, not to say eccentric, character in English politics, William Pitt.

If England had ever been tempted to indulge the mood of uninhibited rationalism, to exile warmth of feeling or moral enthusiasm in favour of mere good sense, the temptation had been decisively overcome by the middle years of the century. Five years before George III came to the throne, an earthquake had killed some 5,000 people in a few minutes at Lisbon, and within a short time similar and associated catastrophes had

[1] See D. G. James, *The Life of Reason*, 1949, Ch. 2.

killed twice as many more. The celebrated eighteenth-century complacency was severely shaken all over Europe. Only the most hardened Pangloss, it seems, could sustain the proposition that all was for the best in the best of all possible worlds. Some were shocked into atheism by the manifest lack of discrimination on the part of the Deity. Others were confirmed in, or finally persuaded of, the belief that God was deeply offended by the wickedness of the human race. But it had not required the Lisbon earthquake to shake the English. As John Milton had delighted to point out, when God intends to impart some new thing in the way of reformation to his people, he imparts it first to his Englishmen. Five years before the terrible affair at Lisbon— at precisely the half-century mark—London had experienced two severe 'quakes in the space of two months. No-one was killed, but Lord Chancellor Hardwicke was shaken in Westminster Hall, Leicester House had seemed to be sinking at the foundations, and even Horace Walpole was persuaded that there was somebody under his bed. People took to camping out in the fields at night, and a thriving trade was done in hackney-coaches, rural lodgings, and 'earthquake-gowns'. The Bishop of London wrote the best-seller of the century, warning a lewd age to mend its ways in time,[1] and the preachers in general made a good thing out of the evident wrath of an outraged Deity. One 'quake might be geological, but two were manifestly theological. There is no reason to believe that the new seriousness that began to overtake the English after the mid-point of the eighteenth century was the first-fruit of a geological disturbance. It is much more probable that it was among the first-fruits of the labours of John Wesley.

It was also among the by-products of certain Acts of Parliament which aimed to make the price of gin prohibitive; of the devotion of a number of philanthropists and medical men who were improving public health; of the good sense of such London magistrates as the Fieldings who were propagating a more socially responsible attitude towards crime.[2] One way or another, large numbers of people were being given better

[1] Bishop Sherlock's *Letter on the Occasion of the late Earthquake*, 1750, sold 105,000 copies.
[2] See Chapter 3, supra, pp. 17–18.

physical opportunities of living decent lives: society, if not yet the State, was beginning to hinder hindrances. Within these brightening horizons of physical health, the English were returning to the free-play of the latent religiosity of the race. With Wesley and Whitefield, the country was in for a religious revival more socially momentous than any in its history. With the Pitts, father and son, the new moralism and idealism were to transform the world of politics. With Henry and John Fielding, Jonas Hanway, John Howard, Thomas Clarkson, and a score more of men and women of feelings, a compassionate concern for the poor, the neglected, and the oppressed was to re-create a social conscience. There was a long way to go, yet. The England of Hogarth, with its passion for brutal sports and its obsession with gambling and drink, was still flourishing in the early years of the new reign. But it is not too much to say that with the accession of George III, care and conscience, domestic virtue and laborious ways, were in the process of capturing the throne itself. The year 1760 did not see the accession of a benevolent despot. Rather it witnessed the meeting of a moralistic King with a moralistic people, the shadowy initiation of a spectacle which was to become familiar in the England of Queen Victoria. Only a blind determination to remain on the plane of 'constitutional' history can obscure the importance of that point in time.

George and Dragon

PERHAPS IT was a mere formality for the King to begin his reign with a Proclamation for the Encouragement of Piety and Virtue, and for the Preventing and Punishing of Vice, Profaneness and Immorality (or for the Better Observance of the Lord's Day). It was not until 1787 that William Wilberforce backed up a similar promulgation with a 'Promulgation Society' and a Vigilance Committee. Nevertheless, it was an appropriate start and accorded well with the new King's personal reputation. More interesting was the report that the King 'intended to introduce a new custom into his family, that of living well with all his family', for the domestic broils of the House of Hanover had been a scandal and a byword from the day of their arrival in England, when the Prince of Wales had stepped ashore in front of his father at Greenwich and had been mistaken for the King. It has often been supposed that there was something pathological about the way that the Hanoverian kings regularly quarrelled with their eldest sons. In fact, given the curious circumstances of the accession of the first two Georges, there is nothing really remarkable about it, unless it be the virulence of the ill-humour displayed on either side. Neither George I nor George II really cared about living in England, nor were they under the slightest illusion about their meagre popularity with their subjects. Middle-aged and irascible princes, longing always for Hanover, and thwarted at every turn by arrogant ministers and (in their view) ludicrous parliaments, threatened for years by the conspiracies of Stuart Pretenders in league with foreign courts for their overthrow, there is little cause for surprise that they came to detest their heirs-apparent as rallying-points for disgruntled politicians and investors in a reversionary interest.

George III, quite apart from his preference for England, was spared for many years the political bugbear of a Prince of Wales. As if to show his thankfulness for the unparalleled security of his Crown, he went out of his way to show the most delicate attentions to those of his kinsmen who stood nearest to the throne. Among these was his uncle, the Duke of Cumberland—'Butcher' Cumberland of Culloden—now a war-scarred and semi-paralytic veteran on the edge of the grave. The King did not wish his uncle's name to come after that of his own brother, the Duke of York, in the Church prayers. After his tutor, Lord Bute, Uncle Cumberland was very much of a father-figure to the self-mistrustful and inexperienced young King. He was to depend on his services in choosing and negotiating with his ministerial servants over the next six years. So he commanded that in future his subjects should pray only for his mother, 'The Princess Dowager of Wales, and all the Royal Family', thus avoiding invidious distinctions. At the same time, Edward, Duke of York, was sworn of His Majesty's most honourable Privy Council, along with John, Earl of Bute, the King's 'dearest friend'.

On the 8th day of September 1761, the King entered into the state of Holy Matrimony with the Princess Charlotte of Mecklenburg-Strelitz, 'a Princess distinguished by every eminent virtue and amiable endowment', as he assured his Privy Council, 'whose illustrious line has constantly shown the firmest zeal for the Protestant religion and a particular attachment to my family.' Mecklenburg was a north-German and Lutheran principality measuring some 120 by 30 miles in extent, and the Princess was a plain young lady of seventeen. The King, always brave himself, had been captivated by the courageous appeal of the Princess to the better nature of the King of Prussia at the time of his invasion of Mecklenburg. Her letter to the great conqueror was forwarded to his ally, the late King George II, as 'a miracle of patriotism and good sense in so young a Princess'. The letter makes pretty reading, but the King's subjects had hoped for a pretty Queen, preferably the Lady Sarah Lennox, younger daughter of the Duke of Richmond, an entrancing creature of sixteen to whom the Prince had lost his heart before his accession. Now, as the young

5. William Pitt the Elder

6. Richard Arkwright

7. John Wilkes

8. Frederick,
Lord North

man put aside his personal feelings at the instance of his mother and Lord Bute, and prepared dutifully to take 'Miss Charlotte of Mecklenburg'[1] to his embraces, the scurrilous London print-sellers began to trade in portraits of Lady Sarah with her name struck out to make room for that of Her Most Serene Highness. The King's dutiful devotion to *la belle-laide* of Mecklenburg-Strelitz was life-long and exemplary, and Queen Charlotte rewarded his affection with fifteen children in twenty-two years. But to the English people she became, and remained, simply 'Old Snuffy'.

She came from the Elbe in the yacht *Charlotte*, escorted by a British fleet under the command of Lord Anson. Storms held the *Charlotte* off Harwich for several days, while the Princess diverted herself with practising English tunes on the harpsichord. Setting foot ashore on 7 September, she proceeded via Colchester and Witham, 'bowing to all who seemed desirous of seeing her, and ordering the coach to go extremely slowly through towns and villages as she passed, that as many as would might have a full view of her'. On the second day of her journey she went by the Hackney Turnpike to Constitution Hill, and thence through St James's Park to the garden gate of the Palace, where the King raised her up from her obeisance and led her within. They were wedded and bedded that night. A fortnight later they were crowned amidst great rejoicings. Lady Sarah Lennox always said that it was the happiest day of her life.

It was a sight that had not been seen in England for many a long year: a King in his early twenties and a Queen in her teens. The average age of English sovereigns at their accession, since 1603, had been forty. Now, it seemed, was beginning the Age of Youth—a notion of itself which was to persist under George III for many years to come. The greatest of the King's servants, William Pitt, was to become Prime Minister at twenty-four (though posterity has found it hard to believe that Pitt the Younger was ever young), and Nelson was to become a post-captain before he was twenty-one. For nearly half a century

---

[1] Vide Henry Fox, who had carried off Lady Sarah's elder sister in 1744 and was now deprived of the advantage of becoming the King's brother-in-law.

the people had been accustomed to the fierce or sullen faces of middle-aged Germans scowling at them from the windows of the state coach at the opening of Parliament. Now they saw the smiling face of a youth who, despite his Hanoverian features, made the most of his claims to Englishry. The amount of English blood in his veins was negligible, but in manners, tastes and attachment he could play the part of a British monarch more convincingly than any man in his position for a century. There certainly was something fresh and delightful in this meeting between a young king and his people. When he went to open the new session in November, the people turned out in unprecedented numbers, 'nor did ever people appear so unanimous in testifying their applause'. Horace Walpole, pert and cynical as ever, began by remarking, 'When you have changed the cipher of George II into that of George III, and have read the addresses, and have shifted a few Lords and Grooms of the Bedchamber, you are master of the history of the new reign . . . which is indeed but a new lease of the old one.' And yet, after attending the levée he was surprised to find that the levée-room had lost so entirely the air of the lion's den. 'This young man', he found, 'don't stand in one spot with his eyes fixed royally on the ground, and dropping bits of German news; he walks about and speaks to everybody.' On the throne, receiving loyal addresses, 'he is graceful and genteel, sits with dignity . . . all his speeches are obliging . . . he seems all good nature and wishing to satisfy every one'. Properly aware of the element of 'performance' inherent in all public behaviour, Walpole concluded: 'the part is well acted', and went on to ask himself what possibilities lay behind the scenes.

And, of course, the King was showing a political face, playing the correct game of historic continuity in conformity with the traditions of a people, and a Constitution whose very nature was conservative. There was nothing villainous in all this. Every monarch professed, on his or her accession, to be at least as English as the English. Queen Anne, in her first speech from the throne, insisted that her heart was 'entirely English'. Even George I had thought it wise to utter a few words in English on his first appearance in his Parliament. George II when he was

Prince of Wales and busy courting popularity by trying to appear as unlike his father as possible, was heard to declare that 'if anyone would make their court to him, it must be by telling him he was like an Englishman'. His son, Frederick, in his turn, impressed upon the future George III that he must 'convince his country' that he was 'not only an Englishman born and bred', but that he was 'this by inclination'. George III's famous profession, therefore, was the fruit of long rehearsal. 'Born and educated in this country', His Majesty was graciously pleased to say in guttural but happy accents, 'I glory in the name of Briton.' He went on to say many other good things: for instance, about the war with France, the latest glorious phase of a contest which was regarded as almost a sacred part of the Constitution itself. He described it as 'both just and necessary' and swore to prosecute it to a victorious conclusion in association with his 'good ally and brother, the King of Prussia'. Few who heard him utter this impeccable sentiment knew that His Majesty had originally intended to describe the war as 'bloody and expensive', but had changed his language under the persuasion of Mr Pitt. It would not have mattered what language he used as long as it was understood that Mr Pitt was to remain at the head of His Majesty's affairs. The Duke of Newcastle, it was reported, had made some show of resigning the Treasury, but Mr Pitt had declared his willingness to remain on the same footing as before. 'Business as usual' was the right motto for a nation on the way to winning the richest regions of the world's trade under the inspired leadership of the greatest war minister in her history.

This man, William Pitt, had stood at the head of public affairs since 1757. It might please Almighty God to call to His mercy the late most high, most mighty, and most excellent monarch, George II, and to set in his place the high and mighty Prince, George III; but the hearts and minds of Englishmen nevertheless belonged to His Majesty's Secretary of State for the Southern Department. Even while the old King's corpse still lay at Kensington Palace, and before the new King was crowned, the City of London had memorialized 'The Great Commoner' at the laying of the foundation-stone of the new Blackfriars Bridge. An inscription 'in large plates of tin', boasted that the new bridge had been undertaken 'amidst the rage of an extensive war', and was to stand to all posterity as:

A MONUMENT OF THIS CITY'S AFFECTION TO THE MAN
WHO BY THE STRENGTH OF HIS GENIUS
AND STEADFASTNESS OF HIS MIND
AND A CERTAIN KIND OF HAPPY CONTAGION
OF HIS PROBITY AND SPIRIT
RECOVERED, AUGMENTED AND SECURED
THE BRITISH EMPIRE
IN ASIA, AFRICA, AND AMERICA
AND RESTORED THE ANCIENT REPUTATION AND
INFLUENCE OF THIS COUNTRY
AMONGST THE NATIONS OF EUROPE.

The new King, the child of Leicester House and its fantasies, saw William Pitt in a different light. Pitt was 'the blackest of hearts', and later—at the time when he thundered against the American policy of Grenville and Lord North—the King was to call him 'a trumpet of sedition'. He began by hating him for deserting the Leicester House opposition in order to defend George II's beloved Hanover on the way to 'winning Canada on the banks of the Elbe', and he ended by hating him as the man to whom the rebel Colonists were to put up statues dedicated to 'the illustrious Mr Pitt, under God and the King the Saviour of Britain and the Redeemer of America', including a white marble one in Wall Street depicting him in a Roman toga. He always feared the dynamic potentialities of the great minister—an 'overmighty subject' if ever there was one—although he need never have doubted Pitt's profound respect for the Monarchy and its lawful independence. When Burke said that Pitt was intoxicated by the least peep into the royal closet, he was indulging in a typically Burkeian over-statement of a plain fact. To Pitt the kingship was no mere historic symbol of national unity, but a present reality. The King was 'the royal Master' to whom his servants owed a personal and individual responsibility. It may have been a slightly old-fashioned view by the 1760s, as was the view of the King himself. With Pitt at his side George III would have been 'The Patriot King' *volens nolens*. But could he ever hope to reign unchallenged in the hearts and imagination of his people while this man occupied his pedestal?

As for the other reigning minister, the Duke of Newcastle, the 'Minister for Majorities' who had made it possible for the Great Commoner to go his victorious way by his management of Parliament, finance, and all those sordid details with which the magnificent war leader could scarcely be expected to concern himself: that ageing expert in the dispensation of the loaves and fishes who had served his apprenticeship under 'the missionary of vice' Robert Walpole, and had scarcely been 'out of employment' for half a dozen years since 1724: he represented all that George III loathed and detested in the vile race of politicians. If the war be brought to an end, Pitt would go out like a candle-flame in the sunshine. Deprived of the Treasury, the great bank of 'interest', the Duke of Newcastle would be like a paralytic robbed of his crutches. The young King was resolved to end the war, take the Treasury out of the hands of the Duke, and to put his dearest friend, the Earl of Bute, at the head of his affairs. Together, he and his 'd. friend' would inaugurate the reign of virtue and religion. 'The successor I have long had in my eye to the D. of N.' he wrote to his 'd. friend' when the D. of N. was at last shivering on the brink of resignation, 'is a man void of his dirty arts, who will think of mine and his country's good . . . not of jobs . . . '

Some twelve months later, the Preliminaries of the Peace of Paris had been carried through the House of Commons by an unexampled exercise of jobbery and proscription, and the Earl of Bute was hastening into retirement amidst the execration of the nation. The King was left gloomily to anticipate the verdict of history upon kings and ministers who desert the cause of virtue. To have 'purged out corruption', he averred, would have won immortality: 'then when we are both dead our memories would have been respected and esteemed to the end of time . . . '

The fact that George III decided to promote political virtue by acting as his own political broker need cause no surprise. When he called in the great parliamentary jobber, Henry Fox, to 'manage' the House of Commons for the carrying of the Peace preliminaries, he had confessed that he had had no alternative but to 'call in bad men to govern bad men'. It is safe to say that no-one, from the King downwards, could have kept a majority together for a fortnight in those days without the 'cement' of 'interest'. He who wills the end must will the means, and since Sir Lewis Namier took the lid off eighteenth-century politics for us, it need no longer shock or surprise anybody that the King succumbed to the exigencies of the age in which he lived. At the same time, it would be unjust to deny the sincerity of the King's vision of himself. The illusions of mankind are no less important to the historian than are the realities which defeat them. Only thus is revealed the true irony which haunts all human endeavour, the commonplace tragedy which transcends the conventionally heroic in its claims on our compassion. That King George III saw himself as a latter-day St George at war with the Dragon of faction may be absurd, but it is none the less true. It is even likely that for a moment, at least, he saw himself as a figure of historic tragedy, thwarted and betrayed by the failure of other men to rise to his own moral eminence. When Bute resigned in favour of George Grenville in the spring of 1763, the sad young King wrote to his 'd. friend' in language which suggested that he felt the eye of history upon him. He was to cling to the mantle of St George long after it had become clear to the rest of the world that the virtuous young King had assumed the role of 'the chief of the borough-mongering gentlemen of England', and that the Dragon was not only alive, but kicking its inevitable way into the nineteenth century.

CHAPTER 6

Wilkes and Liberty!

It is certainly the peace of God for it passeth all understanding.
John Wilkes on the Peace of Paris, No. 5 'The North Briton'

THE PEACE of Paris which ended the Seven Years' War fairly
safeguarded British war-gains and served all reasonable am-
bitions of reasonable men. France ceded both Canada and
Cape Breton, while retaining her fishing rights off Newfound-
land and the St Lawrence, with the islands of Miquelon and
St Pierre as *abris*. In India she ceded all her conquests since
1749. True, she was allowed to recover or retain more of the
West Indian Islands than she had a right to expect: Martinique,
St Lucia, Marie Galante and Guadeloupe. In Africa she kept
Gorée while ceding Senegal. In Europe she gave up Minorca.
Her ally, Spain, recovered Havana, while Great Britain received Florida and was confirmed in her logwood rights in
Honduras. Territorially and commercially it was a rich harvest,
not incommensurate with the extent and brilliance of Britain's
war-effort. On the other hand, in terms of future security
against a revival of French power the treaty was notably
deficient. Within a few years France was in a position not only
to assist in the alienation of a large part of North America from
the British dominion, but once more to threaten these shores
with invasion. Indeed, the calamities of 1778–83 were to be
blamed on the peacemakers of 1763.

The outcry that greeted the Peace of Paris sprang less from
the terms of the treaty than from the nature of the war and the
manner of its conclusion. After all, from the British standpoint,
the Seven Years' War was in some respects the first of 'the
people's wars'. It had been concerned with the attainment of
vast objectives in which the commercial life of the whole nation

was deeply concerned. It had been conducted by a war leader unmatched until the twentieth century. It ended with the people's idol roaring ineffectually on his gout-crutches from the opposition benches, against a treaty delivered to the nation at the hands of a detested Scotchman who was suspected of having poisoned the mind of an innocent young Prince, not to mention seducing his mother.

There can be little doubt, however, that but for it having been made by Lord Bute, the Peace would have passed into history without more adverse criticism than the generality of peace treaties concluded between fairly matched adversaries. Almost everyone, including the parliamentary opposition, wanted peace. The year 1763 saw the first notable economic depression of the Hanoverian age, when unemployment and high prices followed the boom artificially engendered by the war. The recession reflected a credit-crisis which had originated in Amsterdam and was spreading to the European money-market in general and was soon threatening London. Lord Hardwicke put the matter in a nutshell when he wrote, at the end of November: 'I am persuaded . . . that the burden and tedium of the war, and the desire for peace, are so strong in the generality of Parliament, and of the nation (abstracted from the interested or wild part of the City of London) that the very name of peace is agreeable to them, and they would have been content with terms rather lower than all we have yet been told of these Preliminaries.' Let Lord Bute act swiftly, with firmness and courage, Henry Fox said, and numbers would flock to him. Let him show that he could make peace, and he would straightway have the support of 'the Tories, the Scotch, and the loaves and fishes . . .' Once he had these with him, 'they would be joined by so many that his Lordship may possibly be sure of a majority. Let that appear, and the majority will be great.' No-one knew better than Henry Fox that power breeds power, that nothing succeeds like success.

When the debates on the Preliminaries were over, and with a five-to-one victory for the King and his favourite, the anger of the defeated opposition was turned to fury by the malevolent use the victors proceeded to make of their triumph. Again, Henry Fox was in the van. 'Leave none of them', he advised

Bute. 'Turn the tables and you will immediately have thousands who will think the safety of themselves depends upon your Lordship, and will therefore be sincere and active friends.' He wrote and spoke in these days like an Attila on the track of the routed allies of Rome. Nor was the King himself behindhand in the slaughter. He would deal with the bigger victims, 'those proud Dukes' as he called them. He was at last able to expend all the hoarded venom of his embittered youth. He struck the Duke of Devonshire's name from the list of Privy Councillors with his own hand. 'I was determined to dismiss him rather than permit him to dismiss me,' he informed Bute. 'The sword is drawn; vigour and violence are the only means of ending this audacious faction.' They were, Bute agreed, 'the most factious combination of *soi-disant* great men against the lawful right and liberty of the King that ever happened in this country . . .' Thus the King with his schoolboy rudeness and the favourite with his penchant for amateur theatricals, indulged their myths and fought their fantasies. As for the 'proud Dukes', they sat at home and scowled for an hour, and then everything went on very much the same as before.

'A more severe political persecution never raged,' Horace Walpole was to write in his *Memoirs*. 'Whoever holding a place, had voted against the preliminaries, was instantly dismissed. The friends and dependants of the Duke of Newcastle were particularly cashiered; and this cruelty was extended so far, that old servants who had retired and been preferred to very small places, were rigorously hunted out and deprived of their livelihood.' This systematic despoliation of a defeated parliamentary minority, based on division-lists, and extending the long arm of malevolence downwards from Lords and Commons to excisemen, stamp-controllers and tide-waiters was something new in English history. And while the big men scowled and bided their time, the small fry were noisy and immediate in their rage. London, always the most vocal part of the body politic, was in an uproar. Milling mobs embraced Mr Pitt's horses and drew the discarded patriot's carriage through the streets, while Lord Bute was obliged to hire a bodyguard of bruisers when he went to Westminster. Within two months of the Peace of Paris, Bute resigned from the Treasury. 'I am firmly of the opinion', he wrote, 'that my retirement will remove the only unpopular part of the Government.' He left his master with the services of George Grenville, and within another fortnight John Wilkes spoke again in *The North Briton*, this time denouncing the King's Speech at the prorogation of Parliament, a speech which had called the Peace 'this salutary measure'. This amounted, Wilkes declared, to 'the most abandoned instance of ministerial effrontery ever attempted to be imposed on mankind'. Indeed, the minister had put a lie into the King's mouth.

Number Forty-five of *The North Briton* opened a campaign that was to be carried far beyond Parliament and the courts, into the streets and beyond the seas, carrying its reverberations across the Atlantic to swell a storm which would sweep away half the new-born Empire and ultimately transform the destinites of the English-speaking peoples.

John Wilkes was already a middle-aged man when he found himself, somewhat surprisingly, at the centre of a storm which presaged the onset of a reformist epoch. Born in Clerkenwell in 1727, son of a wealthy distiller and his strait-laced Presbyterian lady, he carried the habits of the bawdy, full-blooded, rowdy England of Walpole and Hogarth into a society of increasing moral gravity. He was a polished parvenu of politics, a manufactured gentleman who had adopted as his native heath the beautiful county of Bucks. To a natural wit and superabundant vitality he added a tolerable education picked up on the Grand Tour and a brief residence at the University of Leyden. Tall and muscular in person, with the face of a satyr, a twisted jaw, a flattened nose, and a squint which vastly exceeded that slight obliquity of vision which has so often proved an asset to actors and preachers in confronting large audiences, he liked to say that once he had 'talked away his face' he could cut out any rival for a woman's affections in half an hour. That he was a 'man of parts' in the true eighteenth-century sense of the term, is amply proved by his wide and varied acquaintance. The man who distinguished himself as a debauchee even in the company of Sir Francis Dashwood and the 4th Earl of Sandwich, his fellow-members of the Hell-Fire Club, was likewise a cherished confrère of Pitt and Temple.

In 1763, Wilkes was a middle-aged and silent backbencher on the opposition side of the House of Commons. He seems to have entered Parliament in the true eighteenth-century style, as an indispensable means of making a figure in the world, very much as he had got himself appointed to the county magistracy of Bucks, then to the office of High Sheriff, and finally to the rank of second-in-command to Sir Francis Dashwood, Colonel of the Bucks Militia. As a 'Patriot' and a spirited, if somewhat bogus, country gentleman, he belonged naturally to the following of Mr Pitt, the inspired war leader and patron of his country's commercial fortunes. But it was not Mr Pitt, but Pitt's high-mettled and obdurate brother-in-law, Earl Temple, the cross-grained head of the house of Grenville, who brought John Wilkes into politics. The Earl's magnificent mansion at Stowe was one of the great houses of the old Whig connexion which served in the early years of George III as centres of patronage for the malcontents and anti-ministerialists. In very much the same way the country houses of men like John Hampden had served during the Eleven Years' personal government of Charles I. So Lord Shelburne's house at Bowood in Wiltshire was to harbour Bentham, Priestley, and Benjamin Franklin in the days of Lord North. Wilkes was the kind of witty gadfly that Earl Temple and his circle were looking for in the hour of the discomfiture of 'the proud Dukes' at the hands of George III. Lord Bute had his own gang of pamphleteers and journalists, among them Tobias Smollett of *The Briton*, and Wilkes was set up as a counterblast with *The North Briton*, whose dedicated task it was to flay all Scotsmen, time-servers, courtiers and Jacks-in-Office of the King's 'new order'. *The North Briton* holds no such place in our history as Cobbett's *Register*, with its concern for social justice in an age of revolutionary change. Its purpose was wholly destructive, and its politics wholly ephemeral. But for the storm which arose over its forty-fifth number, it would have been long forgotten save among antiquarian inquirers into the careers of some of its minor contributors, like Charles Churchill. Number Forty-five made it immortal.

Wilkes had found his true *métier*. The hanger-on at Stowe, the profligate but efficient Colonel of Militia, the dumb backbencher of the Commons, now sprang at a single bound into the very centre of the national stage. Hitherto, his gay mud-slinging had brought him no nearer to public chastisement than an abortive duel with young Lord Talbot behind the Red Lion Inn at Bagshot, in consequence of his references to his Lord-ship's over-trained horse, which had entered Westminster Hall backwards as it bore the King's Champion into the royal presence at the Coronation. Lord Bute himself had chosen to disregard even the libellous pamphlet in which Wilkes had likened him to Roger Mortimer. The King, however, had never forgiven the imputation put upon his mother, who figured in this scabrous production as Queen Isabella, Mortimer's para-mour. Now, when Bute had withdrawn 'behind the curtain', and Wilkes proceeded to charge his successor, George Gren-ville, with having put a lie into His Majesty's mouth at the prorogation of Parliament on 19 April 1763, the King decided to strike. No doubt he acted out of a sense of cumulative wrong, but the article in question contained in itself sufficient cause of offence to a Prince who wished his royal words to his Parlia-ment to be regarded as his own. It is sometimes said that Wilkes showed immaculate respect for the King by his insistence that His Majesty, no less than his people, had been made the victim of abandoned effrontery by his ministers. It made things worse, in the King's eyes, that Wilkes should have opened his attack with some unpalatable observations upon our constitu-tional history. 'The King's Speech', he began, 'has always been considered by the legislature, and by the public at large, as the Speech of the Minister.' In fact, Wilkes contrived to give the impression that George III was a kind of ventriloquist's doll on the knee of George Grenville. Nor was the King likely to have been mollified by the closing references to the House of Stuart which had been 'so weakly advised' as to endeavour to put into practice the 'slavish doctrines of the absolute, inde-pendent, unlimited power of the Crown', however carefully such references were balanced by a confident appeal to 'the personal character of our present amiable sovereign . . .' Such a testimonial from the man who had composed the Introduc-tion to *The Death of Mortimer*, was heaping insult upon injury.

'Instead of applying to my Lord Chief Justice to punish him,' said Dr Johnson, 'I would send half a dozen footmen and have him well ducked.' It appeared that they managed these things better in France, where a generation earlier Voltaire had been cudgelled by the footmen of the Chevalier de Rohan. George III, however, bore at least this much resemblance to Charles I, that he liked to have the law on his side. He gave orders that John Wilkes should be prosecuted for libel, and the Law Officers of the Crown were consulted on the question whether or not the privileges of the House of Commons exempted him from arrest. Charles Yorke, the Attorney-General, before submitting his written opinion to the Secretaries of State, sent the document to his father, Lord Hardwicke, the late Lord Chancellor. Hardwicke had no reason to love the King's present ministers, but he confidently supported his son's opinion that the privileges of the House of Commons did not extend to an action for seditious libel. He concurred in the opinion that Number Forty-five of *The North Briton* constituted such a libel. It was, he said, 'the most unguarded and audacious that he had ever seen' Hardwicke, however, had always deplored any discussion of parliamentary powers and privileges by the courts of common law. He was fully aware of the delicacy of Crown Lawyers giving written opinions to the Executive. He later expressed the view that 'the Attorney and Solicitor should have talked with the King's servants first, and endeavoured to conduct the business in a way less liable to clamour'. In the event the way chosen by the Secretaries of State proved the worst possible. On 23 April, Lord Halifax issued a General Warrant empowering four messengers and a constable to search for the authors, printers and publishers of Number Forty-five of *The North Briton*, to seize them and their papers, wherever they might be found, and to bring them before the Secretaries of State. Wilkes's name was not put into the warrant.

The 'generality' of the warrant, however, consisted less in the absence of names than in the very wide powers of search and seizure vested in its executants. It seems that the Secretaries of State had originally intended to charge Wilkes with *treasonable* libel, in which case a Secretary's warrant for arrest might have been couched in the most general terms imaginable. When, after consultation with the Law Officers, the charge was amended to seditious libel, the Secretaries appear to have imagined that a General Warrant would do their business without question. It is certain that neither the Law Officers nor the ex-Lord Chancellor were ever consulted on the form of warrant to be used, but only on the question of the privileges of a Member of Parliament. The Attorney-General later asserted in debate that the General Warrant was illegal, that he had never seen the warrant until after the arrest, and that the question of its use or its legality had never been submitted to the Law Officers by the ministers. The fact is that the Secretaries possessed no evidence as to the authorship of Number Forty-five. Halifax, under examination in court, later admitted that the General Warrant was drawn up three days before such evidence came into his hands. The evidence, indeed, was provided by the messengers who had acted under the terms of the warrant. It was a clear case of *post hoc, propter hoc*. In their anxiety to afford prompt satisfaction to the wishes of the King, whose enthusiasm for George Grenville and his colleagues was fast waning, the ministers had rushed in where angels might well have feared to tread—only to find themselves confronted with the devil: or, in the King's words, 'that Devil Wilkes'.

Within three days, the messengers and constable had arrested forty-nine persons, among them Kearsley, the publisher of Number Forty-five, and Balfe, the printer. Unfortunately, they had also arrested Dryden Leach, who had printed or reprinted several numbers of *The North Briton*, but not Number Forty-five. He was quickly released, and was not hauled before the Secretaries of State. But Leach was to bring actions against the three messengers for breaking and entering his premises, and for illegal arrest, being awarded £400 damages by the Court of Common Pleas three years later. His action was to elicit Lord Mansfield's pronunciation of the illegality of General Warrants when the case went up to the Court of King's Bench on a bill of exception. The arrest of Wilkes himself provided the *chef-d'œuvre* of this feast of ministerial ineptitude. The messengers treated him with almost reverential circumspection. Refraining from an arrest when their quarry arrived at his house in Great George Street 'in liquor' on the evening of 29 April, they awaited his emergence on the following morning, and then suffered him to brush them aside while he went off to a nearby loft where he kept his printing-press and disposed of the types for Number Forty-six of *The North Briton*. On his return, he invited the messengers into his house and delivered them an harangue on the illegality of General Warrants. The messengers, growing weary of Wilkes's lecture in constitutional law, threatened to call for constables, or even soldiers, and ultimately succeeded in persuading him to step into a chair, which carried him to the house of Lord Halifax, who lived a few doors away. There, in the grand apartment, overlooking the Park, the two Secretaries of State awaited their visitor in solemn panoply behind a long table furnished with pens, ink and paper. Halifax was courteous, and Egremont brutal, but neither produced any effect on Wilkes, who airily refused to answer any questions and treated them to a diatribe on the ignorant and despotic cabal of ministers who misgoverned his country. A fresh warrant, embodying Wilkes's name, was now drawn up, and Halifax offered the prisoner a choice of prisons. Wilkes replied that he never accepted favours save from his friends, and by nightfall he was safely lodged in the Tower of London. He begged that he might not be accommodated in a room previously tenanted by a Scotsman, since he feared to contract the itch. On the whole, he stated his preference for the apartment once tenanted by Lord Egremont's Jacobite father, Sir William Wyndham.

There can be little doubt that Wilkes and his patrons had anticipated the course of events. 'Pray, Mr Wilkes, how far does the liberty of the press extend in England?' Madame Pompadour had asked the Editor of *The North Briton* when he visited Paris at the time of the Peace of Paris. 'That, Madame,' Wilkes had replied, 'is what I am determined to find out.' This was typically Wilkesian persiflage. It is probable that he had discussed with Pitt the terms of the retort which the *North Briton* should make to the King's Speech, an advance copy of which was in Pitt's hands. It is certain that he had concerted with Temple the steps that were to be taken in the likely event of his arrest. Temple at once applied to Sir Charles Pratt, at the Court of Common Pleas, for a writ of Habeas Corpus.

Such a writ had not been moved in that court since the reign of
Charles II, but Pratt was a follower and friend of Pitt, and it
was obviously desirable to avoid application to the usual court
for such writs, the King's Bench, where sat Lord Chief Justice
Mansfield, the Scottish scourge of all libellers and the principal
pillar of the Administration in the courts of law. 'Law is
politics,' Lenin was to aver, from slightly different premises, in
a later century. It certainly was so on more than one occasion
in the reign of George III. From the beginning of the Wilkes
affair, and before it, politics and law were inextricably mingled.
Not only was Temple obliged to make two applications for the
writ of Habeas Corpus, but every conceivable device of legal
chicanery was to be employed by the King's ministers during
the next six years in their attempt to overwhelm their obstreper-
ous victim and to evade the consequences of their own high-
handed folly. All in all, it has been computed, their campaign
cost the country £100,000. It is impossible to compute the cost
in terms of discredit thrown upon the kingly government and
Constitution with whose good name they were entrusted.

The first blow fell promptly on 6 May, a little more than a
week after the arrest of Wilkes, when Mr Justice Pratt, after
rebuking the messengers for evading the first writ of Habeas
Corpus, discharged him from the Court of Common Pleas on
the ground that his privilege as a Member of Parliament
exempted him from legal process in all matters save treason,
felony and breach of the peace. Wilkes, in an address to the
crowded court, asserted that upon his discharge rested the
liberty not only of peers and gentlemen, but 'what touches me
more sensibly, that of the middling and inferior set of people'.
What was to be decided that day was 'whether English liberty
shall be a reality or a shadow'. Pratt's decision, in fact, had
only to do with the privilege of a Member of Parliament. He
had, in the opening of his judgment, declared that Halifax's
commitment of the prisoner was perfectly in order, and the
question of the legality of General Warrants was not before the
court. But the crowd in court and at the doors chose to interpret
the discharge of Wilkes as a triumph for liberty in each and
every sense of the word. As the judgment ended, the cry of
'Wilkes and Liberty!' swept for the first time to the confines of

the waiting City and beyond. Among the many tributes which followed from 'the inferior set of people', Wilkes received a request from the club-men of the *Rose and Crown* at Wapping to inform them of the date of his birthday, since the members had sworn to get drunk every year on that date in celebration of his release. The issue of 'Liberty', in terms of the validity or otherwise of General Warrants, yet remained to be settled, and it was not until six months later, in December 1763, that Wilkes was able to secure a verdict in the Court of Common Pleas against Robert Wood, the Under-Secretary of State, for damages in the matter of the seizure of his private papers. In his direction to the court, which awarded Wilkes £1,000, Pratt declared General Warrants illegal. Only in the Easter Term, 1765, did Lord Mansfield make his declaration to the same effect in the Court of King's Bench at the final settlement of the action of Dryden Leach against the messengers.

Both parties in the contest pursued their course with vindictive zest. On the day of Wilkes's arrest, before anything had been formally brought against him, the King expressed his intention of 'having him put out of the Militia'. Temple, executing the royal command as Lord Lieutenant of Bucks, couched the order for Wilkes's dismissal in such condolatory language that he was relieved of his Lord Lieutenancy a week later. Throughout the summer and autumn of 1763, however, the London juries were awarding hundreds of pounds in damages to scores of masters and journeymen of the printing trade for illegal arrest under the General Warrant. The merchants, who predominated on the juries, were—as Wilkes said—'firm in the cause of liberty', more especially where 'the inferior set of people' were concerned. It became almost a matter for national jubilation every time some humble compositor or printer's-devil was solaced with a pocket full of guineas for having been dragged from his well-earned slumbers in Blackfriars or Seven Dials. Wilkes himself was not content with prosecuting Under-Secretary Wood, but proceeded to the prosecution of Halifax himself as the prime mover. The Secretary of State was able to evade prosecution by various unworthy devices until such time as Wilkes had been compelled to flee the country. It was only in 1769, after his return, that he secured damages in the sum of £4,000, a sum which was considered so inadequate by his supporters that the jury had to be smuggled privately from the court. No doubt Lord Egremont would have been mulcted in the same sum had he not passed beyond the jurisdiction of earthly tribunals in August 1763.

The process of hounding Wilkes out of England was set on foot immediately after his discharge by Pratt on 6 May. Against the advice of the Attorney-General, the ministers decided to prosecute him for infamous and seditious libel in the Court of King's Bench. Armed with Pratt's decision in favour of his privilege, Wilkes refused to appear. Thwarted and humiliated by their failure in this clumsy attempt to override Pratt's judgment, the ministers took up the cudgels in a field where politics had no need to assume the mask of common law, and where their prejudices were bound to prevail in the form of resolutions of regimented majorities. When the new session of Parliament opened on 15 November, Grenville delivered a royal message asking the Commons to take into consideration the case of John Wilkes who had lately avoided trial for libel by pleading the privileges of their House. Humble thanks were at once returned for His Majesty's gracious message, and a motion was carried by 237 votes to 111, declaring Number Forty-five of the *North Briton,* 'a false, scandalous and malicious libel; containing expressions of the most unexampled insolence and contumely towards His Majesty, the grossest aspersions upon both Houses of Parliament, and the most scandalous defiance of the authority of the whole legislature; and most manifestly tending to alienate the affections of the people from His Majesty, to withdraw them from their obedience to the laws of the realm, and to excite them to traitorous insurrections against His Majesty's Government.' This motion, with its hint of treasonous intention on the part of Wilkes, was passed after many weeks of public clamour in the streets of an unpoliced capital, and it was perhaps not altogether surprising that General Conway, a member of the Rockingham connexion, was dismissed not only from his Household Office but also from the command of his regiment for voting with the minority. 'The King cannot entrust his army,' George Grenville observed, 'in the hands of those that are against his measures.' On the previous day, the City mob had prevented the execution of the order of the House of Commons, affixed to its motion of condemnation, that Number Forty-five should be burned by the public hangman. The populace not only rescued the copy of Number Forty-five from the hands of the hangman before the Royal Exchange. It burnt in its place a large jackboot and a petticoat for the benefit of the Earl of Bute and the Princess-Dowager of Wales.

In the House of Lords something even more damaging was being hatched for the discomfiture of John Wilkes than a regimented resolution of the House of Commons. The Ministers of the Crown had laid hands upon a printed copy of an exceedingly dull and obscene poem, supposedly composed by John Wilkes as a parody of Pope's *Essay on Man*. The *Essay on Woman* was most probably the work of one of Wilkes's confrères of the Hell-Fire Club, Thomas Potter, probably the lewdest son ever begotten by an Archbishop of Canterbury. Wilkes, however, had supplied 'Notes' to this dreary little composition under the name of Warburton, Bishop of Gloucester. It was now decided to prosecute Wilkes for obscene libel and, since Warburton was a member of the House of Lords, Lord Sandwich—who had replaced Egremont as a Secretary of State—was deputed to bring the matter before their Lordships. Sandwich, one of the coarsest libertines of the day, and an original member of the Hell-Fire Club himself, undertook the task with loathsome relish. As one who had rallied to the support of Grenville's Ministry and had now accepted high office in the government, he was fair game for the sharpest edge of Wilkes's wit and Churchill's pen. It was to Sandwich, who had prophesied that he would die of a pox or on the gallows, that Wilkes had delivered the famous riposte: 'That depends, my Lord, on whether I embrace your principles or your mistress.' It was of Sandwich's activities that Churchill wrote in *The Candidate*:

> To whip a top, to knuckle down a taw
> To swing upon a gate, to ride a straw,
> To play at pushpin with dull brother peers,
> To belch out catches in a porter's ears,
> To reign the monarch in a midnight cell,

To be the gaping chairman's oracle—
Whilst in most blessed union rogue and whore
Clap hands, huzza, and hiccup out *Encore!* . . .

—all these, and many more low banalities, were the favourite sports of this unrivalled Lothario. Now Sandwich had his revenge. Amidst mingled protests and cries of encouragement, and with an occasional pause for expressions of pious horror, he read to their Lordships very faithfully the whole of the offending doggerel, including the 'Notes' ascribed to the Bishop of Gloucester. As Francis Dashwood, now Baron le Despenser, and himself a founder-member of the Hell-Fire Club, audibly observed, it was like listening to Satan rebuking Sin. At the end, Warburton cholerically called upon his God to witness that he had had no hand in the 'Notes', and Lord Temple made an impromptu protest against the manner in which the government had abused its powers in obtaining the text of the *Essay*. Then a resolution was passed declaring the *Essay on Woman* 'a most scandalous, obscene and impious libel'.

There was now a double charge pending against Wilkes in the Court of King's Bench: one of seditious libel and one of obscene libel. When the cases came on, however, Wilkes was in France. On 16 November he received a challenge to a meeting with pistols in Hyde Park from one Samuel Martin, a fellow-member of the House of Commons, whom he had reviled unmercifully in the *North Briton*. Martin was a toady of Lord Bute, an old Leicester House man, who had served as Joint-Secretary to the Treasury under Newcastle. It was he who had 'betrayed' Newcastle in his last days as First Lord of the Treasury by supplying the favourite with Treasury papers behind the back of his chief. Thereafter he had served as a principal agent in Henry Fox's great 'management' of the Peace Preliminaries in Parliament. Rumour had it that Martin had for months past been shooting at a target with a pistol, and it is worthy of note that in his letter of challenge he denied Wilkes his privilege of a choice of weapons. Wilkes, with typically careless courage, proceeded at once to Hyde Park and fell with a bullet in his groin. His principal concern at the moment appears to have been with the safety of his antagonist, whom he advised to flee and keep his mouth shut. He was, he wrote to

his beloved daughter Polly from his sick-bed, perfectly satisfied with the behaviour of Mr Martin, and he promised to join
her in Paris before Christmas. He was cheered, early in December, by the verdict of the Court of Common Pleas which
awarded him £1,000 damages against Under-Secretary Robert
Wood. Jubilant crowds roared the news under his window
before going off to hoot Lord Halifax. Meanwhile, the House
of Commons had divested him of his privileges. On 23 November it was resolved that 'the privileges of parliament do not
extend to the case of writing and publishing seditious libel',
thus giving the lie to Pratt at Common Pleas and prejudging
the issue still pending at King's Bench. Wilkes was now exposed
to the full blast of the law of libel on both counts, and he could
hardly expect to retain his membership of the House of Commons once he had been convicted. To say the least, he needed
a few months respite to take breath and recover his health.
On Christmas Eve he evaded the watch on his house and slipped
away to France. When his case was called at King's Bench on
21 February, Lord Mansfield entered judgment on him in
his absence, and in the following November he was formally
declared an outlaw. He had been expelled from the House
of Commons one month before Mansfield entered judgment
against him for the alleged publication of Number Forty-five.
Politics had not merely been confused with law. They had
forestalled it. Thus was completed, observed *The Annual Register*,
rather prematurely, 'the ruin of that unfortunate gentleman'.

What is the meaning of the 'Wilkes and Liberty' episode of
1763? Who were the people who took up the cry, and what, if
anything, did they mean by it? The Londoners who found a
hero in Wilkes were a very mixed crowd indeed. There can be
no question of a 'working-class' following in the modern sense
of that term, or of 'the people' now entering politics as a distinctive or conscious force. For one thing, London was in no
sense a typical industrial centre. New industries sprang up there,
but with the improvement of communications and the development of a large home market for industrial products they tended
to move rapidly away to areas where coal and iron, water-
power and labour, were cheaper and more readily accessible.
London was rather the home of small businesses, and the

typical Londoner was not a proletarian but a craftsman, a shopkeeper, a retailer, or an employee in some form of distributive activities. The few large businesses which employed wage-paid labour on an extensive scale were engaged in brewing, ship-building, and silk-weaving. The skilled workman was employed rather in the building trades, shoe-making, cabinet-making, clock-and-watch making, tailoring, printing, and baking. Few London businesses were affected by power-driven machinery even at the end of the century. There was, however, a large and often unruly water-side population, fostered by the enormous growth of the port of London during the Seven Years' War. The spearhead of the Wilkite mobs was composed not of the mill, mine, and factory workers who were to supply the armies of Peterloo and the Chartist demonstrations of the following century, but of riverside roughs, handloom weavers from Spitalfields, porters, carters, sedan-chairmen, link-boys, the riff-raff of dubious occupations or none whose faces peep out of odd corners of Hogarth's *Gin Lane* and *Beer Street*. These were the 'mobility', or in Burke's ill-conditioned phrase, 'the swinish multitude'. But Wilkes had also at his back, though not on the streets, a large number of 'the middling sort' of people; people who would never have thought of joining a street-mob; men of commercial standing, sometimes well-to-do, a kind of subaltern rank to the monied interest of the great finance corporations; the people whom Alderman Beckford once called 'a good-natured, well-intentioned, very sensible people who know better perhaps than any other nation under the sun whether they are well-governed or not'.

The recession which began to show itself in 1763 when unemployment followed upon a boom artificially stimulated by the war, the dislocation of trade with the new world, consequent upon Grenville's fiscal policy, rapidly showed themselves in the industrial world of the artisan. The water-side workers of London, some of the toughest elements in the population, were increasingly idle and ready for mischief. The Spitalfields silk-weavers, demanding in vain a revised price-list for their products, were on the streets in rowdy demonstrations in October 1763. There was, as always in that century, a good deal of sheer horse-play in the crowds that turned out whenever rumour told of 'a little 'un' putting up his fists against a 'big 'un'. This is precisely the figure that John Wilkes wished to cut in this, the first of his numerous encounters with King, Lords, and Commons, with his avowed concern with the liberties not only of peers and gentlemen 'but, what touches me more sensibly, that of the middling and inferior set of people', and his impudent nose-thumbing of His Majesty's Secretaries of State in Great George Street. It would be a mistake to imagine, however, that the Wilkites disturbances were nothing more than a chance outbreak of rowdyism on the part of drunken porters and wharfingers. It required something more than sporting instincts inflamed by alcohol to transform a blackguardly journalist with a horrific squint and a tongue like a rattlesnake into a popular leader. Behind the London mob, in town and township in provincial England, and along the Atlantic seaboard of North America, men of very diverse social status and experience were stirred to contribute a distant cheering, inspired by a vague consciousness that someone, somewhere, was at last putting a pin into the pretensions of the old monopolists of political power and private profit. 'Wilkes and Liberty!' expressed something more ubiquitous than concern for the personal fate of John Wilkes, and something far less coherent than concern with a philosophy of freedom. Increasing literacy, economic discontent, an awakening consciousness of executive ineptitude and parliamentary tyranny, these forces—together with the example of resistance on the part of Englishmen in America—were to ensure the increasing presence of popular politics in the landscape of eighteenth-century England in the years which intervened between the foundation of the Wilkite Society or the Supporters of the Bill of Rights in 1769 and the impact of the French Revolution in the London Corresponding Society in 1792. Thus, after the barren years of Noodle, politics were to concern themselves once more with what the late Sir Lewis Namier in his elegant old-fashioned way called Flapdoodle.

CHAPTER 7

George Grenville and the Americans

BUTE HAD sowed the whirlwind. George Grenville reaped the storm. With the unimaginative coolness of a routine lawyer and man of business, Grenville knew that once the Earl of Bute had retired 'behind the curtain' and John Wilkes was either in jail or in exile, the King must win. He told Charles Yorke, who thought 'the clamour of the people' must prevail upon Grenville to broaden the basis of his Administration by 'taking in aids from the opposition', that the uproar was not for any change of ministers, certainly not for the Duke of Newcastle, or even for Mr Pitt, but for Pratt[1] and Wilkes. No government whatever could be expected to suffer Wilkes's libellous onslaught without retaliation, and retaliation always gets a government a bad name, like Voltaire's *animal* which is labelled '*méchant*' simply because *quand on le bat, il se défend*. Most people, once he was out of sight, would probably have agreed with Dr Johnson that Wilkes was 'an abusive scoundrel' best fitted for the horse-trough, or with young Jeremy Bentham who, on hearing his idol, Lord Mansfield, enter judgment against the absentee, wrote to his father in February 1764: 'Wilkes was an object of perfect abhorrence to me, and I abhorred him for his opposition to the King.' The man's profligate private life did ill service to his cause in an age that was turning from Walpole to Wesley. However absurd the spectacle of the English people in one of their periodic fits of moral indignation, Wilkes was no more able to laugh away the reviving moralism of the early years of George III than Oscar Wilde could evade the moralistic hangover from the reign of Queen Victoria. Even Mr Pitt, who had enjoyed Wilkes's bawdy in private, now withdrew his coat-tails from contact with the lecher in public. 'He did not

[1] Mr Justice Pratt, later Lord Camden.

deserve to be ranked among the human species . . . the blasphemer of his God and the libeller of the King.'

Clinging to the hand of his 'd. friend' behind the curtain, the King nevertheless admitted that George Grenville, Bute's successor at the Treasury, was a man of the utmost probity and a most competent man of business. No-one could have approved more enthusiastically than George III of Grenville's unbending respect for the dignity and privileges of the House of Commons. He could have asked for no better servant in the tasks of vindicating royal and parliamentary honour against scoundrels like John Wilkes on the one hand and stiff-necked Americans on the other. The trouble with Grenville was rather his manners, his touchy dignity and self-importance, his pedantic formalism, his clerkly devotion to the details of profit-and-loss accounts. 'That gentleman's opinions,' the King came to think, 'are seldom formed from any other motives than such as may be expected to originate in the mind of a clerk in a counting-house.' With these opinions, imparted in a fussy manner and with legalistic pedantry, he earned the royal detestation as England's prize bore. 'When he has wearied me for two hours,' the King complained, 'he looks at his watch to see if he may not tire me for one hour more.' In the end he declared that he would rather see the Devil in his Closet than George Grenville.

Grenville's defects were at any rate the defects that go with supreme respectability. On the other hand, the defects of his colleagues might have been specially designed to damn the prospects of a Prince who wished to identify his government with the aims of virtue and religion. True, Henry Fox, now Lord Holland, had withdrawn to the House of Lords, but he still retained the paymastership. It was not until the summer of 1765 that the best-hated political buccaneer of his age took himself off to the bleak and ugly mansion he had built for himself on the North Foreland, there to preside as the idolatrous and idolized father of the spoilt, black-headed lad, Charles James Fox, who was to grow up into the best-loved political buccaneer in history. 'Hell-Fire Francis' Dashwood had also withdrawn to the Upper House, as Lord le Despenser. Another member of the Hell-Fire fraternity joined the Administration in the person of John Montagu, 4th Earl of Sandwich, known to his friends as 'Jemmy Twitcher' after 'peaching' on a third member of the fraternity over *The Essay on Woman*. This cold-hearted debauchee was a very able administrator, and now became Secretary of State for the Northern Department. His colleague at the Southern Department, Lord Egremont, was steadily 'digging his grave with his teeth'. Such was the miscellaneous collection of rakes, pedants and dullards which secured the expulsion of John Wilkes from the House of Commons and the imposition of a Stamp Tax on the American colonists. It came to an end when in 1765 it omitted the Dowager-Princess of Wales from the Regency Bill drawn up at the time of the King's first serious bout of the malady that was to haunt his later years, thereby incurring the royal displeasure to such a degree that His Majesty accepted the services of the Marquess of Rockingham, along with the Dukes of Grafton, Newcastle and Portland. *Faute de mieux*, 'the Old Corps' were back again.

And yet Grenville's Ministry, for all its queerly assorted components, was in most respects the strongest, the most closely knit, and the ablest that served the King in the first ten troubled years of his reign. Its strength rested greatly upon the personal abilities of Grenville himself. The promoter of the ill-starred Stamp Act was to go down to history under a cloud of Whiggish, and priggish, denigration; a cloud that was to become a positive mushroom on the other side of the Atlantic. For one thing, he was unlucky enough to incur the venomous hatred of that most influential shaper of historical reputations, Horace Walpole. For Grenville had secured the dismissal from his Council of Walpole's beloved cousin, General Conway, for voting on the wrong side in the Wilkes expulsion affair. There had also been a horrid moment when the celebrated man-of-letters had trembled for his own sinecure at the same malign hand.

And yet, when he came to write his *Memoirs*, Horace Walpole paid tribute to Grenville's great authority in the Commons on account of his 'spirit, knowledge, and gravity of character'. Gravity, in the sense of 'gravitas', was his strongest point. The office of Prime Minister was already beginning to take shape in something like its modern form, and Lord Bristol once described Grenville as 'the phantom of a Prime Minister'. He intended to be more than a phantom. His suspicious nature led him to resent any rivalry to his own predominance as the King's first servant, especially where the control of patronage was concerned. He rather naturally thought: 'If it is his Majesty's pleasure to place me at the head of the Treasury, it is impossible to suppose that he means to withhold from me any part of his confidence.' After the King's attempts to come to terms with Pitt in both 1763 and 1765, he considered that some display of royal confidence was due to him, in order to correct the impression that his master had wished to be rid of him. It was, at least in part, his determination to assert his authority in the matter of appointments that finally drove the King to dispense with him. Grenville's Ministry, in fact, was remarkable among the loosely knit administrations of these years for the efforts made by its members, and more especially by its head, to maintain internal coherence *vis-à-vis* the King. It is true that its members were not precisely a happy family, more especially after the adherence of the Bedfords, but there was still some truth in Grenville's assurance, after his dismissal, that 'union was their crime, not division'.

Undistinguished in the field where philosophy may adorn workaday talents with an imaginative concern for the larger purposes of human life, devoid of those graces which capture the imagination and warm the heart of historic memory, indifferent alike to the splendours and the miseries of our common humanity, George Grenville stares at us down the corridor of time with the frigid features of a watchful bank manager or a well-trained attorney. They are the features which his nephew, the younger Pitt, was to inherit from the stubborn Grenville ancestry; but whereas in the nephew both the features and the temperament of the Grenvilles were crossed with the fiery genius of his father, in his uncle, George Grenville, they were unlighted by any other passion than the small, concentrated force of the precision. Grenville loved 'business' for its detail, its files, and its ledgers, its fine devices. 'He took public business not as a duty which was his to fulfil, but as a pleasure he was to enjoy.' Personally, he lived on his investments and saved his stipend, and he carried his personal financial habits into the conduct of public affairs. He hated red ink, debit accounts,

extravagance in all its forms. It was once said of him that he
preferred 'a national saving of two inches of candle' to all the
glorious victories of his celebrated brother-in-law. It was these
characteristics of thrift and frugality that earned him the scorn
of Pitt, a scorn which Grenville retorted by acid references to
the great war minister's notorious indifference to finance. As a
stickler for forms and the finer points of distinction, his character has been handed down to us by Edmund Burke, another
financial rake-hell. The author of the Stamp Act, wrote Burke,
was apt 'to think the substance of business not to be much more
important than the forms in which it is conducted'.[1] It was
the supreme tragedy of British history in the eighteenth century
that this man set himself, in the winter of 1765, to raise a
revenue in America, mainly by the application of red tape and
sealing-wax.

The American colonies at this time consisted of some two
and a half million people, white and black, dwelling in thirteen
diversely organized communities on the eastern fringe of the
North American continent. The whites were of overwhelm-
ingly British descent. Their forefathers had sailed westward
with the passion for liberty in their hearts, a passion mighty
enough to inspire them to fight the savage and the wilderness,
to tame the wild and set up their cherished landmarks from
the edge of the Atlantic to the Great Lakes and the Alleghany
Mountains. The course of this perilous enterprise had produced
a hardy, brave and vigorous race of men, impatient of rule
and increasingly critical of the bad old Europe from which
they sprang. They were, in all essential respects, seventeenth-
century Englishmen who had made good, and readily open to
the persuasion that old England had gone wrong. As Edmund
Burke put it, with little exaggeration, their religion was 'a
refinement on the principle of resistance . . . the dissidence of
dissent, and the protestantism of the Protestant religion', while
their politics were the politics of freedom. 'They augur mis-
government at a distance, and snuff the approach of tyranny
in every tainted breeze.' In fact, they wanted to be left alone.

Of course, they wanted the impossible. They could not be
left alone; not, at least, until they should submit to some

[1] Speech on American Taxation, 1774.

scheme of common defence and regulation. The colonies had grown from small settlements founded by the initiative of private companies, and for a long time they lived under a great diversity of organization. After the Revolution of 1688, and during the more settled years that followed, the mother country was able to give more attention to her offspring, and by 1760 proprietary colonies living under royal charters had largely given place to crown colonies, living under royal governments. By 1763, eight of the twelve continental communities were royal, only Pennsylvania and Maryland remaining proprietary, only Rhode Island and Connecticut remaining chartered colonies with elected governors. All this was part of a conscious policy of asserting British sovereign authority throughout the King's dominions, a phase of nascent imperialism. The sovereign authority of the Parliament at Westminster had been undergoing a process of widening and deepening for many years. The Parliament at Westminster had extended its legislative authority over Scotland by the act of Union in 1707, and over Ireland by the Declaratory Act of 1719. Since 1688 it had increasingly taken over from the Crown the regulation of the Church, and at the same time it had begun to assume responsibility for the regulation of the 'plantations' or colonies. As early as 1724, the Solicitor-General had issued a decision that the colonial subjects of the Crown could be taxed only by their own representatives or by the British Parliament. The fact that Parliament did not choose to exercise this right directly until 1764 only served to increase the sense of shock which was felt in the colonies at the passing of the Stamp Act. The notion that George Grenville lost the American colonies because, as someone said, he 'read the colonial dispatches', displays a lamentable ignorance of British imperial policy over half a century and more. Grenville's action was no bolt from the blue. Rather it was an injudicious decision taken after the exercise of much patience and deliberation. It was injudicious in its form, not in its principle. The Stamp Act was a justifiable act of sovereign authority carried through by an impeccable lawyer. But as Burke said, the politic question should have been, 'not what a lawyer tells me I *may* do; but what humanity, reason and justice tell me I ought to do'. Grenville had brought sovereign power to the test of action among a people for whom the last word in political wisdom lay with John Locke, the arch-exponent of 'limited government'. And again, Burke put the issue: 'If that sovereignty and their freedom cannot be reconciled, which will they take? They will cast your sovereignty in your face. Nobody will be argued into slavery.'

Throughout the great debate which was now opening upon the world, the stubborn doctrine of parliamentary sovereignty was to confound the best and most generous minds of the age at grips with the problem of organic growth. The paradox of 'The American Question' was the unapprehended conflict between fact and theory which lies at the back of all revolutions. If the historic communities of the American continent were to remain under the sovereign sway of the mother-land, some appropriate mode of imperial organization had to be devised for their containment, for the conciliation of conflicting claims and the promotion of purposes common to the whole Empire. And yet, if constitutional theory were to be brought into conformity with the facts of historic evolution there was a grave danger that the cold hand of legalism might freeze the blood of brotherly communication. It was not an age of brave and vigorous thinking. Rather it was an age of legalistic formalism, on both sides of the Atlantic, and perhaps in the colonies even more than in England. The very fact that the colonies were populated by men whose minds had stopped thinking with Locke, if not with Edward Coke and the lawyers of the seventeenth century, ensured that any debate on a legalistic issue would rapidly wax hot with the passions of the Stuart era. Embers which had grown cold at Westminster were still live coals at Boston and New York. More than this, the English mind had moved on from the largely medieval notions of Coke and Locke, with their belief in the essentially limited nature of government. Not only in practice, but in theory also, England had entered upon the age of limitless secular authority. Of course, philosophers were still prepared to pay lip-service to 'indefeasible natural rights' and the equally 'natural' limits of governmental authority. Whigs of the great tradition like Pitt and Camden, and even Junius (who begged John Wilkes to remember the distinction between a supreme and an arbitrary legislature), were still prepared to maintain that there was a law above parliaments. But the rising tide was not with them. Rather it was with young Jeremy Bentham who, before the American revolution could settle anything, had put himself— and, in consequence, English liberal jurisprudence for a century to come—on the side of that limitless and indivisible sovereignty with which Thomas Hobbes had prematurely invested Leviathan a generation before John Locke put pen to paper. Meanwhile, an omnicompetent Parliament at Westminster had been acting upon the full doctrine without apology or dismay for more than half a century. And when, in 1766, the Rockingham Whigs repealed the Stamp Act, they were to accompany the repeal (to the applause of Burke himself) with an Act declaratory of the British Parliament's sovereign right to tax the colonies. What Burke and his friends wanted to say in 1766 was not that the Parliament at Westminster could not tax the colonies, but that it should not. Whether the Declaratory Act was calculated to soothe the susceptibilities of a people made unhappy by legislative irritation is even more doubtful than the pacificatory effect on a Stuart parliament of James I's testy observation that his prerogative was no fit subject for the tongue of a lawyer.

The American colonists had suffered little if any real oppression from the rule of the British Crown and Parliament, but they had grounds for complaint that their interests were subjected in many particulars to those of the English merchants trading in the New World. Under the old Colonial System, which had been in force since the time of the Navigation Acts of 1651 and 1660, the monopoly of colonial trade in the interests of British merchants and manufacturers was held to be the *raison d'être* of the Empire. Plantations or colonies were conceived as ministering unto the wealth and strength of the mother country by providing her with raw materials and by consuming her manufactures. Such commodities as sugar, tobacco, rice, molasses, cotton, indigo, naval stores, and furs were 'enumerated' as importable exclusively to the United Kingdom, while by the Staple Act of 1663 almost all goods from European countries were exportable to the colonies only by re-shipment from British ports. By 1760, the value of British exports and re-exports to the American colonies was computed at two million pounds per annum, and British merchants carried some four million pounds' worth of American debts on their books. Plainly, British businessmen were intimately concerned in the wise management of the government's commercial policy. They could ill afford to see colonial prosperity and goodwill upset by political incompetence on the part of His Majesty's ministers.

The colonists themselves were by no means the losers by this apparently one-sided arrangement. The same legislation which gave British merchants the monopoly of trade assured to the colonial producers a virtual monopoly of protected markets within the British dominions for their goods. Moreover, the Acts of Trade were laxly administered, exceptions to 'enumerations' were sometimes made by law.[1] And in any case the whole complex system left many doors open to extensive and highly profitable smuggling, more especially during the long years when Sir Robert Walpole firmly winked both eyes at colonial liberties. It was, indeed, as much George Grenville's lawyer-like endeavours to stop up the innumerable breathing-holes enjoyed by the colonial merchants as his formal legislation to raise a revenue in America that brought about the hostility of the 'sixties. As for the colonial manufacturers, they suffered little from the prohibitions placed upon industry in the New World by the British Parliament. Hats, woollens, hardware, all could be imported from England more cheaply than they could be manufactured in America, and Parliament made no attempt to stop the manufacture of shoes, soap, candles, and coaches, all of which flourished in New England. Even the Act of 1750 prohibiting slitting-mills was not greatly resented at the time, although ironmasters were seriously affected by the 'enumeration' of iron in 1767. What really injured American internal economy was rather the prohibition of paper money. The shortage of a circulating medium and the threat of more and higher taxes, rather than industrial prohibitions, were the worst irritants upon radical feelings in America. At the same time, however, the very frequency of inoperative or harm-

[1] For example, in 1730, the Carolina rice-growers were permitted to export their 'enumerated' product to southern Europe.

9. Heveningham Hall

10. Ickworth House

11. The Cognoscenti, young aristocrats on the Grand Tour

less economic legislation passed by the British Parliament undoubtedly served to injure colonial *amour-propre*. There was
always a plenitude of psychological affronts to the colonists,
who steadily came to see themselves as a very junior partner in
every enterprise contributing to imperial prosperity.

It cannot be said that the Americans were driven into rebellion by intolerable economic oppression. The rebellion was
brought about by an irresistible desire for self-determination on
the part of their governing class. The colonies had conducted
a war of attrition against the royal prerogative for several
generations, a campaign which had been made easier by the
mutual jealousies of King and Parliament in the sphere of
imperial control. 'Salutary neglect' on the part of Walpole
and Newcastle had contributed much to the growth of self-
reliance and love of liberty in the colonies, while the development of representative institutions (every colony had an elective
assembly by 1760) provided a focus for concerted resistance
to the royal authority exercised by Crown-appointed Governors
and Councils. The pattern of government which now prevailed
in the colonies, just because it was oligarchic rather than
democratic, was eminently suited for the conduct of such
resistance. The legislatures had persistently denied to the royal
Governors either a Civil List or the uninhibited control of
patronage, so that the executive lacked nearly all the normal
eighteenth-century means of exercising a controlling influence.
The colonial assemblies were as jealous of the power of the
purse as had been the English House of Commons in its contest
with the Stuart Kings. Nor was this jealousy surprising, since
the Governors were often impoverished English gentlemen
foisted on the colonies for 'outdoor relief', nonentities, rakes,
bankrupts, and discarded courtiers. 'Whenever we find ourselves encumbered with a needy Court-Dangler . . .' wrote one
English critic of the system, 'we kick him into an American
Government.' The colonial legislatures had extended their
authority to the initiation of laws and the appropriation of
finance, and when George Grenville began to assert parliamentary authority in America it must have seemed that the
victory achieved over the royal prerogative had now to be won
all over again at the expense of the British House of Commons.

King Log had been replaced by King Stork. The King had been a parent, always remote, sometimes stern, but genuinely concerned with the prosperity and contentment of his subjects overseas. The House of Commons was a jealous and malevolent elder brother. Long before open hostilities broke out, a colonist could avow: 'I would much more willingly see my Property arbitrarily disposed of by a Privy Seal than extorted from me by the unwarrantable Power of a Parliament whose Members would naturally endeavour to lessen their Burthens.'

The British government certainly had good reason to ask the colonies to contribute to the cost of their defence after the Seven Years' War which, it was argued, had been fought on behalf of the whole Empire. The American colonists were inclined to maintain that Britain had dragged her colonies into a war of imperial aggrandizement for her own profit. Having burdened herself with debt by her own extravagance and ambition, they thought, she had no right to demand that the colonists should help to foot the bill. As a matter of fact the Americans were never asked directly to contribute towards the lessening of the British National Debt but only to assist in the cost of maintaining an army of 10,000 men in North America against the resurgence of French power and the depredations of the Indians. These were both very real dangers. The peace terms of 1763 had left France in a position to recover for a war of revenge, if not of reconquest. Pitt had predicted that another war would be necessary to curb her power within ten years. Choiseul predicted that France would be ready for revenge in half that time. The British government realized that it was useless to rely upon the spontaneous energies of the colonists. The recent war had showed them to be indifferent to everything but their own immediate and local interests. Now that the French menace had been removed, their co-operation was likely to prove more illusory than ever. When at the Peace of 1763 the British government had decided to take Canada and leave the valuable island of Guadeloupe to the French—a policy primarily determined by considerations of colonial security—Vergennes had prophesied that 'they will ere long repent the removal of the only check that kept their colonies in awe'. For fifty years the French had been predicting that if the French left Canada the

English North American colonies would become independent.

As for the Indians, the English colonists on the spot professed themselves to be less worried than the government at far-away Westminster. They had been fighting the red-man on and off for generations and had acquired all the arts of cruelty and duplicity in robbing him of his land and avenging themselves for his savage acts of reprisal. They greeted the Peace Treaty of 1763 as a signal for a fresh epoch of westward expansion, unhampered by the French. At once, however, they were to be reminded that the path of westward expansion was still the war-path. The Pontiac rising of 1763 made it clear that the Indians, with or without French instigation, were yet capable of barring the white man's westward course with blood and fire. It was to deal with this situation that the British government issued a Royal Proclamation in that year, forbidding the purchase or settlement of land beyond the Alleghanies.[1] The Proclamation was not intended to lay down a final boundary-line for British expansion. It was a hurried expedient to check the frightful feuds perpetually raised by rugged individualism on the frontiers of the wilderness. In future, the vast *ci-devant* Indian empire of the French was to be under direct British control, unhampered by colonial self-government, regardless of frontiers previously assigned to the colonists and of grants of land already made to individuals. In fact, as the colonists saw it, the natural inheritors of the west were to be confined within a ring-fence east of the mountains. Their feelings of angry frustration were scarcely mollified by their realization that it was part of Great Britain's intention to exclude them from the fur-trade of the Ohio Valley in the interests of the monopoly of the Hudson's Bay Company and to put a stop to the evasive action of colonial debtors who might prefer the western wilderness to the long arm of the law. The land speculators of Pennsylvania and Virginia—such families as the Washingtons—took it particularly hard.

It was into this situation, already fraught with jealousy and mistrust, that George Grenville intruded his policy of raising a revenue in America. He had behind him the full force of English opinion that the colonists had for long enough evaded

[1] See *Sources and Documents of American History*, ed. S. E. Morison ,pp. 1–4.

their share of the burden of imperial defence, and that it was
high time the British taxpayer should be afforded some relief.
The financial facts were all on Grenville's side. The National
Debt stood at £140,000,000 in 1763. The public debt weighed
to the extent of £18 per head per annum on Englishmen and
only 18s. per head per annum on the colonists.[1] After the
Chancellorship of Hell-Fire Francis Dashwood, a man of business was sorely needed at the Exchequer, and Grenville was
properly concerned to initiate a policy of retrenchment and a
more equitable distribution of burdens. Within the financial
perspectives of that age, when the imposition of an excise on
cider could produce the threat of parliamentary revolt among
the lords and gentlemen of the 'cider-country', and an addi-
tional ha'penny on a pint of porter could raise roars of protest
from tinkers, tailors, and cobblers, the English regarded themselves as the most grossly over-taxed people in the world. The
country gentlemen believed themselves to be shockingly exploited by a war-time Land Tax of 4s. in the pound for the
prosecution of a war which chiefly benefited the merchants,
planters, nabobs, and Americans. Neither George Grenville, nor
Lord North, would ever need to resort to bribery in order
to recruit parliamentary majorities for a policy of taxing the
American colonies. The sound of American taxation was sweet
music to their ears. All that Grenville had to do was to decide
upon ways and means.

Grenville's Stamp Act, which was designed to raise a revenue
by a straightforward process of taxation within the colonies,
was only the culmination of a larger programme of economical
reform. Grenville, the cheeseparing economist, proceeded from
the first principle of efficient collection of existing duties.
'Salutary neglect' came to an abrupt end. The gaping holes in
the mercantilist fabric were plugged by a number of measures
to stop smuggling. When he took over the management of the
revenue, it was reckoned that it cost £8,000 to collect £2,000
worth of customs duties in American ports. For years, revenue
officers had been feathering their own nests, while nearly three-
quarters of a million pounds' worth of merchandise was
smuggled in and out of North America per annum. Grenville

[1] These are Lord North's figures.

undertook to save £130,000 by economical and administrative reform during his Chancellorship. It was to be done, so far as America was concerned, by tying up the colonial merchants in a mesh of red-tape, bonds, dockets, warrants, and affidavits, and by increasing the powers of the hated Admiralty courts which dealt with evasion. Thus Grenville gave to the collection of revenue 'the air of hostile combination', and the Americans regarded the whole policy as designed to enhance the monopoly enjoyed by British merchants. In 1764 Grenville proceeded from 'improved collection' to the imposition of fresh duties. Higher imposts were levied upon imported French lawns and cambrics, and more commodities than ever were included in the category of 'enumerated' articles. The Molasses Act of 1733, which had imposed a duty of sixpence per gallon on foreign molasses, was due to expire at the end of 1763, and Grenville replaced it with a Sugar Act reducing the duty to threepence. On the face of it, the Sugar Act might appear, from the American angle, to be an improvement upon the Molasses Act, but in fact it was nothing of the sort, for whereas the Molasses Act had been practically nullified by wholesale smuggling during the period of 'salutary neglect', the Sugar Act was accompanied by an evident intention to enforce it. The Americans wanted either free trade or unimpeded smuggling. Grenville gave them a high duty and an improved customs service.

The Sugar Act of 1764, unlike the Molasses Act of 1733, was a revenue act. It marked a departure from the avowedly traditional mercantilist legislation of the British Parliament, which limited itself to the purposes of regulating colonial trade. John Dickinson (the Pennsylvanian Farmer of the celebrated *Letters*) called it 'the first comet of this kind that glared over these colonies since their existence'. Yet it was passed easily and with little constitutional comment, by a House of Commons hungry for revenue and resentful of colonial intransigence during the Seven Years' War; while the colonists themselves, with a few notable exceptions, seem to have been distracted from the constitutional principle by their overriding concern with the 'sinister interests' which had inspired it. They regarded it as a triumph for their old enemies, the planters of the British West

Indies, the latest trick played by the powerful 'Sugar-lobby' at Westminster, which would sacrifice the happiness and posterity of the Empire to the greed of a 'few dirty Specks, the Sugar Islands'. This feeling was particularly strong among the merchants and rum-distillers of New England, whose prosperity depended upon the supply of cheap molasses from the French, Dutch, and Spanish islands of the Caribbean. They were now to be compelled to buy the higher-priced molasses of the British islands in order to put money into the bulging pockets of absentee planters who spent a large proportion of their time and fortunes in corrupting the House of Commons in the interests of their monopoly. Things had been tolerable as long as North American merchants and producers had been able to nullify British legislation by smuggling. In future, strict enforcement of the West Indian monopoly bade fair to ruin northern American trade and industry for the benefit of a corrupt gang of nabobs and political wire-pullers. The fact that the West Indian 'Sugar-lobby' was insufficiently powerful at Westminster to do all this without the willing initiative of George Grenville's Ministry made no difference to the intensity of North American feelings on the subject.

The Sugar Act made it certain that Grenville's next move in the interests of British finance would meet with a storm of disapproval. That he hit upon the device of a Stamp Act made certainty doubly sure. The Stamp Act itself was no novel expedient, either in form or principle. Englishmen themselves had been paying a duty on stamped paper for long enough. It was the regular source of more than £100,000 for the national Exchequer. Nor was the idea of introducing the levy into the colonies a brain-child of George Grenville. It had been proposed in Pennsylvania itself as early as 1739, and had been discussed by the Treasury Board in 1754 and 1757. Grenville seems to have been influenced in the matter by a Scot, one Henry McCulloch, who had also advised him in the policy of the Sugar Act. Anyway, the Stamp Act had a number of obvious attractions to a Chancellor of the Exchequer. It was a simple tax to collect, for the onus of buying stamps lay upon the citizen who wished to give validity to his transactions. It took a toll upon litigation, a luxury in which Americans indulged at the slightest provocation.[1] It would fall especially upon the literate classes, and the Americans were then, as now, profligate consumers of newsprint. In England, the upper and middle classes were used to taxing themselves, and accepted the privilege of footing the national bills of expenditure. Unfortunately for George Grenville, the impact of his cherished scheme was greatest upon the most vociferous classes of colonial society, the lawyers, newspaper-men, merchants,and publicans.

In itself, the Stamp Duty was not unreasonable. Seen by the literate, legalistic, argumentative classes of colonial society it was one more, and the most odious 'badge of slavery'. It brought to a head long-standing and widespread resentment against a whole policy—the policy of imperial reconstruction. It was like the policy by which Philip II raised the Revolt of the Netherlands and that by which Laud and Strafford had once awakened the worst suspicions of the propertied and literate classes in England. It was the sign and symptom of an intention to govern a people who had for long been left very much to their own devices, a people moreover who never had—and never have—submitted readily to government. The American revolt was the precipitation of the inherent anarchism of the New World. The most dangerous moment, the true flashpoint of revolution, is the moment when an ancient government decides to govern a young people. It is the crisis-hour of statesmanship. By a sorry concatenation of circumstances, England at that hour was peculiarly short of that commodity.

[1] It is noteworthy that almost as many copies of Blackstone's *Commentaries* were sold in the colonies as in Great Britain itself.

CHAPTER 8

The Stainless Friends

WHEN THE Marquess of Rockingham replaced George Grenville at the Treasury in July 1765, the issue which was to divide
the first British Empire was already joined. Patrick Henry and
his friends had passed the famous Virginia Resolves through
the House of Burgesses in scenes which resembled, in both tone
and language, those of Sir John Eliot's famous Three Resolutions in the House of Commons in 1629. But it was not legislative, or popular, resolves, here or in America, that brought
about the replacement of Grenville. The Ministry died because
the King found it intolerable, and for no other reason. In the
summer of 1765, the Marquess of Rockingham came in with a
Ministry of old and young Whigs of the 'great tradition', the
King having failed to bring in Mr Pitt, now the Earl of
Chatham, who was living down in Somerset, often ill, always
weary, and resolved to be (as he put it) 'a man standing single'
and attached to no party. Pitt had been disgusted by the slight
resistance to the Stamp Act, and by the failure of the opposition
to secure a resolution condemning General Warrants. He had
become the possessor of the estate of Burton Pynsent in Somerset
at the hands of Sir William Pynsent, an old-fashioned Whig
gentleman who was reviving a fashion among rich men in the
last period of the Roman Republic to seek posthumous honour
by leaving legacies to eminent patriots who deserved well of
their country. Sir William was moved by the great war leader's
stubborn opposition to the Peace of Paris. Twenty years earlier,
Sarah, Duchess of Marlborough, had left him £10,000, along
with valuable reversionary rights in appreciation of his patriot
opposition to Sir Robert Walpole. So, while his brother-in-law
Grenville planted the seeds of discord in the New World won
by the Great Commoner's brilliant efforts, Pitt went on plant-

ing trees in martial rows about the beloved home which was to make him for the first time an English country gentleman. He hoped, he said, 'to pass not a little of the rest of my days' in the happy seclusion of Burton Pynsent, 'a Somersetshire bystander'.

While it is never possible to affirm positively that the course of history was fatally determined at some specific point in time by the occurrence, or the non-occurrence, of some specific event, it is inconceivable that an Administration headed by William Pitt would have lost the hearts of both the American colonists and the electorate of Middlesex, with all the sorry consequences for the harmonious development of the English-speaking world. At no time in the reign of George III was a strong, united, and able Administration more desirable than at that moment, when the Americans were magnifying irritations into anger, and when John Wilkes was squaring up to the task of tempting the governors of his country to make fools of themselves afresh. The minds and hearts of the people, here and in North America, would always be with Pitt while Pitt remained true to himself and his visions of imperial destiny. It required no more than some unequivocal sign that government was in strong, clean and popular hands to win all, and more than all, that had yet been lost, for the King's just authority in the affairs of his subjects, at home and overseas. The opportunity was lost in that summer of 1765. The short-lived Rockingham Administration, the sorrows of the Duke of Grafton, and the long agony of Lord North were yet to prove that much else than the hearts and minds of the people still held sovereign authority in England.

It was plain from the beginning that the Rockingham Ministry represented no party triumph over the King. Not only was it composed of disparate elements; even its truly Whiggish core was infirm. True, the Marquess had set on foot the reconstruction of a principled and disciplined Whig party by bringing together Newcastle and the younger men under his banner, and in future years, his private secretary, Edmund Burke, was to embroider upon the slender claims of this Ministry to have re-founded the Whig tradition in terms of his own noble definition of party. As a classic example of hindsight, 'A Short Account of a Late Short Administration' is rivalled only by his own 'Thoughts on the Causes of the Present Discontents'. At the time, during the thirteen months of the first Rockingham Administration, 'the knot of stainless friends' were full of doubts, divisions, and misgivings, both on account of the alien elements of the King's old servants in their midst and the unresolved tensions within their own ranks. Nor did the King ever think of the first Rockingham Ministry as more than a rather unpleasant interlude until he could make other and better arrangements.

The Marquess and his following liked to call themselves 'a knot of stainless friends'. They believed themselves to be the only honest men in English politics. They claimed to be consistent in both principle and policy; they constantly avowed their superiority to the 'dirty arts' of placemen, favourites, and political jobbers; and they were never tired of asserting their exclusive claim to represent the great Whig traditions of liberty and constitutional government. So often and so earnestly did they utter these professions that they succeeded in imposing their peculiar myth on a long line of distinguished historians. But there has for a long time been abroad a suspicion that the gentlemen did protest too much, and at the present time the Rockinghams are in danger of suffering the fate that overtook Aristides the Just. More than a hundred years ago Coleridge was wont to point out the violence of the operation of 'the moral law of polarity', so that 'when the maximum of one tendency has been attained, there is no gradual decrease, but a direct transition to its minimum, till the opposite tendency has attained its maximum . . .'[1] This has now happened to the reputation of the Rockingham Whigs. Their purity has been impeached by the progressive revelation of the financial affairs of Edmund Burke, their greatest prophet and propagandist. And even if the Marquess himself remains more stainless than his servants, anyway—as Becky Sharp observed—it is easy to be good on £5,000 a year, which represents a very small fraction of the income of Charles Watson-Wentworth. As for consistency of principle, we are told that the Marquess was consistent only in his resistance to the power and influence of Lord Bute and in his opposition to the conduct and the measures of George Grenville. Finally, the claim of the Rockingham Whigs to the

[1] *Table Talk*, 25 April 1832.

apostolic succession of Revolution Whiggery has become something more suitable for apology than for boastfulness, involving, it seems, the intention to enthrone King Rockingham in place of King George. In all this change of 'climate' as regards the historical reputation of the group of 'stainless friends', the central element is the dislodgement of Edmund Burke from his pedestal as the great and good prophet of a resuscitated constitutionalism, and his relegation to the limbo which properly awaits political myth-makers of malignant imagination. And yet, when all has been said in denigration of the over-righteous Rockinghams, the fact remains that they succeeded in imposing their peculiar myth, partly by historical hindsight, and partly by the ineluctable fact that after the failure of George III's policy in the age of Lord North they were to prove the first reforming ministry of the reign. Burke's Economical Reform Act of 1782, and the emergence of Charles James Fox from their ranks as the great tribune of liberty in the age of the French Revolution, set the seal of positive achievement on their pretensions in the age of revolution in America. Justice to the Rockinghams requires the historian to remember that what men believe, rightly or wrongly, is of no less importance than what the historian may think of their motives, and no less formative in the making of history.

Charles Watson-Wentworth, 2nd Marquess of Rockingham, was at this time a lean, attenuated, somewhat shadowy young man of thirty-five. He had inherited his title, his wide estates, and his Whig principles from his father, who had gone profitably with Walpole and the Pelhams. Hereditary wealth and prestige gave him great influence with the country gentlemen of Yorkshire, although his estates extended also to many broad acres in Northamptonshire and Ireland. To these advantages he brought decent morals and a blameless mediocrity of intellect. 'A weak, childish, ignorant man', Horace Walpole called him, 'by no means fit for the head of Administration.' Fortune, friendship, family tradition, the reflected glory of men of genius and talent among his followers: all served to hoist him to an elevation in the politics of his time which his own abilities scarcely could have brought him to attain. Coming to the first place in the royal service by the good offices of the Duke of

Cumberland in 1765, he came to like it, and to take it for granted that it should be his place to take the lead whether in office or in opposition ever after. Like most men of second-rate powers and uncritical self-identification with the cause they serve, Rockingham was devoured by jealousy and mistrust of abler men than himself. He had no reason to dislike Newcastle, who was on his way out, or Edmund Burke, a parvenu, and his protégé, who was on his way in. But he could never forgive a favourite like Bute, a genius like Chatham, or a first-rate man of business like Grenville. It would be going too far to say that he raised his prejudices to the status of principles,[1] for the Marquess had his quite genuine beliefs, even if they were for the most part evolved from personal prejudices and maintained on a basis of obstinate self-esteem. While it may be true that he only succeeded (where he succeeded) because other men had failed—notably in taking over the leadership after the defeat of the King and Lord North in America—he showed quite sufficient dumb devotion to his rather negative idealism to deserve success. Even a few consistent and self-righteous dislikes, embroidered upon by the genius of Burke and luckily justified by the failure of George III, may wear the air of essential superiority when steadily adhered to over a period of twenty years. Perhaps Rockingham has suffered some diminution in the eyes of posterity from the fact that most people know his small, rather frail, features only from the sketchy obscurity of the unfinished portrait by Sir Joshua Reynolds, where the Marquess looks out from beside the Irish pudding-face of his immortal secretary. Reserved and remote indeed he was. His shyness made him shun speaking in the House of Lords whenever he could avoid it. He was happiest in the elegant groves of his home at Wentworth Woodhouse, or among the gentlemen-riders on Newmarket Heath.

In taking the Treasury in July 1765, Rockingham had the whole-hearted blessing of the Duke of Newcastle, who himself took the Privy Seal. 'The putting my Lord Rockingham at the head of the Treasury,' wrote the old oligarch, 'was done without my immediate knowledge, but very much with my appro-

[1] Though this appears to be the opinion of Mr Brook in his treatment of Rockingham in *The Chatham Administration, 1766–1780.*

bation . . . he is the person in all England I wish there.' And this despite the fact that Rockingham had brought beneath his pale banner the High Whigs of the great tradition and the younger men who were concerned to revitalize the tradition from broader and deeper sources in the national life. On one occasion, the old Duke referred to the new Ministry as 'an Administration of boys', but he could feel fairly confident, it seems, that it would be an Administration of good boys. With the Marquess at the Treasury, everything possible would be done to strengthen the party with youthful energies while yet placating the conservative prejudices of the old brigade. This attempt to drive a team of old and new Whigs in double-harness was to prove a serious cause of weakness in the new Ministry, yet the attempt had to be made, and posterity owes a tribute to the Marquess for making it. In his brief tenure, which lasted for twelve months and twenty days, 'the knot of stainless friends' could do little more than set an example of good intentions. Yet those who stood and fell with the Marquess of Rockingham at this time were to serve as a steady, if sometimes inept, centre of opposition during the long years that followed. The reformation of English political life over which the King had thought to preside in the pride of his youth was to bear fruit twenty years later, when Burke had endowed reforming Whiggery with something like a philosophy. By that time, however, the Marquess was within a few months of his early death.

In 1765, Edmund Burke was as yet a nobody in the political scene. It is hard to believe this of a man of whom Dr Johnson said, that to take shelter with him under a shed from a shower of rain would cause anyone to put him down as a remarkable man. But so it was. Since 1757, when he became the political annalist of *The Annual Register*, he had been a mere 'chiel amang ye, takin' notes'. He had no seat in Parliament until the winter of 1765–6, and his fame in the great world was to date from his American Speeches in 1774–5. He was a man of thirty-five when he left 'Single-Speech Hamilton' for the personal service of the Marquess of Rockingham. A graduate of Trinity College, Dublin, he had come to London to read law at the Middle Temple and turned instead to the trade of letters.

His first published work, *A Vindication of Natural Society* (1756), was a satire on the romantic nature-worship associated, perhaps erroneously with the name of Jean-Jacques Rousseau, whose *Discourse on the Origins of Inequality* came out in the same year. The *Vindication* was readily mistaken for a posthumous work of Lord Bolingbroke, whose polished periods Burke took off with the deadly skill of an inspired journalist. His second was *A Philosophical Inquiry into the Origins of our Ideas of the Sublime and the Beautiful*, much admired in its day, but insufferable to a later taste.[1] David Hume, meeting him for the first time in September 1763, takes note of him as 'a very ingenious Irish gentleman, the author of a tract on the Sublime and Beautiful'.[2] Six months later, Hume could refer to the authority on Beauty and Sublimity as 'all-powerful' and now acknowledged as such by 'all the world'. Hume had already recorded his opinion that Burke was 'a very good man, a better man than a politician'— a judgment which history seems to be in the process of reversing. Nothing that Burke did before his attachment to the Marquess, however, can compare with the brilliant annual summaries of contemporary history which he wrote for the *Annual Register* during these years. Anonymous as they are, they are yet signed all over with their author's matchless flair for swift and penetrating analysis. The world that read the *Register* in the days of the Seven Years' War, the high-tide of Pitt and the low-water politics of Bute, must surely have suspected that a new and unnamed planet had swum into their ken.

Burke was not unaware of his own powers, and his fervent spirit and mind were already fully alive to the opportunities afforded to an aspiring young politician, by the crucial issues of the age that was opening. 'There was never a season', he wrote of the spring of 1765, 'more favourable for any man who chose to enter into the career of public life.' Yet, neither at this time, nor at any later stage of his career, did Burke attain to high office. His two brief periods at the Paymaster's Office in 1782 and 1783 were to prove his sole experience of public

---

[1] The work was at once influential in Germany (Lessing's *Laokoon*, 1766, was an early example) and is still treated respectfully by such writers on Aesthetic as Ernst Cassirer (*Die Philosophie der Aufklarung*, 1932).

[2] *Letters of David Hume*, J. Y. T. Greig, 1932, Vol. I, pp. 400, 404, 439.

3²548

employment in an official capacity[1] during a political life of
thirty years. This is not wholly to be accounted to his comparatively humble birth.[2] A parvenu could yet rise high in that age
of aristocratic patronage. But Burke was an Irish parvenu. He
spoke with a strong Irish brogue. He had a number of shady,
and needy, Irish friends and kinsmen, to whom he remained
shamelessly kind and loyal. He had a Papist mother, his wife
was a convert from Popery, and Edmund was openly sympathetic to both Irish and Papist claims to fair treatment. He
was suspect from the beginning as a Jesuit in disguise, and, in
the early days of the Rockingham Administration, the Duke of
Newcastle tried to discredit him with the Marquess as a secret
Jacobite and Papist. It is very much to the credit of Rockingham's good sense that he withstood this kind of malignity. But
the eloquent Irishman in a coat like a cassock and a hat like
a biretta, spectacles on nose and nose high in the air, refining
away before the House of Commons like any Schoolman, was
a gift to the lampoonists and caricaturists for many years. The
truth about Burke's exclusion from Cabinet office, however, is
far simpler than any suspicion about his supposedly sinister
affiliations. It is simply that he was not fit for it. Priceless as
an advocate, he was far too intemperate for routine ministerial
employment. Passionate, violent, dogmatic, often arrogant, he
was perhaps the greatest artillery-man of debate that the House
of Commons has ever known. As a minister at the head of a
department, he would have been a disaster, and his best friends
knew it. The Paymaster's Office was the best they could do
for him.

Perhaps it is only just that Edmund Burke should have been
the victim of a myth, for he was himself one of the great myth-
makers of English history. He was to invent, almost single-
handed,[3] the Whig interpretation of George III and his sinister

---

[1] It is important to stress the word 'official', since Burke seems to have
been present, despite his lack of office, at a meeting of the Cabinet on at
least one occasion in 1793. See W. A. Miles, *Correspondence during the French
Revolution*.

[2] For an important discussion of this question, and much else concerning
Burke's life, see T. W. Copeland, *Edmund Burke: Six Essays* (1950).

[3] Almost; for Horace Walpole had some share in it.

designs upon the Constitution. This was set forth in his *Thoughts
on the Causes of the Present Discontents* in 1770. His 'prentice hand
had already shown its cunning in 1766. Within a few days of
the fall of the first Rockingham Ministry, he had invented the
legend of the stainless virtue of the Marquess and his friends,
and of their incomparable services to England: 'a set of men
far the best that probably ever were engaged in the public
services of this country'. In *A Short Account of a Late, Short
Administration*, the world received an eight hundred word com-
muniqué of 'plain facts . . . neither extended by elaborate
reasoning, nor heightened by the colouring of eloquence', and
summing up the achievements of a single year under seven
heads: the repeal of the Stamp Act, the passing of the Declaratory Act (designed to compose and yet secure the dependence
of the colonies), the repeal of the inquisitorial cider-excise duty,
the condemnation of both General Warrants and the seizure
of private papers, the wise regulation of American trade, and
the improvement of both domestic manufacture and inter-
colonial commerce by the Free-port Act for Dominica and
Jamaica. All this had been achieved without backstairs influence or corruption of any kind. 'With the Earl of Bute they
had no personal connexions. They neither courted nor per-
secuted him. They practised no corruption; nor were they
suspected of it. They sold no offices. They obtained no reversions or pensions.' At the same time, they had been 'traversed
by an opposition of a new and singular character, an opposition
of placemen and pensioners'. However, corruption had been
unable to prevail against virtuous men backed by the people.
'They were supported by the confidence of the nation,' and
more especially had they sought and gained the co-operation of
the commercial community. 'That administration was the first
which proposed and encouraged public meetings and free consultations of merchants from all parts of the kingdom; by
which means the truest lights have been received; great benefits
have been already derived to manufactures and commerce;
and the most extensive prospects are opened for further improvements.' As for the King, 'they treated their sovereign
with decency, with reverence'. They had not been dismissed
prematurely, although they had held their offices under many

difficult discouragements. They left their offices 'at the express command, as they had accepted them at the command, of their royal master', and had 'left their king and country in a much better condition than they had found them'.

It has been necessary to deploy at some length the content of this, Edmund Burke's first essay in party propaganda, in order to take the full measure of a new phenomenon. Here, for the first time, was an aristocratic Whig connexion setting itself up—or being set up by its cleverest spokesman—as a party after the modern style. True, it was not until four years later that Burke promulgated his famous definition of party. Yet, in 1766, with the seals of office still warm from their hands, the Rockingham Whigs had been furnished with an apologia and a manifesto addressed to the nation at large. For sixty years and more, ministries had come and gone after their kaleidoscopic fashion, by re-shuffling and reinforcement, and men might fairly say: 'Plus ça change, plus c'est la même chose.' But here at last, men were being told, was an Administration which possessed a real identity, which had come to power in order to carry through a programme, and which now contemplated with satisfaction a record of planned achievement. The very fact that these claims were made, quite apart from their basis in reality or otherwise, was a portent. It is of the nature of myth that it is immune from the criticism of facts, even though the myth-maker may adduce a select corpus of facts in the course of its elaboration. The facts that Burke adduced were, indeed, as he claimed, 'plain' enough, but their plainness concealed as much truth as it revealed. The *Short Account* is compact of those half-truths that serve the propagandist better than lies, and its total impression is belied by any but the most superficial examination of the history of the first Rockingham Administration.

In the first place, the Rockingham Administration never enjoyed sufficient internal cohesion or security of tenure to enable it to carry out a planned and unified policy. Not only was it tormented by the tension between its own disparate elements. It was troubled by the surviving elements of the preceding Administration. Again, it had to contend with a Sovereign who disliked its prevailing tone, not to mention its predominant members, and with a House of Commons containing a large

number of placemen and pensioners created by earlier Ministries. This was the 'opposition of a new and singular character',
of which Burke complained, although there was nothing new
and singular about it. Indeed, it is possible to detect a flavour
of sour grapes, as well as of boastful virtue, in his claim that the
Rockinghams 'practised no corruption . . . sold no offices . . .
obtained no reversions or pensions'. Better for them, indeed, if
they had been able to employ the normal, indeed, the indispensable cement of eighteenth-century Administrations.

More than this, they had to contend with the independent
attitude of the most influential Whig of the age, for Pitt was
not only absent from their counsels, but let it be known that he
took a poor view of their transactions. Again and again, Rockingham sought the great man's suffrage for his measures, more
especially after the death of Cumberland in October 1765 had
deprived the Ministry of its mainstay at Court. True, Rockingham sometimes gave the impression of ignoring Pitt's finer
susceptibilities, notably when he gave up the policy of treaty-
alliance with Prussia, and again when he made Lord George
Sackville Vice-Treasurer of Ireland. When he approached Pitt
for his views on the proposed repeal of the Stamp Act in
December, Pitt gave him to understand that he would join the
Administration if Newcastle were excluded and Temple were
at least offered the Treasury. Newcastle, to his great credit,
professed his willingness to stand down, but Rockingham would
not hear of such wholesale concession, nor could he contemplate
his own replacement by so mean a figure as Temple. He has
been accused of appealing to Caesar and then refusing to take
Caesar's answer. The fact is, however, that short of submitting
to an entire re-modelling of his Ministry, with Pitt as its master,
he could hope for nothing but 'an answer answerless'.

When Parliament reassembled in the New Year, and the
Houses debated the address from the Throne, Pitt took up the
cause of the American colonies with the first notes of that
blasting eloquence which caused George III to denominate
him at a later time as 'the trumpet of sedition'. He denounced
the Stamp Act as not only inexpedient, but illegal, developing
the distinction which was to become a favourite line of attack
during the next phase of the contest: the distinction between

internal and external taxation. 'I rejoice that America has resisted,' he declared. And then, after expressing approval of the Ministry's intentions towards the colonists, he went on explicitly to deny them his confidence. He could not, and would not, he said, with embittered reference to the past, give the ministers his confidence, for 'confidence is a plant of slow growth in an aged bosom'. It was after this damaging declaration of independence that Rockingham and Grafton waited on Pitt with a royal invitation to join the Administration, either with or without Temple. Pitt once more stipulated for the exclusion of Newcastle. At any rate, the ministers now knew where he stood on the American question, and that they must proceed to the outright repeal of the Stamp Act if they were to avoid increasing his displeasure. By proposing to accompany the repeal with an Act declaratory of the right to tax the colonies, however, they brought down his wrath once more. They had now asserted 'England's right to do what the Treasury pleases with three millions of free men', for the Stamp Act had not been merely inexpedient, but a gross and tyrannical violation of the original contract between sovereign power and the people.

By this time, Rockingham had succeeded not only in affronting Pitt on the vexed issue of legality. He had offended the King, who had wished rather to modify than to repeal the Stamp Act. He had to contend also with the animosity of Grenville, Bute, the Bedfords, and large numbers of peers and country gentlemen, not to mention placemen and pensioners: everyone, indeed, to whom the Stamp Act stood as the cherished begetter of an American revenue, a beloved brain-child, or a symbol of England's righteous determination to have at a bunch of stiff-necked and purse-proud colonists. In this appalling situation, Rockingham made a third desperate attempt to secure Pitt's goodwill. It met with the same uncompromising reception. Grafton, who had only joined the Ministry on the understanding that his hero should somehow be brought into its ranks, now threatened to resign, and a final attempt to win Pitt's support had to be made in order to retain him. The attempt merely provided Pitt with another opportunity to castigate the Ministry as at present constituted. He made it perfectly plain that the sole hope of the country lay in an Administration free from all factitious 'connexion': in short, a coalition of all the wise and virtuous who would rally round the King in support of such measures as proceeded from the patriotic wisdom of William Pitt. Burke called this 'the cant of Not Men, but Measures, a sort of charm by which many people get loose from every honourable engagement'; in fact, a device 'to throw an odium on political connexion'. Pitt had, indeed, conjured up the shape of things to come: that 'very curious show', as Burke called it, which within a few weeks was to supplant 'the knot of stainless friends' with a 'tessellated pavement'. Meanwhile, Grafton carried out his threat of resignation from a government which, he declared, lacked 'authority, dignity and extension', and was replaced by another nobleman of the Stuart blood in the person of the Duke of Richmond. Apparently as Lord Buckinghamshire acidly observed, it was 'necessary always to have a Secretary of State of the race of Charles II'. Not that it mattered greatly, for the Ministry had barely two months to live.

The recalcitrance of Chatham was of enormous importance to the fortunes of the Rockinghams. It was not based simply on a difference of principle, with regard to 'Party' or 'Connexion'. The doctrine of 'Not men, but measures' was not really the 'cant' that Burke called it, any more than was the doctrine of party that Burke was pleased to pretend had replaced the oligarchic pretensions of the Old Corps. The fact is that the Rockinghams were trying to win the suffrage of those widespread commercial interests whose confidence Chatham alone had won and deserved. In a sense—a very limited sense, perhaps—it was a contest for the mantle of Sir Robert Walpole. But Pitt had the advantage of being the man in possession. Driven from office, and cultivating the rural tastes of a newly fledged country gentleman, he was nevertheless the grandson of 'Diamond Pitt', the friend of 'Sugar-King' Beckford, the darling of the City of London, the inspired war leader who had hounded the French from the richest commercial regions of the world. He had known, as no-one else had known, how to invest a gigantic commercial enterprise with the aura of a patriotic, and even a Protestant, crusade. To take office in a crisis over

American trade and taxation without the suffrage of William Pitt was 'the most rash experiment that ever was made'. Poised on the flank of the contest with the gloomy, prognosticatory hauteur of the elder statesman, Pitt was still the idol of the nation. He could, and now did, speak freely of the men with whom he had been obliged to maintain an uneasy and supercilious alliance when in power. Not that he had ever underrated the importance of the old Whigs. Perhaps he had even tended to overrate it, in that he stood so unforgivingly upon the exclusion of Newcastle. Moreover, the younger generation of the great connexion were of another temper than that of the high-and-dry Whigs of the Newcastle tradition. Men like Grafton and Shelburne, and indeed Rockingham himself in his frigid fashion, were consciously adjusting themselves to the outlook and interests of the mercantile and 'popular' world which Pitt had drawn to the heart of Whiggery. To some of these younger men, especially to Grafton and Shelburne, Pitt was the hero and the prophet of that wider Whiggery which was to find its apogee in his son, twenty years later.

The first Rockingham Ministry, struggling to maintain itself without the support of Chatham, and in the teeth of discarded ministers like Bute and Grenville, would in any case have been compelled to look beyond the doors of the House of Commons for support. They looked for it, and they got it, and in the end they failed to control it. Bidding tentatively for at least the appearance of support from those widespread bodies of opinion in the country which cared nothing for places so long as commerce flourished, they found themselves in danger of becoming the catspaw of a commercial policy dictated to them by the clamorous committees of West Indian and North American merchants. The truth was that the Rockinghams never had a plan of commercial reform. Nor did they inaugurate a new commercial policy. They acquired these things piecemeal, and not without misgivings, at the behest of their commercial supporters, and they found themselves carrying through some of the most fundamental changes of the century in British trading policy. They possessed neither the internal solidarity nor the conscious conviction of principle to impose a programme. The programme came afterwards in the form of the skilful rationalizations of Edmund Burke, whose gift for writing history was rivalled only by his genius for inventing it. And plainly, Burke was the man to do it, for he played the part of chief liaison officer between the Ministry and the business world throughout. The active and enlightened commercial policy which Burke was to claim as the chief title of the first Rockingham Ministry to the gratitude of the nation was in fact a series of solutions carefully adjusted to the prejudices of their own conservatives and to the clamour of their commercial supporters out-of-doors—and indeed to the conflicting interests within the ranks of the commercial men themselves. For there was no single 'commercial interest'—save for a short period when the main objective was the repeal of the Stamp Act. The Rockinghams were not only under fire from the Court, the opposition, and their own right wing. They were frequently subjected to a cross-fire from the great rival interests of North American and West Indian merchants, whose demands clashed at a number of important points.

The North American and the West Indian interests were united at least in their desire for a relaxation of Grenville's anti-smuggling regulations. Grenville himself had secretly issued orders to moderate the stringency of his measures as regards smuggling between the Spanish and the British islands in the Indies; and the Treasury Minute of 13 November 1765, which Burke was to cite with proud approval as a first-fruit of the wiser policy of the Rockinghams, and which was certainly received with satisfaction by the American merchants in England, was in fact of little importance. In any case, something far more constructive was wanted than a piecemeal relaxation of 'those fatal orders of Mr Grenville'. The North Americans wanted a further reduction of duty on foreign molasses, and the opening of certain 'free-ports' in Dominica and Jamaica. These demands, at the expense of the British West Indians' monopoly, at once threatened to produce a commercial conflict, and the rift was only temporarily closed in face of the common danger presented to the whole British trade in the New World by the colonial disturbances over the Stamp Act. News of the disturbances reached London in October, although colonial merchants had been addressing appeals and protests to the British government for some weeks past. By December, the London merchants trading with North America were organizing themselves in order to bring pressure to bear on the government. Under the leadership of Barlow Trecothick they set up a committee of twenty-eight prominent traders to manage a national campaign against the Stamp Act policy. The Stamp Act issue was one which enabled them to forget, at least for the time being, their conflicting interests in other respects. It provided a single point of focus and engendered a strong sense of confidence and a valuable experience of organized effort. Largely through the enthusiasm and energy of Edmund Burke, this extra-parliamentary organization, with its network of local committees in such important commercial centres as Liverpool, Bristol, Manchester, and Glasgow, was brought to bear directly upon the Rockingham Administration. 'That Administration', Burke was to write, 'was the first which proposed and encouraged public meetings and free consultations of merchants from all parts of the kingdom; by which means the truest lights have been received . . .' Concerted petitioning and the marshalling of witnesses made the case against the Stamp Act irresistible. Not that the Rockinghams wished to resist it. But with the organized and unanimous opinion of the commercial classes behind them, they could force the hand of the King and their own conservatives with 'the clamour of the merchants'. The Stamp Act was repealed in February, Conway's motion for leave to bring in an appeal measure being carried by a majority of 108 after an all-night debate in a House besieged by an excited crowd of merchants trading with America.

Thus, while it is true that Pitt's eloquent denunciation of the Stamp Act was an important element in forcing on the reversal of Grenville's policy at the hands of the Rockingham Whigs, there is no question of Pitt's having forced the Rockinghams to act.[1] They could claim to have acted on their own independent conviction and upon what Burke chose to call 'the truest lights'

---

[1] When Burke said in his speech on American Taxation in 1774 that 'it is now given out for the usual purposes, by the usual emissaries, that Lord Rockingham did not consent to the repeal of this Act until he was bullied into it by Lord Chatham', he was for once justified in dismissing the opinions of his opponents as 'artifices of a desperate cause'.

vouchsafed to them by deliberate consultation with the parties
most vitally interested. That, however, is the full extent of their
independence and of their authority. Their caution had mani-
fested itself from the beginning in their decision to precede
the repeal of the Stamp Act with an Act declaratory of the
sovereign power of King and Parliament over the colonies in
all matters.[1] The Declaratory Act was intended to propitiate
both the opposition and those government supporters who
feared the possible implications of a policy of concession. It
was also a measure of propitiation to the King, who, while he
had assented to the ministerial policy, could hardly have been
expected to rejoice in an implied surrender of sovereign rights
over his subjects by his faithful Commons. It was widely
imagined that the King was compelled at this time to acquiesce
in a policy of which he disapproved.[2] This was untrue. The
King would have preferred to modify rather than repeal the
Stamp Act, but he refrained loyally from embarrassing them
by insisting upon it. True, he declined to punish placemen who
had voted against the repeal measure, and he was certainly
annoyed at the indiscretion with which the government made
use of his name in their anxiety to justify their policy. The
Declaratory Act should at least have cleared up any doubts
about the Ministry's care for the royal authority. Unfortunately, it increased the hostility of Pitt, and was to prove a
further rock of offence in America when the colonists, after their
first jubilant gratitude over the repeal, had time and inclination
to discover precisely what had happened. The Act in itself was
perfectly proper. It declared what everyone knew to be true
and no-one in England cared to challenge except Pitt and his
followers, and even they failed to divide the House on it. It
was passed unanimously by the Commons, and with only five
dissentients in the Lords, and its passage undoubtedly smoothed
the way for the Stamp Act repeal. Burke, who was later to

---

[1] Explicit reference to taxation was avoided, perhaps out of consideration
for Chatham's attitude.

[2] Cf. Lord Chesterfield: 'The repeal was carried in both houses by the
ministers against the king's declared inclinations, which is a case that has
seldom happened, and I believe seldom will happen.' (*Letters*, ed. Bradshaw,
III, 1836.)

blame the American troubles upon the undesirable habit of
'urging subtle deductions . . . from the unlimited and illimit-
able nature of supreme sovereignty', was one of its most
enthusiastic advocates both inside and outside Parliament.

Once the Stamp Act was repealed, the rift between the North
American and the West Indian interests again became apparent, and the machinery of extra-parliamentary pressure became perilous to the government's already precarious command
of the situation. Even before the repeal, they were making
demands which threatened to rob the Ministry of its initiative,
and as they pressed on with these demands the centre of gravity
of activity tended to be moved from the Ministry to the extra-
parliamentary committees of the merchants. The contest by
which the North American interest secured the opening of free-
ports in the West Indies for foreign ships, and the reduction of
the duty on foreign molasses from 3*d.* to 1*d.* per gallon, was
fought over the dying body of the Rockingham Administration
rather than by its free agency in the House of Commons. The
West Indian interest, strong in the patronage of Pitt and Beckford, threatened to resist the North American demands to the
last ditch. The Cabinet was divided, and Rockingham and his
intimates inclined to accede to the full demands of the North
Americans, Newcastle and his friends hesitating to do so in the
face of the growing hostility of the West Indians. Burke waited
upon Pitt in an attempt to dissuade him from encouraging their
obduracy, but in vain. Pitt only withdrew his support from the
West Indians when he saw that his popularity was likely to
decline if he persisted in opposition to the North Americans,
and in the end a compromise was reached. The Ministry merely
gave the compromise their approval and provided the legislative forms, although Burke contrived to secure an address
from the West Indians, in which they acknowledged the government as their patrons and benefactors. It was too late. The
legislation embodying the reduction of duty on foreign molasses
and the opening of free-ports in Dominica and Jamaica was
passed in May and June, as the government was tottering to
its doom. On the thirtieth of July, the seals of office passed from
the Marquess of Rockingham to the Earl of Chatham. Edmund
Burke completed his onerous task as liaison officer in the difficult

traffic between the Rockinghams and the fratricidal world
of commerce by putting it on record that 'under them, the
interests of our northern and southern colonies, before that time
jarring and dissonant, were understood, composed, adjusted,
and perfectly reconciled'. Nor did he neglect to declare: 'They
were supported by the confidence of the nation.'

There is no means of judging. The nation was not consulted
either in the formation or the dissolution of the first Rockingham Administration. It is safe to say that the Administration
deserved the confidence of all lovers of liberty by its record.
It had passed strongly worded resolutions against General
Warrants and the seizure of private papers by the officers of
the Executive. It had repealed the Cider Tax which had led to
the rough handling of excise-men as minions of inquisition, an
example of successful resistance to taxation which is said to
have influenced American resistance to the Stamp Act. It had
firmly asserted the legislative superiority of Parliament over the
colonies while withdrawing the obnoxious measure in which it
had lately been exercised. It had acted as the agent, if not the
principal, in advancing freer trade between North America and
the West Indies. In fact, if good intentions and good works are
sufficient claims to a nation's confidence, the Rockinghams
deserved that confidence more than most. Unfortunately, however, they lacked almost everything else. Their leader had never
raised his voice in the House of Lords throughout the conflict,
and their ranks were in perpetual peril of dislocation. As a
Ministry, they represented an uneasy compromise between the
new Whigs and the old; between men who were prepared to
seek the reinvigoration of the Whig cause from wider bodies
of opinion in the nation's life, and the guardians of the great
traditions of the Pelhams, the Cavendishes and the Russells, who
had ruled securely for so long as the self-appointed heirs of the
Glorious Revolution. This uneasy combination, nurtured by
recent and novel experience of opposition, and tested by the
crises encountered during thirteen months in office, was to produce the 'Party' of the future, the rejuvenated connexion which
hardened into maturity during the ascendancy of Chatham,
Grafton and North, to emerge replete with its historic myth at
the hands of Edmund Burke.

Burke, the future philosopher of conservative Whiggery, won his spurs at this time, not as a theorist, but as a man of business, a propagandist, an indefatigable organizer. The pragmatic cast of his philosophy in later years, and the preservation of his strongly intellectual nature from the *pseudodoxia epidemica* which lie in wait for the intellectual in politics, were largely guaranteed by the solid, not to say sordid, character of this, his earliest experience of the real world of politics. It is not true that he came to act 'under a perpetual system of compromise' because he felt his 'measureless superiority to those about him'. But it is true that he first learnt the nature of politics 'in a Noah's Ark, with very few men and a great many beasts'.

CHAPTER 9

A Tessellated Pavement

You may strike up your sackbut, psaltery, and dulcimer, for
Mr Pitt comes in . . . 'Tis a great aera, my dear Sir, and a new
birthday for England!

Horace Walpole

He made an administration, so checkered and speckled . . . such
a tessellated pavement without cement . . . that it was, indeed,
a very curious show; but utterly unsafe to touch and unsure to
stand on.

Edmund Burke

THE MOMENT it was known that the King had sent for Mr Pitt,
it was possible for any man who wished, or affected to wish, to
turn his back on politics to declare with Horace Walpole:
'I leave them happily and gloriously settled, and an exclusion
given to the public's and my private enemies.' Now the King
might be happy, for Mr Pitt had sworn never to set foot in the
Closet but in the hope of 'rendering the King's personal situation not unhappy, as well as his business not unprosperous'.
Only the great families would grieve, Walpole predicted. As
for the colonists, they were already putting up statues to 'the
illustrious Mr Pitt, under God, and the King, the Saviour of
Britain and the Redeemer of America'. Not the least impressive
of these, depicting Mr Pitt, in white marble and wearing a
Roman toga, had been put up in Wall Street by the people of
New York. It was Mr Pitt, not the Marquess of Rockingham,
who received American thanks for the repeal of the Stamp Act,
and it was regarded as morally certain that Mr Pitt would not
have accompanied the repeal with the enactment of a Declaratory Act.

One way and another there was plenty of support for an
Administration headed by William Pitt, and assured of the

royal favour, by the summer of 1766. King and country alike were weary of weak ministries coming and going like a succession of transient and embarrassed phantoms. It was bad for trade, bad for foreign relations, bad for the reputation of government itself. The King's unpleasing experience of George Grenville and the Marquess of Rockingham had served only to increase his devotion to the royal independence. He was resolved that the existing ministry should not be totally displaced, but that it should serve as a basis for remodelling. Anything else would amount to that fearful contingency, 'the storming of the Closet'. Mr Pitt had set his fears at rest by saying that 'no Man was an honest Man who recommended none but his own friends, as that must be to form a Phalanx to disable the Crown from dismissing them when it judged it proper'. Pitt went to work 'chalking out' his Administration by taking 'the subsisting administration as the basis and making such alterations in it as would give it more stability'. He professed to wish 'as far as it was possible to dissolve all factions and to see the best of all parties in employment'. He was even disposed to speak well of Lord Bute 'as a Private Man and Man of Honour'. It was entirely proper, he said, that the King should 'not allow Ministers to presume to meddle with his private acquaintance . . .'

Pitt set out from Somerset on a Wednesday morning in July at a speed which terrified Lady Chatham when she heard that he had been seen 'four miles on the other side of Marlborough, Lud-a-Mercy, going at such a rate . . .' He was in town on the Friday morning, less than three days after leaving Burton Pynsent, a journey which took the *Taunton Flying-Machine* four. Resorting to the house of his kinsman, Captain Hood, in Harley Street, he let a little of his own blood in order to allay the threat of a fever. Next day he had audience of the King at Richmond Lodge, returning to Harley Street for a 'five o'clock chicken'. Three nights in town in the heat of July sent him out to North-end, Hampstead (still known as 'the country'), where he lodged in the house of his friend, Charles Dingley, 'a bower of refreshment' to which he was to have recourse increasingly as his health deteriorated. Indeed, the whole tragedy of Pitt's Administration is hinted in these, its opening scenes, at Harley

Street and Hampstead in the hot July days of 1766. Often prostrated by the fevers of his recurrent gout, his debilitated body rebelled increasingly against the strains imposed by the cares of office, bringing upon him the horrors of the manic depression which was to make the last years of his life little but a living death. He was still two years short of sixty when he returned to the direction of public affairs. His heart in these later days was ever with the wife of his bosom and the five children in their beloved Somersetshire home.

Despite the fatigues of his journey, Pitt was soon able to infect the political world with a sense of boundless optimism and vigour. He told Hester that he trusted to his oldest patron, Divine Providence, to carry him through the 'unlaborious work before me'—unlaborious compared with the tasks of former times. Friends and enemies alike seem to have regarded Mr Pitt's health as the most important question in the world just then. When he went down to Bath, in the autumn, the crowd in the Pump Room stood up when he entered and remained standing while he drank his glass of water. 'I hope your Majesty's health is better,' one Somersetshire man called out to him as he passed through the throng. Only one man in England could rival his authority over the minds and hearts of his countrymen in those lovely autumn days. Within a stone's throw of the world of fashion gathered in the 'mimic capital' of the West, a lean, elderly man, his fresh-coloured face framed by smoothly combed hair 'with a soupçon of curl at the ends', spoke his sermon with parts and eloquence, only raising his voice towards the close, when he 'acted a very ugly enthusiasm'. To Horace Walpole, a connoisseur of all the arts, John Wesley preaching in a Gothic chapel at Bath was 'as evidently an actor as Garrick'. The notion of Mr Pitt and Mr Wesley in the same town, the detestable little city 'all crammed together and surrounded with perpendicular hills' beside a river 'paltry enough to be the Seine or Tiber', was like living in a fair.

The new Administration was, as Burke said, 'picked and culled from all quarters'. Of the men who had served under the Marquess, the most notable survivors were Henry Conway, Walpole's beloved cousin; Charles Townshend, the brilliant and unstable character who had held the Pay-Office; and

Augustus Henry Fitzroy, 3rd Duke of Grafton, who had actually left the Marquess some months before Pitt took over. Pitt was the god of Grafton's idolatry, and the god now insisted upon the acolyte taking the Treasury, which meant that Grafton would be deputy Prime Minister were Pitt's health to entail his retirement, which it soon did, with disastrous results for the historical reputation of Grafton and for the integrity of the Empire. The best men in the new Ministry were both friends and personal followers of Pitt: Charles Pratt, 1st Lord Camden, who had been the hero of the Court of Common Pleas throughout the affair of Wilkes and *The North Briton*, and whom Pitt now made Lord Chancellor; and the young Earl of Shelburne, 1st Marquess of Lansdowne, who rivalled the Duke of Grafton in personal devotion to Pitt, and vastly exceeded him in intellectual calibre. 'Let him stick to measures' Pitt had said of Shelburne when the young man was tempted to serve under Rockingham, 'Connexions as to men are mean, but on measures commendable.' At which Shelburne had told the Marquess: 'As to my future conduct, your Lordship will pardon me if I say "Measures and Not Men" will be the rule of it . . .' The doctrine, according to the Marquess's secretary, Mr Burke, was cant, or a 'sort of charm by which many people get loose from every honourable engagement'. It was certainly a charm with Pitt, who could always put measures before men, since there was only one man involved, and his name was William Pitt.

That, in the event, proved to be the tragedy. This brilliant Administration, which contained within its ranks—in the persons of Grafton, North and Shelburne—no less than three future Prime Ministers, had no other principle of unity than devotion to the author, the cabinet-maker, mosaic-maker or joiner who, at the moment of its construction, withdrew to the House of Lords as the Earl of Chatham, occupying a decorous sinecure as Lord Privy Seal. It was indeed a tessellated pavement without cement, and as Burke put it 'a very curious show . . . unsafe to touch . . . unsure to stand on'. The prophecy came true. 'If ever he fell into a fit of the gout, or if any other cause withdrew him from public cares . . .' confusion would follow. 'When his face was hid for a moment, his whole system was on a wide sea, without chart or compass . . . Deprived of his guiding influence, they were whirled about, the sport of every gust . . .' It was the familiar fallacy of Enlightened Despotism, enacted within a parliamentary system. When the presiding genius departed, chaos was come again.

Chatham's withdrawal to the House of Lords was to prove disastrous to the coherence and control of government business in the lower House, for not only was he the head of the government in the House of Lords but the First Lord of the Treasury was there too. Government forces in the House of Commons were delivered over to the infirm leadership of Henry Conway, a Secretary of State whose department (the Northern) had only a minor share of patronage to administer. In an age when the direction of Treasury patronage was all-important for the management of majorities, it was fatal for the leadership of the Commons to depend on a Treasury chief who sat in the upper House. Either Grafton would have to delegate patronage to Conway, to the detriment of his power and prestige as First Lord, or Conway would have to go short, to the detriment of his authority in the Commons. When it is realized that Grafton was often obtuse or inert, and Conway distracted by his allegiance to the Rockinghams (now in opposition) and inclined to bury his head in the affairs of his department like an unhappy ostrich, while Chatham was for long periods incapacitated by illness at Bath, Marlborough or North-end, it is not to be wondered at that the great hopes of 1766 were soon dashed.

Not the least element in the oncoming chaos was supplied by the brilliant fooleries of the Chancellor of the Exchequer, Charles Townshend, who had decided to go down to history as the man who had settled the affairs of the Empire, East and West. Settle them he did in America with his American Import Duties Bill of 1767, a measure by which, he boasted, he would be able to tax and please the colonists at one and the same time, but by which in fact they were driven over the edge into revolt. His plan for tapping the wealth of the East India Company, whose riches now inflamed the minds of politicians with similar visions to those engendered by the El Dorado possibilities of the South Sea Company half a century earlier, was only a bolder, more direct version of the numerous devices for 'raiding' John Company's pocket which occupied the minds of most men con-

12. Portrait of the Wedgwood family by Stubbs

13. Samuel Johnson

14. Edward Gibbon

cerned with the problem of the National Debt in this period of
anxiety about post-war finance. The renewal of the Company's
Charter was about to arise, and opportunity to extract money
from a rich corporation dependent upon the State for its
privileges was hardly to be resisted. To take that opportunity
was, as the King himself bluntly put it, 'the only safe method of
extracting this country out of its lamentable situation owing to
the load of debt it labours under'. Chatham talked about its
necessity as 'the redemption of the nation'. George Grenville,
the father of imperial economy, and a stickler for strict
legality, having burnt his fingers over the Stamp Act, was all
for measures to reduce the debt, but not by a policy involving
the violation of charters. Townshend was for doing a deal with
the Company in advance of parliamentary inquiry into the
Company's affairs and legislative haggling. As usual, he was in
a hurry, intent on achieving a *coup de foudre*, the more so because
Chatham, ill and often absent, dragged his feet and did nothing
but talk. He was hand in glove with Laurence Sulivan and a
powerful faction among the Directors of the Company, in whose
General Court a group of speculators had managed to pass a
motion to raise dividends from 10 to 12½ per cent. The government, under the wise and well-informed guidance of Shelburne,
at once brought in a Dividend Bill, prohibiting the Company
from raising its dividend for a period of twelve months without
consent of Parliament. It was on the night when the Dividend
Bill passed the Commons that Townshend made his famous
'Champagne Speech', not to denounce the measure but to
deliver a wild and witty denunciation of the government in
general. As far as anyone could make out what he was saying,
he was proposing the return of the Marquess of Rockingham
and his friends to power, with himself at their head. He treated
the existing Administration as already non-existent, and called
for the restitution of the first post in Administration to the
House of Commons. The speech destroyed any credit its author
still enjoyed as a serious statesman. 'The net result of his intervention in East Indian affairs was totally to discredit him as a
politician,' Sir Lewis Namier has said. The same authority
treated his subject more than generously when he gave his
opinion 'that his conduct may have been guided by no more

rational motive than his own pecuniary interest'. It were too generous altogether to add *in vino veritas*. Few men have done so much mischief in so short a time as Chancellor of the Exchequer. Fortunately for the coherence of governmental affairs, Charles Townshend (destined to a dubious immortality as 'Champagne Charley') was to die of inflammation of the bowels before the summer of 1767 was out.

Not the least happy element in the pleased anticipation of Englishmen in the autumn of 1766 had been the hope, indeed the confidence, that Pitt's return to mastery would put Europe, and more especially France, once more in awe of Britain. 'You know I love to have the majesty of the people of England dictate to all Europe,' wrote Horace Walpole. 'Nothing would have diverted me more than to have been at Paris at this moment.' Continental observers, however, were rather less impressed. Frederick the Great, who ruled Prussia with a staff of clerks compared with whom Pitt's colleagues were free men bristling with initiative, remained unconvinced that British policy would prove any more consistent under the new régime. He 'talked of the instability of our measures and sudden changes in our administrations, which made it almost impossible to transact business with us with any sort of security', reported Sir Andrew Mitchell from Potsdam in September, after sounding the King on the renewal of closer relations between the two governments. Mitchell assured him that 'a new plan was formed and government had acquired a consistency' which would put an end to 'unsteadiness of measures', but he had to report that Frederick still remained 'diffident and backward to enter into engagements'. As for the French, Choiseul thought the only danger was that 'cet homme altier et ambitieux' might enter upon a course of war and conquest in order to recover the popularity he had lost with the people by accepting an Earldom. 'Nous ne pouvons comprendre ici quel a été le dessein de My Lord Chatham en quittant la Chambre de Communs.'

All hopes of reviving grandeur swiftly faded with the onset of the winter of 1766–7 when Chatham departed for Bath once more on account of his gout. 'Political gout', unsympathetic critics called it, and the King himself was heard to remark on the lack of fortitude some people showed under its onslaughts.

When he set out on his return to London in February, he was obliged to take to his bed at the Castle Inn at Marlborough, and it was not until 2 March that he reached town. There he found the Administration smarting under a defeat of 206 to 188 in the Commons on an opposition motion to reduce the Land Tax. It was said to be the first time that a government had been defeated on an important measure since the reign of Sir Robert Walpole, and for a breathless moment it seemed that the opposition might push its advantage to the point of overturning the government. They threatened to withdraw Henry Conway and the other Rockinghamite elements in the Ministry. For long enough they had regarded Henry Conway as a hook either to drag themselves into the Administration or to drag the Administration down. Chatham, however, showed himself scornfully indifferent to such threats, even when they began to take shape in the form of the resignation of Sir Charles Saunders, First Lord of the Admiralty, and two other members of the Admiralty Board, Admiral Keppel and Sir William Meredith, in November, even though Conway still stayed. It was on such occasions as this that Chatham was wont to imitate Cardinal Richelieu's mode of putting some spunk into Père Joseph. 'Courage my Lord Grafton,' he would say, 'the Closet is firm . . . All will yet be well.' And indeed it was. The disparate factions of the opposition Whigs failed to unite, partly because their most effective leader would have been George Grenville, whom few could stand, and partly because their most numerous clan was the Bedford Whigs, or 'The Bloomsbury Gang', who always insisted on the promise of all the most lucrative jobs. When Parliament was dissolved on 10 March 1768, it was not on account of any success on the part of the parliamentary opposition, but simply because the statutory term had been reached. It was very rare indeed for an eighteenth-century parliament to fall short of its full seven years' life.

The most ominous event of the early spring, however, was neither adverse votes in the Commons nor resignations from the Ministry, but the arrival of John Wilkes once more on his native shores. Intent upon battle 'out-of-doors', he had written to the Duke of Grafton, expressing his hopes that his 'long unmerited exile' might end now that his former allies were in office, and that he might be allowed 'to continue in the land and among the friends of liberty'. His advances had been brushed off. When the general election came on (in the spring of 1768) he stood for the City of London, his old stamping-ground. He was received with customary enthusiasm by 'the poorer sort', but with insufficient suffrage from the wealthier city magnates. When he tried again, this time for the county of Middlesex, he headed the poll. The old cries for 'Wilkes and liberty' rang out again, and the sacred number 'Forty-five' was chalked on every door from the Royal Exchange to Brentford. The Austrian Ambassador was taken out of his carriage to have the 45 chalked on his boot-soles. As the Duke of Richmond put it, 'whatever men may think of Mr Wilkes' private character, he has carried his election by being supposed a friend of liberty'. It was an event, his Grace added, which 'must produce something . . .' Within a few months it was to produce the birth of Radicalism.

The Tessellated Pavement Ministry came to an end with the resignation of Chatham in October 1768. In effect, it had been defunct since Chatham's health had given way after his return to London in March 1767, necessitating his withdrawal to seclusion at Hampstead in a state of total incapacitation for the least concern with public business. There he had lived for many months in a condition of manic depression, receiving his food through a hatch and riding out by night, scarcely able to bear the sight of his fellow-men and driven to something like frenzy at the slightest mention of politics. It fell to Grafton, devoted as ever to his master, to take the nominal headship of the Administration, hoping against hope that the sick god would return if only he could hold on. Hold on he did, but he could do little more. At the end of May he had laid his griefs before the King, and the King had secured him an interview with the invalid. With his habitual obdurate courage, George assured the sick man that for his own part, he would never 'truckle' to the 'hydra faction' which was intent, as ever, upon storming his closet. 'Be firm, and you will find me amply ready to take as active a part as the hour seems to require.' Grafton's purpose in meeting Chatham had been to secure his consent to overtures to one or other of the opposition factions for an alliance which might strengthen the Administration. Either the Bedfords or the

Rockinghams it must be, and Chatham listlessly made it plain that he preferred the Bedfords—as the lesser of the two evils. Grafton tried both, and when it became clear that Rockingham would not join, but would only replace, the Ministry, he came to terms with the Bedfords.

The adhesion of the Bedford Whigs both strengthened and weakened the Administration: strengthened it in numbers and weakened it in quality. It was not long before Chatham's favourite disciple, and the most competent man in the ministry, Lord Shelburne, was threatened with dismissal. Shelburne did not wait. Like the man in the Dickens novel, he preferred to be kicked at the top of the stairs and to fall down of his own accord. No sooner had Shelburne left than Chatham resigned the Privy Seal, and Grafton now found himself in fact, and no longer merely in name, at the head of the government. Lord Camden, who was, next to Shelburne, the firmest and most loyal Chatham-ite in the ministry, remarked somewhat bitterly to Grafton: 'the administration since Lord Chatham's illness, is almost entirely altered, without being changed'. The alteration had come about in the kaleidoscopic fashion typical of ministerial alterations in that age of aristocratic politics. Only in those terms likewise is it possible to understand the survival of the Duke of Grafton's government over the next two years, indeed until the day in 1770 when Frederick, Lord North, came to the King's rescue, inaugurating a ministry of twelve years' duration, the longest of the reign before the coming of the Younger Pitt. 'Wilkes and Middlesex', *The Letters of Junius*, *Thoughts on the Causes of the Present Discontents*, such classic phenomena of opposition crowd the two years of the Duke of Grafton's ministry. 'You have taught me to look elsewhere than to the Commons for the sense of my subjects,' George II had once said to William Pitt. In the days of Lord Grafton, George III might have said the same to John Wilkes, to Sir Philip Francis[1] and to Edmund Burke. But then, like the Bourbons, George III never learnt anything.

[1] The most likely author of *The Letters of Junius*.

The Birth of Radicalism

> Mr Wilkes' success is an event which, I think, must produce
> something . . . I am not sorry that the ministry should see that
> there is in the people a spirit of liberty which will show itself on
> proper occasions, as in the choice of their members . . . I think
> it will show the administration that, though they may buy lords
> and commons and carry on their measures smoothly in parlia-
> ment, yet they are not so much approved of by the nation.
>
> *The Duke of Richmond, 1768*

THE ADOPTION of the word 'radical' as a substantive instead
of merely as an adjective in the vocabulary of politics belongs
to the last years of George III's life. It was in 1819, Harriet
Martineau tells us, 'that the Reformers first assumed the name
of Radicals'.[1] But as an adjectival expression of reformist
politics it went back at least to the days of John Wilkes and the
uproar over the Middlesex Election of 1768. For it was at this
time that the reformism of Whig gentlemen who followed the
Marquess of Rockingham and harkened unto his secretary,
Edmund Burke (who wrote his *Thoughts on the Present Discontents*
in 1770), began to be shown up in certain quarters for what
Catherine Macaulay called it in her *Observations* on Mr Burke's
'pernicious work'—briefly, a sham. Mrs Macaulay was a sister
of Alderman Sawbridge, one of the most radically minded
politicans in the City of London, a disciple of Chatham and
Shelburne, and a confrère of John Wilkes. She was a lady of
generally Republican sentiments, and she had a shrewd idea
that Whig reformism of the Rockingham–Burke type was
simply one more manœuvre of one more aristocratic faction
inspired by concern not for popular causes but for 'the loss of
their own power by the king's independent behaviour.' People

[1] *History of the Thirty Years' Peace.*

like Burke, she suspected, were really trying to argue mankind into opposition for their own peculiar interests alone. Their success would only be to consolidate the position of an aristocratic clique and could in no wise serve the interests of the people. The people's interests could only be served by an effective Place Bill, more frequent parliaments, and 'more extended and equal power of election'. She stressed the necessity to pledge parliamentary candidates to work for this programme. In fact, the gaff was being blown on gentlemanly Whig reformism.

Catherine Macaulay went so far as to denounce Burkeian reformism as a sinister design to forfend *effectual* reformation. It was not that, although it is always a little difficult to acquit reformism from John Locke to Lord John Russell of a certain equivocation. When Locke wrote in 1690[1] that Old Sarum might very well be reformed by an act of royal prerogative, the reader must pray for a willing suspension of disbelief. Similarly, when Burke argues against more frequent parliaments and more effective Place Bills, putting his faith in a stricter supervision of members of parliaments by their constituents—in other words, 'the interposition of the body of the people itself'—the reader recalls that Burke reckoned 'the people' in any political view to comprise about 400,000 persons 'of tolerable leisure . . . of some means of information, above menial dependence'. He would add that 'the rest, when feeble, are the objects of protection; when strong, the means of force'.[2] Major John Cartwright, who was later to be the doyen of radicalism and a scathing critic of 'Burkism'[3] and to sum up the equivocal nature of Whig reformism in his celebrated pamphlet 'Mock Reform, Half Reform and Constitutional Reform' in 1810, had already published his first reform tract, 'Take Your Choice' by 1776. Much of the strong wine of English radicalism as it was to be poured forth in the days of the Regency, was brewed in the days of John Wilkes, Horne Tooke, and Catharine Macaulay in the City of London in the 1770s.

---

[1] *Second Treatise of Civil Government*, Ch. XIII, sect. 158.
[2] *Letters on a Regicide Peace*, 1796, Letter I.
[3] 'Never speaking on the Constitution . . . but in trope or figure, in simile, metaphor, or mysterious allusion.'

Wilkes himself was in these years a difficult and dissolute leader, if he was ever really a leader at all. He was indeed something a good deal more valuable to infant radicalism: the Injured Man with a hide like a rhinoceros. He simply could not be either shut up or put down. The Duke of Grafton tried first to ignore him and then to suppress him. He would not be ignored. Technically an outlaw since his departure from France while charged with both seditious and obscene libel in the winter of 1763, he had blithely got himself elected for Middlesex on his return in 1768. After that his outlawry had been quashed on a technical point, but he was sentenced to imprisonment for two years and the payment of a substantial fine. In the King's Bench prison he was well housed and suffered no denial of the company of his friends, male or female. Friends and admirers from all over England, and America, solaced him with tokens of admiration and sympathy in the form of food-parcels, hogsheads of tobacco, and live turtles. Even the most comfortable species of inactivity was not for him, however. He petitioned the House of Commons for redress of his grievances. He published a letter to the Secretary of State, Lord Weymouth, accusing him of inciting the 'massacre' of some half a dozen persons shot down by the miltary at a riot which ensued when a mob of his supporters, disappointed at his non-appearance at the opening of Parliament on 10 May, threatened to storm the prison and carry him to the House in triumph. His language ('a hellish project . . . brooded over by some infernal spirits, without one moment's remorse') determined Grafton to secure his expulsion from the House of Commons.

This was not the worst of it. At the by-elections for Middlesex that ensued, he was re-elected over and over again, until the House took the ineffably foolish step of seating his opponent, Henry Lawes Luttrell, on an insignificant minority of votes. By declaring Wilkes incapable of election in future, and by choosing Luttrell to represent Middlesex in his place, the House of Commons had legislated single-handed (creating a new disqualification) and replaced election by co-option. While it is true that the House could not have allowed Wilkes to take his seat in the same session that had seen his expulsion, it could, and should, have refrained from creating a new disqualification and seating his defeated opponent. Impeccable constitutional lawyers, including George Grenville, warned of the consequences. Only after endless wrangling, and the most ingenious—and disingenuous—twisting of precedents, did the House depart from its false position in 1774, when Wilkes was allowed to take his seat and the record of the House's folly was expunged from its journals.

The case of 'Wilkes and the Middlesex Election' threw a lurid light upon the ancient institution which men were soon to call 'the unreformed House of Commons'. Some went so far as to deny the sovereign authority of an assembly which contained a co-opted member while the wishes of the electors of Middlesex were ignored. This high-handed behaviour, together with the levying of taxes on colonial subjects of the Crown who lacked representation in the House, seemed to amount to a double-barrelled assault on the elementary principles of representative government. It is hardly surprising that the American colonists saw in John Wilkes a champion of their own cause, or that many Englishmen came to think of the colonists as Englishmen overseas fighting again the battle which their ancestors were imagined to have won in their struggle with the Stuart kings. 'The feelings of the colonies were formerly the feelings of Great Britain,' Burke told the House of Commons. "They were formerly the feelings of Mr Hampden . . . the people of the colonies are descendants of Englishmen . . . We cannot, I fear, falsify the pedigree of this fierce people, and persuade them that they are not sprung from a nation in whose veins the blood of freedom circulates.' The practical outcome of this alliance in freedom of the Old World and the New was the foundation in 1769 of the Society of the Supporters of the Bill of Rights. The Society may be fairly described as the first parliamentary reform society in English history, though it was much else besides, notably a society for the support of John Wilkes, or at least for the payment of his debts.

The founder-members[1] of the Society were Wilkes's wealthier and more influential friends in the City of London, the Borough of Southwark and the County of Middlesex: Aldermen and Members of Parliament. The declared purposes of the Society

[1] John Horne, later to be known as Horne Tooke, took the initiative.

were (1) the defence of the constitutional rights of the subject, and (2) the support of 'Mr Wilkes and his cause'. The most pressing business, the raising of money for Wilkes, was put in hand at once. The Society sent him £300 for immediate use, endowed him with an annuity of £1,000 and eventually paid out about £20,000 on his behalf.[1] More important, however, was its framing of Eleven Articles for parliamentary reform, which included the promotion of 'full and equal franchise', and the pledging of candidates to the Society's purposes. The Society backed Wilkes's motion for the reform of representation in 1776. Little or nothing was achieved, but the Society deserves to go on record as linking the name of Wilkes, however equivocally, with the history of parliamentary reform clubs which were to proliferate in both London and the provinces over the next half-century and more. Far more practically important was the Yorkshire Association founded by Christopher Wyvill in 1780, consisting of the gentry, clergy and freeholders of the county, and concerned to petition Parliament for economical reform. The Yorkshire Association was joined by other County Associations, and at one stage seemed likely to grow into a nation-wide movement. The County Association movement lent support to the Younger Pitt's abortive measure for parliamentary reform in 1784. There are a number of links between these attempts and the Middlesex Election uproar in 1769, bringing the Wilkite movement into the main stream of the English radical movement as it gathered strength in the latter years of George III and the early decades of the nineteenth century.

Perhaps Wilkes's most tangible achievement towards the advance of democracy was the blow he struck in 1771 for the basic condition of free government, the freedom to publish parliamentary debates. He conducted the fight in a typically impudent Wilkite fashion, as a magistrate of the City of London. He got certain printers brought before him on the charge of having published debates of the House of Commons, which exclusive body took the view that the electorate had no right to know what their representatives said. Wilkes discharged the printers, and (it is hardly too much to say) congratulated them and begged them to do it again. He brought the City into

---

[1] This cleared about two-thirds of what he owed.

conflict with the House so effectively that the Lord Mayor, Brass Crosby, was arrested under the Speaker's Warrant before the dispute ended. The House, of course, never surrendered its right to prohibit publication, but in effect it ceased to exercise it in future. Thus Alderman Wilkes fought the battle of the fourth estate of the realm, to whose liberties he had a life-long attachment as a rogue journalist.

He was always finding things out by trying them on his pulses, or perhaps his senses, for he was that rare character in English political life, the inspired sensualist. Gayer than Charles Bradlaugh in the nineteenth century, a great deal less cold-hearted in his roguery than Horatio Bottomley in the twentieth, he had most of the virtues and the vices of Charles James Fox and the society of mingled squalor and bravura that gave him birth. But for his personal courage and wit, he might appear as nothing but a patch of scum dancing on the broad current already beginning to hasten towards the rapids of a revolutionary age. Around his hideous person gathered the frustrated feelings of thousands for whom the *ancien régime* was beginning to be a bore and an abomination. Ironically, yet appropriately, he retired from parliamentary politics in the year of the outbreak of the French Revolution, an event which he regarded with distaste and utterly failed to understand. He died a loyal follower of the Younger Pitt, whose understanding of it was no greater. To die as a Pittite Tory in the year of the battle of Cape St Vincent and Camperdown was no curious conclusion for a man who was never less than a patriot and whose memorial tablet simply and truthfully bears the statement that he was 'A Friend of Liberty'. A braver man than his adversaries and more magnanimous than most of his allies, he may perhaps be best remembered as the first 'card' to make a mark on the history of modern England. Like Arnold Bennett's great prototype, Edward Henry Machin, he deserved a medal for his manifold services to 'the great cause of cheering us all up'.

The broadening and deepening of the current of radicalism associated with the name of John Wilkes owed much to forces and events far distant from the City of London and utterly alien to the mind and morals of its hero. It owed most to events in America and to the reviving moralism of the age. 'As to politics' William Cobbett wrote when looking back to his childhood in rural Surrey (he was born in the year of the Stamp Act), 'we were like the rest of the country people in England: that is to say we neither knew nor thought anything about the matter.'

> The shouts of victory or the murmur of a defeat, would now and then break in upon our tranquillity for a moment; but I do not remember ever having seen a newspaper in the house . . . After, however, the American War had continued for some time, and the cause and nature of it began to be understood, or rather misunderstood by the lower classes of people in England, we become a little better acquainted with the Americans . . . Here Washington's health and success to the Americans were repeatedly toasted . . .

At last something more and other than the politics of Noodle, Foodle and Quoodle, or 'who shall have the places', was involved. Here was a concern for right, for Rights, for something which resembled a principle. As Lord Acton somewhat oddly remarked, after the Boston Tea Party in 1773, 'the dispute had been reduced to its simplest expression and had become a mere question of principle'.[1] As another great exponent of moral forces in politics, S. T. Coleridge, once said:

> At the enunciation of principles, of ideas, the soul of man awakes and starts up, as an exile in a far distant land at the unexpected sounds of his native tongue. These alone can interest the undegraded human spirit deeply and enduringly because these alone belong to its essence and will remain with it permanently.

This was now happening, as the colonists were driven from their objection to the concrete measures of George Grenville to base themselves on a principle of natural justice.[2] 'No taxation without representation' is more than a lawyer's maxim. It reflects the fundamental human principle that persons are not merely things: that they must be consulted in deciding their own fate. When the quarrel emerged on to this level it could be discerned that politics were once more beginning to be about something, that the long years in the wilderness—the years of Walpole and

---

[1] *Lectures on Modern History*, p. 311. For Acton to call something 'a mere question of principle' must ever remain peculiar.

[2] See Ernest Barker, *Traditions of Civility*, VIII.

the Duke of Newcastle—were coming to an end. 'Flapdoodle' was again in fashion.

It had never been out of fashion with that vast middling section of English society which filled the chapels of Protestant Dissenting religion, the public for which Samuel Richardson wrote *Pamela, or Virtue Rewarded*, and for which King George III was always 'Good King George'. These were the people who loved a moral sentiment, more especially one that could be expressed in a motto, almost as much as they loved a sportsman or a gambler. The people who loved George III for his duller domestic virtues also gave their hearts with no less reserve to the man whom George III loathed, that prince of gamblers, Charles James Fox. No-one can ever hope to understand why the reputation of the Duke of Grafton survived all the malice of the *Letters of Junius* unless he also knows that his Lordship died at a ripe old age in the odour of sanctity as the author of 'Hints for the serious Attention of Clergy, Nobility and Gentry' (1789) and 'Serious Reflections of a Rational Christian' (1798). Even John Wilkes, some thirty years before he achieved Christian burial in Grosvenor Chapel, managed to achieve a reputation for extreme piety in Paris. 'I never see Mr Wilkes here but at Chapel', wrote David Hume in May 1764, 'where he is a most regular, and devout, and edifying and pious attendant.' It seems, indeed, that the way to win the hearts of the English in the age of the American Revolution was by combining the manners of a marquess with the morals of a Methodist.

In their religion the English have always maintained a preference for a type of theology that approximates to the divine sortilege of Jean Calvin. After all, there was a thousand to one chance against a man's being 'called' or 'chosen' or otherwise distinguished in the divine lottery, and nothing could have bored the ordinary Englishman more than the teaching of Pierre Cuppé in his *Le Ciel ouvert à tous les Hommes*.[1] The risk of Hell-fire lent an enormous attraction to the preaching of Wesley and Whitefield. 'He's going—he's going—he's GONE!' they groaned in ecstasy as Whitefield drew for them the picture

[1] Pierre Cuppé was an Augustinian Canon and Curé of Blois. His book was extremely popular in France, where it circulated in manuscript. It was written in *c.* 1716.

of the sinner sinking into the quicksands of sin and damnation. To judge from the columns of the *Annual Register,* people
rejoiced in fantastic wagers every day: a Fulham fish-porter who
undertook to run from Hyde Park Corner to Brentford in an
hour bearing 46 lb. of fish on his head, a gaggle of Welsh women
who undertook to walk from Westminster Bridge to Deptford
and back in less than two hours for £20, two gentlemen who
wagered to dive into seven feet of water and undress against
each other, while another wagered a thousand guineas that he
would ride twenty-nine horses over 2,900 miles in twenty-nine
successive days. A minister of the Crown, then as in most
periods of English history, stood a better chance of popular
favour if he took Newmarket as seriously as he took Westminster, while a demagogue like Wilkes who backed his personal
fancy against the embattled powers of Church and State, could
be doubly sure of the tumultuous suffrage of an unenfranchised
people. In whatever field the national genius took its pleasure
in the days of Pitt and Wesley and Wilkes, it delighted in the
knife-edge and the tightrope. All-to-lose, all-to-win, might have
been the people's watchword, whether they went to war with
Wolfe and Hawke, to sermons with the field-preachers, or to the
Middlesex hustings with Wilkes, and in every case—Pitt against
the Bourbons, the King against the Proud Dukes, Wesley
against Satan, or George Washington and the embattled
farmers against Lord North—the sporting contest found expression in the personal qualities of a man, preferably some Jack the
Giant-killer.

This paradoxical society with its gaming and its fits of avid
moralism, its equal passion for cockfighting and for sermoniz-
ing, comprised a serious and extensive public opinion. Burke's
estimate of 400,000 persons capable of taking a minimally
informed and intelligent interest in public affairs was too low
even for the middle of the century. It fails to take into account
the increasing literacy of the respectable artisan, not to mention
the vast class of domestic servants. It underrates the new seriousness inculcated into the small shopkeepers and craftsmen in
town and village by the spread of dissenting religion. It ignores
the impulse given to the less cultivated intelligence of large
numbers of unskilled workers by the recurrent pressure of

economic hardship. Illiteracy was never so widespread as was once believed by the pioneers of state-provided schools. The Victorians, who so often deplored the illiteracy of their fore-fathers, were living at a time when an earlier literacy had been stultified by the growth of mechanized industry. Not only had the smaller grammar schools remained, until close on the nine-teenth century, open to the children of working men, but since 1700 there had been an important extension of elementary education of the children of the poor at the hands of the Charity Schools founded under the aegis of the Society for the Promo-tion of Christian Knowledge. Even if a bare literacy was all that these schools afforded in the matter of book-learning, their training in manners and morals—the virtues of industry, thrift, and sobriety—ensured that a great many more children than ever before grew into adults with a serious and responsible attitude to the duties and responsibilities of social life. No doubt the virtues inculcated were callow, and generally concerned to safeguard the persons and the pockets of 'the better sort' who patronized charity as an insurance policy, but they took the edge off savagery and opened the way to better things.

Moreover, wherever a dissenting chapel existed—and they were exceedingly numerous after the Toleration Act of 1689 and the slackening of the spirit of persecution in the reigns of the early Hanoverian kings—there also existed a centre, however crude, for the crystallization of a social consciousness, even for the rudimentary experience of self-government. It was a French-man, accustomed to the monolithic religious life of a Roman Catholic society, who first revealed the vital part played by the multiformity of Protestant congregations in helping to make the England of George III 'in very truth the country of self-gov-ernment—the country which in the deepest sense—the moral and religious sense—of the phrase "governs itself" . . .'[1] The growth of Methodism, that strangest phenomenon of 'The Age of Reason', contributed enormously to this increase of self-consciousness in the masses of the people, even though its founder was an autocrat and a Tory. Finally, there was a vast number of dame-schools. These obscure and unnumbered

[1] Elie Halévy, *A History of the English People in the 19th Century*, Vol. 2, 'The Liberal Awakening', Introduction, p. vi.

centres of private adventure for the spread of literacy come to light at every turn in any inquiry into local history in eighteenth-century England. A widow, a spinster, a village shopkeeper, even a baker or a cobbler, was content to keep an eye on a row of small boys and girls chanting the alphabet or the multiplication table in some dim back-kitchen or workshop in return for a penny a week or a few turves to keep the fire.

Dr Johnson observed that the English in his time had become 'a nation of readers' and it is fairly clear that this had become most noticeable since the middle of the century. It is calculated that there were seventy-five printing-presses in London in 1724. By 1757 there were probably two hundred. The newspaper-buying public had multiplied itself by three during the first half of the century, and it was reckoned that every newspaper bought was read by at least ten persons. There was no mass book-reading public yet. For one thing, the price of a novel would have kept most families in food and shelter for a week. But there were already Circulating Libraries—a term which appears to have been invented in 1742. The enlarged public for any more strenuous reading than newspapers was made up of farmers, shopkeepers, tradesmen and servants. Servants of one kind or another composed the largest occupational group in society, and maid-servants and footmen with time on their hands were large consumers of low-grade literature.[1] They are unlikely to have taken to politics by reading, but it is noticeable that other servants of the 'waiting' variety, such as sedan-chairmen and porters, figure prominently in the Wilkite disturbances.

It is pleasant to think that the things which interest historians have not often been the things which most interested the people who lived with history. Even a cursory reference to the volumes of the *Annual Register* reveals that the nation as a whole was not greatly concerned with the manœuvres attending the fall of Pitt, the ascendancy of Bute, the retirement of Newcastle, or the fact that 'Chatham and Rockingham, Shelburne and North, with their Coalitions or their Separation Ministries, all ousted one another; and vehemently scrambled for the thing they call

[1] And not so low-grade. Richardson's *Pamela*, 1740, was the story of a waiting-maid, avowedly written for her sisters in real life.

the Rudder of Government but which was in reality the Spigot of Taxation'. Instead, we discover a keen interest in the wrecking of Drury Lane Theatre in protest against the attempt to abolish the 'Half-Price Rule'; the shocking murder of Lord Dacre's butler at his Lordship's house in Hill Street; or the ingredients of a game-pie weighing 22 stone which was being drawn to London from Westmorland by two wagon-horses as a present to 'a certain great personage', who was almost certainly Mr Pitt. Fruit-trees in bloom in a mild January, a ruined hay-harvest in an unusually wet June, and a gentleman setting fire to gunpowder, paper, and linen by the refraction of noonday sunshine through a five-inch disc of ice in February: these things went on record along with the fledgling flight of King George and the vicissitudes of ministerial fortune. Who shall say they were any more worthy of oblivion?

CHAPTER II

The Age of Lord North

That well-known statesman was, in the most exact sense, a representative man . . . Germans deny it, but it is true that in every country common opinions are very common . . . Profound people look deeply for the maxims of his policy, and it being on the surface, of course they fail to find it. He did not what the mind but the body of the community wanted to have done; he appealed to the real people, the large English commonplace herd.

Walter Bagehot

HISTORY IS written by the successful people, and for long the successful people were the English, among whom the most successful people were the Whigs. When the Americans became the successful people, they took over English history, imposing upon it their own peculiar myths, greatly to the disrepute of those who ever had the temerity to stand in their way. Among these, Lord North is the saddest, though not the most tragical, figure. His blown-out cheeks and goggle eyes have left him stranded on the shores of history like a deflated frog. That he was in his best days a brilliant debater (which is so much more important in a House of Commons man than being a brilliant orator), a first-class Chancellor of the Exchequer, above all a man of the sweetest temper and the nicest honour who ever spent his days and nights in the parliamentary Noah's Ark— these things are easily forgotten. 'He lost America' is written on his brow (not on his heart, for it is unlikely that he ever loved America). That most Englishmen of his day and generation thought he was right, and that he was received everywhere with warm-hearted applause when he travelled about England after his resignation, are other facts easily forgotten or, if remembered, readily attributed to the sentimental English habit of cheering the loser.

He was at the Treasury (which means that he was Prime Minister) for close on twelve years. The King took him over from Grafton along with a good deal else, including Charles James Fox and a phalanx of place-seekers recruited from among the followers of the Duke of Bedford when Chatham resigned late in 1768; and in the hour of the King's peril, when the opposition Whigs seemed about to unite over American taxation and the expulsion of Wilkes, he had stepped into the breach and saved the day. There were numerous reasons why the opposition failed to impose themselves on the King in 1770, apart from the tactical genius of the Chancellor of the Exchequer, but George III (not habitually a grateful master) adopted Lord North forthwith as the Heaven-born Minister, the servant who was content to be (as North himself once put it) the person who held 'the place next to the director of Publick Affairs at this time', which was, after all, a just and accurate description of the position of a Prime Minister at that stage of constitutional development. It is untrue that the King wanted Lord North as his tool, let alone (in the less elegant phrase) a stooge. His letters in these years are full of urgent appeals to North to show more energy, to prepare plans, to take the lead, indeed—as things worsened—to ride the whirlwind and control the storm. All that can be said of Lord North is that he clung to the storm-tossed ship until it went on the rocks off Yorktown on 17 October 1781, the fourth anniversary of General Burgoyne's surrender at Saratoga Springs. On the former occasion, North had said 'the sooner Britain is out of this damned war the better'. At the news of Yorktown he threw up his hands and cried 'My God, all is over' in mingled misery and relief. At last he could resign with some hope of the King's letting him go. He had been trying to go for ten years.

A strange story, strictly beyond belief in the mid-twentieth century; a minister carrying out a policy in which he did not believe, at the King's command or conjuration. 'I will be responsible for nothing that I do not direct', Pitt had said on leaving office in 1761 because he could not have his war with Spain. 'Lord North's War', as men called it, was not Lord North's, but he could not disclaim it, nor evade responsibility for its conduct. Again and again the King wished to know

whether the wretched man was going to desert his royal master
in the base manner of the Duke of Grafton? Again and again
Lord North protested his fidelity after the manner of Mrs
Micawber. As a man of honour, Lord North was keenly conscious of his manifold indebtedness to the royal friend and
master. He was, for a Minister of the Crown in those days, a
poor man. He had a large family, and his financial abilities (like
those of the Younger Pitt) were applied exclusively to the
management of the nation's finances. Throughout his long
martyrdom his health steadily deteriorated. So limpet-like was
the attachment of the King and his minister that there arose a
certain amount of base, and baseless speculation on the possibility of their common paternity. They were not unlike in
physical feature, and George's father, Frederick Prince of
Wales, had stood godfather to Lord Guilford's eldest son and
given him his own name. A more reputable explanation is to be
found in the King's deluded but undying hope that Frederick
North, given time, would recover his magnificent form of the
year 1770 if only, like Mrs Dombey, he would 'make an effort'.
He did not, apparently could not, make an effort, and early in
1782 went down in defeat, confessing—indeed boasting—that
he had left undone the main thing that he ought to have been
doing for years: interfering in the departments of his colleagues.

In these years many plump English gentlemen sat behind the
Prime Minister in bag wigs, flowered and quilted waistcoats
and little toy swords that they had no intention of using on
anyone, least of all on American colonists; gentlemen closely
resembling Lord North in face and figure and opinions; so that
there can hardly be any extravagance in calling the 1770s 'The
Age of Lord North'. One of these was the Member for the
pocket-borough of Liskeard, a man of almost absurdly similar
aspect with his bag-cheeks, his double-chin, his buttonhole
mouth, his little pot-belly and his short legs. The first volume of
his great history of *The Decline and Fall of the Roman Empire*
appeared in the spring of 1776. The last volumes were to be
published twelve years later, replete with compliments to Lord
North's vigorous intelligence and matchless good humour. The
publication accompanied, step by step, the loss of the colonies
and the defeat of the mother country by a European coalition

of a kind that she has been more accustomed to lead than to meet in arms. It was said, indeed, that the King contemplated offering the historian a 'place' in order to deter him from composing a sequel on the decline and fall of the Empire of Great Britain. However, the Member for Liskeard, like so many in the serried ranks behind Lord North, never opened his mouth but simply sat—and voted correctly. Of course, as a scholar he suffered both insolence and ambiguity from the lips of more active men. When he presented a volume to the Duke of Gloucester, he met with the celebrated query: 'Another damned thick square book! Scribble, scribble, scribble, eh Mr Gibbon?' He misheard Sheridan's reference to 'the luminous pages of Gibbon' at the trial of Warren Hastings as a reference to his 'voluminous pages'.

Not that Gibbon's silence in the House of Commons signified approval of the Prime Minister's conduct of affairs. Despite his later compliments and his respect for the man's mind and temper, he never had much of an opinion of Lord North as a statesman. Of course, he knew the colonists were in the wrong, but there soon came a point where he found it 'easier to defend the justice than the policy of our measures . . . I shall never give my consent,' he was to write in 1777, 'to exhaust still further the finest country in the world in this prosecution of a war from whence no reasonable man entertains any hope of success. It is better to be humbled than ruined.' The words might have been those of any, or all, the lesser Gibbons in Lord North's majority. Indeed, they might have been those of Lord North himself. Gibbon's more celebrated remark that nothing could save the country but the heads of six ministers laid on the table, however, was not made in the House of Commons, but at Brooks's. And, in the summer of 1779, when the Bourbon monarchies of France and Spain had entered the war on the side of the Americans, Gibbon was employed to write an answer to their manifesto (which, of course, he did in the impeccable French of a cosmopolite Englishman), and in July he was appointed to a Lordship of Trade at £800 p.a. When, introducing his Economical Reform Bill, in the following year, Burke proposed to abolish the Board of Trade, describing it as 'perhaps the only instance of a public body which has never degenerated' since it had begun as a job and never lost the health and vigour of its original institution, he made greatly merry about 'the learned leisure' of its members.

1776, the year of the American Declaration of Independence and the first volume of *The Decline and Fall*, saw also the publication of *The Wealth of Nations*. Never was a book by a professor which showed so profound a knowledge of the real occupations of mankind. It supplied the rationale of capitalism in advance of the thing itself. No reference was made to steam-engines or cotton-mills, nor anywhere did the author employ the term *laissez-faire*. When Smith wanted to illustrate the principle of the division of labour, he took as his example the manufacture of pins. While he assumed that the economic system was, like nature, a self-regulating system, and that free competition enabled it to maintain its internal equilibrium, it should be remembered that he was addressing himself to a commercial, but not as yet a properly industrial, state. It should also be remembered that behind his book on political economy stood the larger features of a comprehensive work on moral philosophy. *The Wealth of Nations* was only a fragment of a vast plan, the nature of which can best be perceived in its predecessor, *The Theory of Moral Sentiments*. As Walter Bagehot put it, 'he produced an enduring particular result in consequence of a comprehensive and diffused ambition'. Like Saul, he went in search of his father's asses, and found a kingdom. In looking for 'the natural progress of opulence' he discovered the laws of wealth; and he investigated the progress of opulence as part of the growth and progress of all things.

Bagehot also points out that *The Wealth of Nations* is 'a very amusing book about old times', a book crammed full of curious particulars of a world that was passing away; a book for historians, even for the antiquary, it is also a book of prophecy. In its closing pages, we hear a contemporary voice, when an Empire was in dissolution, descanting upon the troublesome and expensive nature of colonies, more especially such colonies as refuse to submit to British taxes. 'The rulers of Great Britain have, for more than a century past, amused the people with the imagination that they possessed a great empire on the west side of the Atlantic. This empire, however, has hitherto existed in imagination only.' It was time that our rulers made this expensive dream pay off, or that they should awaken from it. 'If the project cannot be completed, it ought to be given up.' Great Britain should then free herself from the expense of defending these provinces in time of war, or of supporting any part of their civil or military establishments in time of peace. In short, she should 'endeavour to accommodate her future views and designs to the real mediocrity of her circumstances'. These are the last words of *The Wealth of Nations*. They surpass all else in the year 1776, and most in the year 1967, for contemporary relevance. Gibbon had composed the epitaph of one Empire. Adam Smith had forecast the destiny of another.

Besides deliverances of such portentous weight as these, the third classic work published this year wears a slightly impertinent air. It was called *A Fragment on Government* and was the work (although it was originally published anonymously) of Jeremy Bentham, a briefless young barrister of Lincoln's Inn.[1] It opened with the words:

> The age we live in is a busy age: in which knowledge is rapidly advancing towards perfection. In the natural world, in particular, every thing teems with discovery and with improvement.

It went on to ask why, since the age was teeming with discoveries and improvements in the world of nature, there was yet so little advance in the moral world, the world of law and government? Who were the enemies of such improvement? Where lay the obstruction? And the young man proceeded to identify the chief enemy to reformation in the celebrated author of the *Commentaries on the Laws of England*, i.e. (although Bentham does not name him) Sir William Blackstone. Jeremy Bentham had gone down from Oxford in 1758 when Sir William, as Vinerian Professor, first delivered his lectures on the Laws of England, but in 1763 he had gone back on purpose to hear him. He listened, he tells us, 'with rebel ears'. He had been unable

---

[1] Briefless because he had begun his career as a barrister by advising his client to go home and save his money. Such was the state of the law that no honest man could condescend to make a living by it. Bentham set out to make a law fit for Bentham to practise. Fortunately he had a small private income. He was to spend the rest of his very long life as a law reformer.

to take any notes 'as my thoughts were occupied in reflecting on what I heard'. In fact, he was already enjoying one of his life-long amusements, the detection of fallacies.[1] He very soon decided that he must clear the ground for reform by exposing the fallacies of the author of the *Commentaries*, that classic work which enshrined the English Constitution as the Ark of the Covenant. Young Bentham, though often disrespectful, gave Sir William his due as a writer. He was the first, he said, 'to teach Jurisprudence to speak the language of the Scholar and the Gentleman'. In a sense that was the trouble with the celebrated *Commentaries*, for 'the enchanting harmony of its numbers' had given 'a certain degree of celebrity to a work devoid of every other. So much is man governed by the ear.' Bentham was to undertake the task of disenchantment. He wrote his *Comment on the Commentaries* (of which the *Fragment of Government* was only a part, hence its title) with the avowed intention of diminishing the regard paid to Blackstone by showing that his ideas were vague, confused, inconsistent—or simply platitudinous. He also wished to show that Blackstone was absurdly complacent about things as they were, basing his complacency on personal and professional prejudice rather than a rational examination of the public good. In short his was very much a young man's intention: 'to do something to instruct, but more to undeceive, the timid and admiring student: to excite him to place more confidence in his own strength and less in the infallibility of great names; to help him to emancipate his judgment from the shackles of authority'. Here was the eighteenth-century's champion 'debunker'. After Jeremy Bentham published his *Fragment* there was really no excuse for anyone who had read it to indulge in habitual and unthinking genuflection at the mention of Our Glorious Constitution. Needless to say, the good old habit was to go on for long enough yet, even though some thousands of Americans were putting

---

[1] His *Book of Fallacies*, 1824, came out when he was seventy-six, and had something of a vogue among the clever young men of the time. It even cropped up in *Pelham* (1827), a popular novel by the dandiacal Bulwer Lytton. 'True, my dear mother, said I with a most unequivocal yawn, and depositing on the table Mr Bentham on Popular Fallacies . . . ' Lytton was, at that time, suffering from a mild attack of Benthamism.

thumbs to noses and fingers to triggers at the self-same utterance. The principal 'undebunker', if the term may be forgiven, was Edmund Burke who, stung to fury by the denouement of the American drama on the soil of France, revived the habit of what old Major Cartwright was to call 'never speaking on the Constitution . . . but in trope, or figure, or mysterious allusion . . .' Burke was turned sixty when he wrote his *Reflections on the French Revolution*. When he brought out his *Fragment on Government*, Bentham was twenty-eight. 'Knowledge of the speculative principles of men in general between the age of twenty and thirty is the one great source of political prophecy,' said Francis Bacon.[1]

The 1770s resembled the 1760s in this, that their quality is likely to be obscured by an excessive attention to politics. Politically considered, the years of Lord North's Administration are bad, sad years, years of a broken empire, defeat in arms, a melancholy struggle to survive. That they issued into an age of national revival under a second Pitt is no heroic tale like that of the first Elizabeth or of Churchill. In these years there was neither a darkest nor a finest hour. If anyone had a finest hour, it was the King, who behaved throughout with John-Bull courage and resolution. When the French and Spanish fleets threatened invasion in the summer of 1779, British sea-power being then at its lowest ebb, it was the King, almost alone, who welcomed the prospect of bringing them to close action without 'the smallest anxiety' about the outcome, given the favour of Divine Providence and as long as 'the officers and men of my fleet will act with the ardour the times require'. Firmness, he reiterated, was the 'characteristic of an Englishman', and he congratulated himself (a little rashly perhaps) on having infused into Lord North and his ministers 'some of that spirit which I thank Heaven ever attends me when under difficulties'. Next year, John Dunning proposed, and carried, his resolution: 'that the influence of the Crown has increased, is increasing, and ought to be diminished'. But then, as somebody said, the minds of the opposition were as narrow as the necks of vinegar-cruets. Even when Yorktown had come and gone at the end of 1781, the King was praying Heaven 'to guide me so to act that

[1] The aphorism was attributed to Bacon by S. T. Coleridge.

posterity may not lay the downfall of this once respectable empire at my door'. Like Winston Churchill at the time of the partition of India, he could not see that he was called upon to preside with equanimity over the dissolution of the British Empire. And lo! before the Peace of Versailles signalized the final independence of the United States of America, Rodney's defeat of De Grasse in the West Indies ensured the restoration of most of what had been lost there to the House of Bourbon, and General Eliott's salvation of Gibraltar after a three years' siege enabled His Britannic Majesty to end the war in a blaze of glory.

The Age of Lord North, however, shines brightest in the memory of Englishmen as the age of Dr Johnson, the great subject who preserved his age, single-handed and for ever, from the monopoly of the political historian. Nor is Johnson's pre-eminence an illusion of historical perspective which afflicts the minds of later generations suffering from a poverty of giants in 'the century of the common man'. It was acknowledged and sometimes resented, at the time. Whatever may have been happening at the other end of the capital where the King and his ministers had their being, it was what happened—most of all, perhaps, what was said—in the little courts off Fleet Street that gave the form and pressure of the time. For here was assembled, informally and in day-to-day discourse, the liveliest brains of an age and a society second to none in that great century of civility. Johnson had been the Great Lexicographer for twenty years, and the author of *Rasselas* for more than ten, and in the crisis-year of 1779 he was embarking on his great edition of *The Lives of the Poets*. The Great Cham of literature had borne the title of King of the Tartars since the year before King George's accession. After the Hebridean Tour of 1773 he was to bear also the nickname given to him by Alexander Boswell, Ursa Major. The tartar and the bear signify the gruff despotism of the man which evokes the howls of pain and delight of posterity, but which often repelled contemporaries of a more polished, not to say feminine, mould. Samuel Johnson and Thomas Gray were the antipodes of the literary world and, fortunately perhaps, they never met, for Johnson made no bones about his opinion of the poet of the *Churchyard*. 'Sir, he was dull in a new way, and that made many people think him GREAT.' David Hume, who was better able to bear the heat of the day, disliked Johnson's despotism with an aversion which must remain the most serious criticism of the whole society. The society of Johnson's London repelled him principally by its almost unalloyed masculinity. For all its rugged charm, when compared with the salon-society of the contemporary France which Hume knew so well, it lacked the gentler moods dispensed by the presidency of *les grandes dames.*

With Burke, Goldsmith, Reynolds, Garrick, all the great company of 'The Club' portrayed and recorded by the voluminous papers of James Boswell and given to the world in the present century, it is easy to forget for a while the troubled sky of Lord North's political malfeasance. A man might live out his life in that society under the persuasion not only that America was well lost but that history itself had stopped upon *une douceur de la vie* which eludes the treasonable hand of time itself. Not that Johnson forgot Lord North and America. 'He had long . . . indulged most unfavourable sentiments of our fellow-subjects in America . . . a race of convicts who ought to be thankful for anything we allow them short of hanging.' That was in 1769. Six years later he wrote *Taxation no Tyranny.* And Lord North, in the middle of his American troubles in 1775, did not forget Johnson. As Chancellor of Johnson's old University, he wrote to the Vice-Chancellor commending to his honourable attention the great *alumnus,* with the consequence that Samuel Johnson was to be known for ever as Doctor Johnson. North commended him for his 'Essays, excellently calculated to form the manners of the people,' and made no reference to the subaltern subject of politics. As for Dr Johnson, 'he did not vaunt of his new dignity, but I understood that he was highly pleased with it'. Boswell's chief item of record for that honourable day concerns rather the great man's habit of secreting orange-peel in his pockets, and his mysterious refusal to throw any light on the matter:

JOHNSON: I have a great love for them.
BOSWELL: Sir, what do you do with them? You scrape them, it seems, very neatly, and what next?
JOHNSON: Nay, sir, you shall know their fate no further.

BOSWELL: Then the world must be left in the dark. It must be said . . . he scraped them, and let them dry, but what he did with them next he never could be prevailed upon to tell.

JOHNSON: Nay, sir, you should put it more emphatically: he could not be prevailed upon, even by his dearest friends, to tell.

CHAPTER 12

The Discovery of England

They recognized that the most brilliant discovery of a brilliant
age was the discovery of their own country.
A. L. Rowse: 'The England of Elizabeth'

IT IS something that happens about once in a century, and it
all began with the *Itinerary* that John Leland wrote for King
Henry VIII. After Leland came Lambarde and Camden,
Harrison and Speed. Then, after the great triumphs of war
and revolution under the Stuart kings, when William III and
Queen Anne presided over a settlement which men wished to
believe everlasting, once again men—and women—thought it
time to take stock. Daniel Defoe rode out on his Tours, and
Celia Fiennes quartered England on a side-saddle. A century
later, when another revolution was changing the land, England
was not only inspected by curious continental travellers who
wanted to find out how a people could achieve both wealth and
liberty, but by home-grown tourists like John Wesley and
Arthur Young who knew the answer but were not content with
the condition of either souls or turnips.

Shakespeare's England was a realm becoming vividly conscious of itself as an 'empire'. The precious stone set in the silver
sea was aware of itself not only as a fair and precious jewel, a
subject for poetry, but as a unique and self-standing political
entity, an empire not in the sense of expansion (though this too
was about to begin) but as contracting upon its own distinct
and separate sovereignty. By the time of the Hanoverians, the
success of this vigorous nation in bridling kings and instituting
responsible government was making it the cynosure of all eyes,
and by the time of the third of them it was presenting phenomena unique in human experience, signs and portents of an

epoch which, within a century, was to transform the face of the world and to change the course of history. This was the first and heroic phase of the Industrial Revolution.

Let there be no mistake about it: men recognized it as something mighty and majestic and even beautiful, whatever they were to think of it when another century brought forth the wilderness of Manchester and Leeds and Birmingham. They spoke of it in terms of the Sublime, and because theirs was a classical age, when the languages and images of the ancient Mediterranean cultures came easily to the lips and the imagination of educated persons, they spoke of it in terms of empire. The ruins of Greece and Rome had lately been revealed to them by the uncovering of Herculaneum, and by the lucubrations of a whole fashionable world of scholarship, and antiquarianism. Josiah Wedgwood, founding his pottery works at Burslem in 1769, naturally enough christened it Etruria. He would, he boasted, throw pots in Staffordshire at least as handsome as those of the Etruscans. Was not England on the way to establishing a second Roman Empire after the triumphs of the Seven Years' War? In 1756, the year of its outbreak, Edmund Burke had published his book, *A Philosophical Inquiry into the Origin of our Ideas of the Sublime and the Beautiful*, much after the style of Longinus *On the Sublime*, and the cult of the Sublime was the cult of 'whatever is fitted in any sort to excite the ideas of pain and danger, that is to say, whatever is in any sort terrible'. And certainly, as forge and furnace, fire and flame lighted the night-sky over Coalbrookdale with the industrial exploits of Abram Darby, and as the sparks set off similar spectacles all over the West Midlands and the Lowlands of Scotland, Sublimity was made manifest in the works of man. Even 'stenches' came into Burke's catalogue of the ingredients of sublimity, and the stenches of industry were likewise manifest. Promptly enough, Arthur Young, visiting Coalbrookdale in 1776, called the spectacle 'horridly sublime'. The frisson was worthy of expression in poetry and painting.

Both these arts celebrated the industrial triumphs in the classic style. Perhaps the poetry were better described as poetizing. It mostly originated in the clergy. The Rev. John Dalton's 'Descriptive Poem addressed to two Ladies at their returning

from Viewing the Mines near Whitehaven' (1755) explained
in octosyllabic couplets the mechanics of the stationary steam-
engine for pumping water out of coal-pits, a device patented by
Savery as early as 1689 and improved by Newcomen in 1712
(James Watt's steam-engine did not arrive until 1769). Dalton
included a properly classical paean to Savery and concluded
with a couplet asserting the superiority of his triumphs over
those of Rome itself.

> Man's richest gift thy work will shine;
> Rome's aqueducts were poor to thine.

When a few years later Arthur Young saw Barton Bridge, with
barges sailing in mid-air by means of Brindley's artificial water-
way, he predicted that it would 'exceed the noblest work of the
Romans when masters of the world'. Most instructive of all,
perhaps, was the Rev. John Dyer's celebrated poem on the textile trades, *The Fleece* (1757). Dr Johnson included Dyer in the
Lives of the Poets, although in his scorn for technical accomplishments he seems to have resembled Cobbett, who once said that
he never cared to see machines in case he was tempted to try
to understand them. Greatly to Boswell's disappointment the
Doctor declined to accompany him on a visit to Matthew Bol-
ton's Soho manufactory when they were in the neighbourhood
of Birmingham in 1776, for, Boswell thought, 'the vastness and
contrivance of some of the machinery would have matched his
mighty mind'. So, when he came to Dyer on *The Fleece*, while
he was willing to acknowledge the poet's earnest endeavour 'to
interest the reader in our native commodity', he was sure that
such endeavours must fail because of the discordant natures of
the woolcomber and the poet, 'the meanness naturally adher-
ing, and the irreverence habitually annexed to trade and
manufacture, sink him under insuperable oppression; and the
disgust which blank verse, encumbering and encumbered,
superadds to an unpleasing subject, soon repels the reader,
however willing to be pleased'. This from a born Midlander
must always disappoint us. Perhaps it indicates another of
Johnson's shortcomings as a true representative of the England
of his age. He need, after all, have had no fear of Dyer's sinking
himself into coarse or vulgar modes, for he was celebrating an

ancient, one might almost say an aristocratic industry before
the onset of the machine-age and mass-production. The engine
described in *The Fleece* is the water-wheel and its modern acces-
sories. 'The spiral engine' on a hundred 'spoles, a hundred
threads with one huge wheel, by lapse of water twines, few
hands requiring'. And Dyer can never bring himself to write of
artisans; his operatives are 'artists', and his masters are 'careful
factors', industry throughout is called 'art' and the poem is full
of 'beauteous shapes . . . freize and column . . . sacred domes'.
All the same, Dyer warns the reader against assuming a snob-
bish attitude:

> To censure trade
> Or hold her busy people in contempt
> Let none presume . . .

Such instances of 'poetizing' industry belong to the decade
before George III's accession. Within less than a generation,
when Erasmus Darwin published his *Botanic Garden*, the tone
had changed. Dr Darwin, another Midland man, prominent
at one time in both Lichfield and Derby, has as his avowed
purpose 'to enlist the imagination under the banner of science'.
It is true that his verse is full of classical figures and images, and
he even brings in 'the nymphs of the steam-engine' for factory
girls, but it is also true that there is no better, or more enlivening, way of discovering the exact state of science and technology in the last decade of the eighteenth century than from
the text, and notes, of *The Botanic Garden*. The poem was immensely successful, being published in two parts in 1789 and
1791 respectively, and reprinted four times before the end of
the century.

Painting, as a visual art, was rather bolder from the start in
adapting its idiom to the world of industry. By a number of
devices, not the least effective of which was the use of chiaroscuro, painting could deliver upon the eyes and the nerves of
the beholder an almost physical assault scarcely less forcible
than that of the original object portrayed. It is perfectly true
that an artist of the Paul Sandby tradition, like Edward Rooker
(1712–1774), could do justice to the luminous classical manner
even to the sublimities of Coalbrookdale, but the subject found

15. Conversation piece by Zoffany

16. The Gordon Riots, after a painting by Wheatley

a more appropriate master in a painter like Philip James de Loutherbourg (b. 1740), who had been a scenic designer for Drury Lane Theatre and in a later time would have been a pioneer of motion-pictures in technicolor. By 1787 George Robertson's pictures, which fulfilled most of Burke's prescription for sublimity, were plainly making smooth the path to the dramatic excesses of Salvator Rosa. The great exponent of chiaroscuro was Joseph Wright of Derby (1734–1797), who, like L. S. Lowry in the present century, spent almost the whole of his artistic life on his native heath. Wright made the conventional Italian journey in the years 1734–5, and he also made the mistake of trying to set up in Bath as successor to Gainsborough in the years 1775–7, but the industrial Midlands in the neighbourhood of Derby were to provide him with subjects best suited to his genius as a painter of light: the fire and darkness of an iron-forge, the flaring windows of Arkwright's mill in the night over Cromford gorge, the white-heat of a glasshouse, the candle-lit faces of men of science experimenting with an air-pump or exhibiting an orrery. He also painted the hardheaded men of the Midlands who were making the new world: Richard Arkwright with his hand resting on a model of his spinning-machine; Samuel Crompton, inventor of the self-acting mule (a cross between the spinning-jenny and the water-frame); and Dr Darwin, who turned it all into verse. Wright was a poet in paint whose subject-matter was the physical world coming to life around him, even though there are obvious stylistic traces in his pictures of the traditional subjects of religious painting, notably, the nativity-like features of his blacksmith's shop with the blacksmith's wife with her child in her arms beside the smith at the beam-hammer.

Much of the work of the early phases of the industrial revolution was carried on in romantic surroundings, in narrow gorges, remote regions of rock and fast-flowing streams where water-power could be harnessed. For a long time to come, the areas affected by such activities were not regarded as ruined, desecrated, or squalid, but rather as romanticized further by man's energies, or at any rate as rendered more interesting. As Thomas Hardy once noted, 'the baldest external objects in a picture are "infused" with emotion by the presence of a human figure among them, or by the mark of some human connexion with them'. Such objects as pit headstocks, canals, bridges, mill-chimneys were to be admired. There was even something attractive about the discord set up between such objects and the surrounding landscape. It is evident that a painter like Joseph Wright was untroubled by intimations of two cultures when he went from painting Dovedale in sunshine around 1782–5 to painting Cromford mills by moonlight in 1789. That 'plain, almost gross, bag-cheeked, pot-bellied Lancashire man, Richard Arkwright' as Thomas Carlyle once remarked, 'was not a beautiful man', while Elizabeth Sacheverell Pole (the widow espoused by Erasmus Darwin) was almost a Madonna in the style of Gainsborough: but Joseph Wright painted them both in all their native worth against the background of Midland culture at the dawn of the industrial revolution, the one for £52 10s., and the other for £63.

Wright's title, 'Wright of Derby', is almost a boast. It would be absurd to refer to Sir Joshua Reynolds as 'Reynolds of Plympton' or to talk of 'Lawrence of Devizes', let alone 'Hogarth of London'. Provincial life in the reign of George III was still a real and vital thing. London had not yet drawn into itself the constellations of genius like a central sun, though the term 'The Provinces' appears first in 1789[1] as a term indicating the non-metropolitan England instead of 'the country'. Of course, hopeful youth had always made for London 'where the streets are paved with gold' in the first excitement of genius. Under George III, however, it did not always stay there. Thomas Bewick, the genius of the woodcuts, made for the Thames on a collier in 1776, the *annus mirabilis* of Gibbon, Bentham and Adam Smith. After nine months he was back on Tyneside, resolved never to return. London was 'a province covered with houses', overcrowded, dirty, unfriendly, in fact 'the Great Wen' as Cobbett was soon to call it. Norwich, Birmingham, Bristol, Newcastle and many another 'provincial' city might have as much, or more, to offer of intellectual stimulus and energizing scenes. In these centres flourished the spontaneous local institutions of an undivided culture, calling themselves Literary and Philosophical Societies, many of them to

---

[1] See Donald Read, *The English Provinces*, opening paragraph.

have long and distinguished lives. The most notable of them was the Lunar Society of Birmingham which started in 1765 and whose bi-centenary has recently been celebrated with an exhibition and the publication of a History.[1] The 'Lunatics' took their name from the habit of certain professional men of the Birmingham area of dining at each other's houses on nights when the moon was sufficiently full to make travel safe against the perils of footpads and execrable roads. Dr William Small, a Scottish man of science who had been Professor of Mathematics and Natural Philosophy at Williamsburg in Virginia, came with letters of introduction to Matthew Boulton, the button-maker of the Soho works. He brought together for the sociable exchange of ideas a group of diversely gifted men, including Boulton himself, James Watt, Francis Galton, Josiah Wedgwood, Erasmus Darwin, and a number of others. They formed the nearest English equivalent to the dinner-table society of the Baron d'Holbach, known as *le café de l'Europe* in *La rue Royale-Saint-Roche* in Paris. They were indeed in certain limited respects, the English opposite numbers of the French Philosophes, with whose works some of them were familiar. The intellectual intercourse thus engendered was in strong contrast to that of Dr Johnson's 'Club' in the capital. It had no presiding despot or Great Cham. In tone it was not autocratic, but egalitarian, the fruitful outcome of diversity, although the prevailing interest was technological, the application of science to industrial purposes. It has been said that the Lunatics represented the vanguard of scientific thinking in England for a quarter of a century, and constituted 'the scientific General Staff of the Industrial Revolution'. Informal societies like the Lunar Society of Birmingham actually succeeded to the initiative once enjoyed by the Royal Society of London in promoting the application of science to social purpose.

By contrast with the Royal Society, these provincial associations were stationed on the very scene of industrial development itself. They owed their vigorous life to the strong self-consciousness of men actively engaged in industry, men who felt themselves—often without any real justification—debarred from the

[1] The Exhibition was held at Birmingham, and the book is Robert E. Schofield's *The Lunar Society of Birmingham*.

culture of the 'Establishment'. Many of them were Protestant nonconformists who had established their own educational institutions in the form of those ubiquitous organs of dissenting religion in the century of Wesley, the Academies, schools and colleges whose curricula tended to be more utilitarian or 'practical' than the classics-ridden studies of Oxford and Cambridge and the ancient public schools. There was here, as Herbert Butterfield has put it, 'a fissure which at times almost seems to amount to a cleavage between two forms of civilisation'. Not that a class interpretation of the phenomena on the lines of a supposititious conflict between town and country, manufacturer and landowner, has much illumination to offer. A great deal of the intellectual energy engendered in provincial England at this time arose out of the cultural, and agricultural, interests of the landed gentry, great and small. Landed gentlemen patronized the topographical literature of the age, looking with particular favour upon 'estate-poems' and the varied forms of work which held up to admiration their latest building operations, advancing the already considerable interest in 'stately Homes'[1] and 'Seats' and 'Retreats'. In the years of the dull Hanoverian Courts, gentlemen preferred to spend a large proportion of their time on their estates, making their country houses into miniature 'courts' where they themselves presided over the local life of county town and countryside. Many of them belonged to the ranks of 'gifted amateurs' in not only the arts, but the sciences as well. They often had good practical reasons for taking an interest in soil-science. Their explorations for mineral wealth beneath their fields led them to advance both geological and archaeological studies, somewhat as engineers were to open up the archives of the earth when they made the railway cuttings in the next century. One way and another they did a good deal of damage to archaeological treasures with their gentlemanly 'digs', mostly conducted without technical skill and carried through by field labourers wielding spade and pickaxe with more rude vigour than knowledge of, or respect for, what they were likely to find. The treasures

---

[1] They were not known as 'stately' until after Mrs Felicia Hemans' popular poem of that title, composed in the 1820s.

retrieved were carried off to cabinets and wall-racks in manor-house and hall, sometimes to be lost for ever by some domestic accident in an age of primitive fire-fighting appliances.

The country houses to which were carried the injured arte-facts turned up by the spades of amateur gentlemen archaeolo-gists among the long barrows of their ancestral lands were also the repositories of the *objets d'art* which these same gentlemen brought back from their travels in Europe, and more especially from their most expensive educational experience, the Grand Tour.

CHAPTER 13

The Discovery of Europe
or
the Grand Tour

MANY A young man of family was sent on the Grand Tour because his parents or guardians felt a wholesome distrust of the Universities which in the middle of the eighteenth century were at a pretty low ebb in both scholarship and morality. In 1771 Lady Leicester of Holkham Hall in Norfolk, for instance, having lost her own son in consequence of a career of debauchery, offered her great-nephew and presumptive heir, Thomas Coke of Longford in Derbyshire, £500 per annum if he should 'chuse to travel' instead of going to 'one of those Schools of Vice, the Universities'. Her late husband had gone on the Grand Tour of Europe to complete his education some sixty years before, and her Ladyship was still living out her widowhood in that Italianate palace beside the North Sea which Lord Leicester had built to embody the fine classical taste, and the multitude of books and manuscripts, pictures and sculptures, acquired in his youthful years of travel.

Young Thomas Coke did not hesitate. He set out at seventeen to explore that large and fascinating place known as 'abroad', to be welcomed everywhere as 'le bel Anglais' or, despite his life-long preference to remain simply 'Mr Coke', the English 'Milord' with a passport to the best society of Europe. Many elderly persons living beneath the Italian sun still remembered his great-uncle, 'Il Cavaliero Coke', who had passed that way sixty years ago with his coach-and-six, his guineas, his attendant carriages and his retinue of chaplain, gentleman-of-the-horse, steward and valet de chambre. That was in the last year of the

War of the Spanish Succession and the first years of the Peace of Utrecht, the sunset of the reign of Le Grand Monarque, of Queen Anne and the great Duke of Marlborough. Now it was the age of George III, Lord North and John Wilkes, of Richard Arkwright and John Wesley, of Jean-Jacques Rousseau and Tom Paine.

It was all very grand, and very expensive. Young Thomas Coke had a basic allowance of £700 a year, and he was away for three years. Other travellers on the Grand Tour—his great-uncle, 'Il Cavaliero' for instance—commonly spent five times the amount. £10,000 to £15,000 expended over three, four or five years, was quite common. The Grand Tour was the expedient of a wealthy aristocracy. It was what may be called 'significant expenditure'—intended to signify that you could afford it in terms of both time and money. To do it on the cheap would have deprived it of its social prestige-value. The elders and betters who footed the bill obviously thought it well worth while. It was a caste-mark within the aristocracy itself. Of course, for a younger son, especially if he were destined for the Church, a period at Oxford or Cambridge, costing only a fraction of the amount, was considered suitable and adequate. But for the young man who was to inherit great properties, and to play his part in politics, war and diplomacy, it was generally considered essential that he should learn manners and the arts of living in France, that he should acquire a correct taste for the fine arts in Italy, and that he should rub off any remains of English rusticity and insularity in the cosmopolitan courts and salons and noble houses of the Continent in general. In France he would learn to speak French (it was hoped) like his mother tongue—French, the language of diplomacy, of 'enlightened' philosophy, of universal 'politeness'. There, too, he would learn fencing and horsemanship; ballroom dancing and deportment; the latest style in sartorial elegance. He would practise the social graces in the masked-balls and festivities of Venice. In Italy he would learn to admire the domestic architecture of Palladio, Italian marbles, the stately style of Roman antiquity, along with the great master-painters of the Renaissance.

It would all be quite easy and perfectly delightful, for the

English Milord, with his far-famed liberality, was welcome everywhere. Doors opened to him at something less than a knock. Letters of introduction took him at once into the society of those who ruled the world of politics, diplomacy and fashion. His path was smoothed by prearrangement, established routes by land and sea, welcoming hostelries, relays of transport laid on in advance—unless he travelled in his own coach, which he often did. Not for him the uncertainties and discomforts experienced by the mere 'Englishman abroad', stumbling along on hired hacks or the public stage, from one village-inn to another, taking pot-luck among the fleas and the burnt ragoûts.[1] The first stage, from Dover to Calais, and the penultimate stage over the Alps from France and Switzerland into Italy, were the worst he would encounter, but once he was at Calais, there was M. Dessein's famous inn, the greatest establishment of its kind in Europe, with its hundred and thirty beds, and more than sixty indoor servants. M. Dessein catered almost exclusively for English travellers, and he ran an excellent post-chaise hire-service. From thence to Amiens, Chantilly and Paris, the route was well worn. After the quite obligatory visit to Versailles, Marly and Trianon, one might make for Rheims, Chalons and Dijon, or take the direct route through Burgundy to Lyons, and thence along the Rhone to Provence and the Riviera. Crossing the Alps, if one chose to confront the mountainous route from Geneva, was the penultimate stage of peril and discomfort. It could be quite terrifying, as Horace Walpole and Thomas Gray found when they went that way in 1739 on mule-back or in chairs swung on poles. Most travellers in the eighteenth century avoided it, their taste being for cities, preferably Roman cities, rather than unregulated scenery. There was no question of haste, or of making a bee-line across France to Italy. Many months would be spent in touring the cities of the Loire, or Languedoc. One might even venture from Bordeaux to the Pyrenees and into Spain, but this was not usually a success, for the Iberian Peninsula was a place of dirt and discomfort. There were plenty of guide-books to warn and encourage in all this. Thomas Nugent's *Grand Tour* was already

[1] Arthur Young's *Travels in France* provide a vivid account of what this kind of travel was like.

on sale by the middle of the century. By 1770 there was *The Gentleman's Guide in his Tour through France*. There was the semi-official *Livre de Poste*, an annual publication, to serve as a kind of Bradshaw to the post-chaise services. Once arrived in Italy, one could go with Jonathan Richardson's Account in hand. This little work, published in 1722, was the Baedeker of the Grand Tour for the art treasures of Italy. It would be an exaggeration to say that the Grand Tour ever became a European industry, like modern Tourism. All the same, as time went on, and Milord on his Tour himself became one of the sights of Europe, the thing took on some of the character of a ritual, with its well-worn routes, its familiar inns and stages, its classic hunting-grounds for antiques. Young Thomas Coke seems to have danced his way through France and Italy, although he did all the right things like climbing Vesuvius and visiting the excavations at Herculaneum. Like his great-uncle, 'Il Cavaliero Coke', the builder of Holkham, he brought back a number of spoils of the Renaissance and the classical world in his baggage; a bas-relief by Michelangelo, an antique mosaic, a magnificent antique of Minerva, and two fine mosaic tables from Hadrian's villa at Tivoli. All these were to be added to the wonderful collection with which 'Il Cavaliero' had stuffed his palace at Holkham half a century earlier. He also made away with the famous red opal ring which was discovered in the tomb of the Senator Nonius, a jewel which is mentioned by Pliny and which is said to have been wanted by Anthony as a gift for Cleopatra, and valued at somewhere around £20,000. Thomas Coke happened to be there when the tomb was opened. He got hold of it before anyone else had seen it, and he always declined to say what he had paid for it. Thus young Thomas collared his share of classical swag. He could hardly have been said to have made the Grand Tour otherwise. But it was infinitesimal when compared with the amount acquired by 'Il Cavaliero'.

It is difficult to resist the impression that Italy must have been running out of genuine antiques by the 1770s. For several generations, English gentlemen on the Grand Tour had been carrying off marbles, mosaics, pictures and manuscripts. Never had there been such a locust-swarm of art-hungry visitors since

the classical mania of the Renaissance. Of course, the middle-
men employed by the English buyers coped with the situation
with suitable ingenuity, and many a clever fake went back in
Milord's luggage to adorn some Palladian mansion set down
in England's green and pleasant land. The English art-dealer,
stationed in Italy, was an expert at 'restoration'. Joseph
Nollekens, the great sculptor, made a good thing out of it
during his residence in Rome in the 1760s. 'The patrons of
Nollekens', writes his biographer, 'being characters professing
taste and possessing wealth, employed him as a very shrewd
collector of antique fragments; some of which he bought on
his own account; and, after he had dexterously restored them
with heads and limbs, he stained them with tobacco-water, and
sold them, sometimes by way of favour, for enormous sums.'
On one occasion, he bought a head of Minerva from a fellow-
dealer and, having acquired a trunk of Minerva for fifty
pounds, invested some twenty pounds in stone and labour in
order to produce a complete Minerva, which he sold for a
thousand guineas. His repute as a sculptor in his own right
served him well in transactions of this kind. He also made quite
a profitable sideline out of smuggling Italian silk stockings,
lace ruffles and gloves inside hollow busts which he sent back
to England, sealing up their backs with a coating of plaster.
'There,' he once said to Lord Mansfield, pointing to the cast
of his celebrated bust of Laurence Sterne, the novelist; 'there,
do you know, that busto, my Lord, held my lace ruffles that
I went to Court in when I came from Rome.'

Whether the English gentleman on the Grand Tour, or doing
business with agents in Italy after his return, got genuine value
for his money or was fobbed off with a fake, largely depended
upon the extent of his own knowledge and cultivation. 'Professing taste and possessing wealth' implies a nice distinction, and
undoubtedly there were many who possessed more money than
sense. But, after all, the Grand Tour was, at its best, an educational enterprise. It quite often justified itself as an alternative
to a university education, and it might include within its
itinerary a period of residence at a foreign seat of learning.
Thus Thomas Coke, Earl of Leicester, 'Il Cavaliero', was sent
abroad to complete his education at the University of Turin,

and the Grand Tour was intended to be an enlargement of this primary academic experience. This young man supplies us, indeed, with the example *par excellence* of that combination of wealth and taste and scholarly interests which alone could make the Grand Tour a thoroughly profitable enterprise. Although he was little more than fifteen when he set out, he took with him not only a train of carriages and a retinue of servants, but a keen intelligence and a passionate devotion to literature. He was no mere collector of classical loot, a snob-victim of sharks and swindlers, but a scholar. He read his classical authors methodically as he travelled. He specialized in the works of, and anything connected with, the great Roman historian, Livy. He collected the works of most of the great Italian painters of the Renaissance, from Michelangelo to Titian. His knowledge and perspicuity, not to mention his great wealth, enabled him to purchase genuine, and genuinely beautiful examples of classical sculpture. True, he had the great good fortune to travel in Italy with the supreme arbiter of classical taste and wisdom, Lord Burlington; and for a time, at least, he travelled in the company of William Kent, the most celebrated architect in the Palladian style. For many years after his return to England, he was engaged in the planning, building and adornment of the great house on the coast of Norfolk which still remains, somewhat incongruously, perhaps, the finest monument to the art of Palladio among the country-houses of England. Holkham Hall might equally well be described as England's memorial of the Grand Tour, or of the education of English aristocratic taste.

Why this cult of the ancient civilizations of Greece and Rome?[1] In the great days of the Grand Tour, educated Englishmen believed themselves to be living in a second Augustan age. The wars of religion were over. Civil strife in its bloodier forms was coming to an end. England was believed to have arrived at a satisfactory and stable compromise in civil government and religious toleration by the Glorious Revolution of 1688–9. The

[1] It was very largely a cult of Rome, for few travellers ever reached the Greek lands in those days, owing largely to the Turk and other menaces to health and hygiene.

great figures were no longer Cromwell and Milton, but Walpole
and Pope. It was possible to believe that civility and politeness
were fast reaching the point where they might be seen to link
hands with the last great ages of moderation, equability and
peace—the ages of the Emperor Augustus and of the Antonines
—after so many centuries of 'Gothic barbarism', unrelieved
save for the brief glory of the Italian Renaissance. Moreover,
the Augustan age believed in 'Europe', and in a single 'European civilization' historically bounded by the frontiers of the
Roman Empire. Edmund Burke was to express this belief in the
basic unity of 'Europe' when he wrote in his *Letters on a Regicide
Peace*, in 1796, of 'the similitude throughout Europe of religion,
laws and manners'. Europe, he declared, was something more
than a mere aggregate of nations. It was a single commonwealth 'virtually one great state having the same basis of
general law, with some diversity of provincial customs and local
establishments'. No citizen of Europe could be altogether an
exile in any part of it. 'When a man travelled or resided abroad
for health, pleasure, business or necessity from his own country,
he never felt himself quite abroad.' No doubt there is some
exaggeration in this, as there is in most of Burke's nostalgic
statements. But there is some truth in it, especially at the higher
social levels. There certainly was something that might be called
an Aristocratic International in the eighteenth century, however little of it there was among peoples in general. 'Fraternity',
one of the watchwords of the French Revolution, was far less
in evidence among democrats than among aristocrats, as any
study of the *émigré* movement clearly reveals. To put it at the
lowest—the level of mere self-preservation—all aristocracies, in
all ages, are primarily concerned to keep the world safe for
aristocracy. The qualities they will cherish are necessarily the
qualities of stability, moderation, restraint: the qualities we
sum up in the vague term 'classical'. Roman antiquity embodied
them all.

Thus the cult of classical antiquity was as natural to the
aristocracy of the eighteenth century as the cult of the Middle
Ages was to become in the century that followed. It was as
natural to the aristocrat on the Grand Tour to visit Herculaneum and to bring home marbles and mosaics from the

disinterred temples and palaces of classical antiquity as it was
for the nineteenth-century tourist to go and visit fair Melrose
a-right by visiting it by pale moonlight, or for the tourist of the
twentieth century to bring home a camera full of snaps of
romantic scenery. These last are representative of the cult of the
romantic view of life, natural to middle-class or working-class
democracy. The aristocrat on the Grand Tour disliked the wild
and unregulated features of 'romantic' scenery, or nature untamed by the hand of man. It is said that Lord Chesterfield
used to draw down the blinds of his carriage when he came in
sight of the Alps. The poet, Thomas Gray, as early as 1739,
could record on his journey among the mountains to the
Grande Chartreuse: 'not a precipice, not a torrent, not a cliff,
but is pregnant with religion and poetry'. Gray heralded the
romantic response. Wordsworth, writing in *The Prelude* of his
youthful tramp to Italy as an undergraduate in 1790, was to
celebrate his first view of Mont Blanc and the majesty of the
mountains as affording men sublime insight into the heart of
truth. Chesterfield was an aristocrat, Gray was the son of a
scrivener, Wordsworth liked to think of himself as the adopted
son of Cumberland peasants. With these three we can see
tourism transformed from a stately progress in search of classical
antiquity to a hike in search of the beauties of nature.

The Grand Tour had always its critics. Criticism generally
turned upon its utility as an educational device for the youth
of an essentially commercial nation like the English. Was it
proper that young men should spend their formative years
frivolling at the courts of Europe, staring at Palladian façades,
or chasing after antiques? Certainly not, Adam Smith declared
unequivocally in *The Wealth of Nations* (1776). The popularity
of the Grand Tour as an alternative to a university education
simply indicated how low the Universities had fallen. 'Nothing
but the discredit into which the Universities are allowing themselves to fall, could ever have brought into repute so very
absurd a practice . . .' A young man who went abroad at seventeen, or eighteen, simply returned home, at one-and-twenty,
some three or four years older. Foreign languages? He might
have picked up a smattering, 'seldom sufficient to enable him
either to speak or write them with propriety'. Manners? 'He

commonly returns home more conceited, more unprincipled, more dissipated, and more incapable of any serious application, either to study or to business, than he could well have become in so short a time had he lived at home.' Beyond sight of his parents, 'spending in the most frivolous dissipation the most precious years of his life', every useful habit formed in his earliest years becomes weakened or effaced. As one might expect, the keynote of Adam Smith's comments is the test of utility— utility defined according to the standards of a man of business in the dawn of the industrial revolution.

Not that the application of such standards had to wait upon the increasing speed of industrial and commercial change in eighteenth-century England. John Locke was accredited with holding similar views nearly a hundred years before Adam Smith published his famous book. In 1764, Richard Hurd, Bishop of Worcester, published his *Dialogues on the uses of Foreign Travel, considered as a Part of an English Gentleman's Education.* Hurd put the argument into the mouths of Lord Shaftesbury and Mr Locke in a debate supposed to have taken place in 1700. While Shaftesbury, the dilettante philosopher and aesthete, champions foreign travel with all the customary arguments for the Grand Tour as a mode of higher education, Locke enters his caveats very much in the style of Adam Smith. He deplores the waste of time, the superficiality of the accomplishments attained, the lack of homely solidity and moral strength, the smattering and the premature sophistication. In the courts of Europe a young man learns servility rather than liberty, manners (of a kind) instead of sound morals, the civilization of gentlemen rather than the culture of men. Better a modest home-bred youth than a travelled and over-confident booby. And if knowledge of the world is in question, how much of the world is constituted by 'Europe'? Locke would retort upon those who advocated the Grand Tour as a means to know human nature: 'To study Human Nature to some purpose, a Traveller must enlarge his circuit beyond the bounds of Europe. He must go and catch her undressed, nay quite naked in North America and the Cape of Good Hope,' not to mention China and Japan. 'These, my Lord, are the proper scenes for the Philosopher, for the citizen of the world, to expatiate in. The tour of Europe is a paltry thing; a tame, uniform, unvaried prospect, which affords nothing but the same polished manners and artificial politeness, scarcely diversified enough to take, or merit our attention.' And if it is objected that these wider scenes 'impose too great a task on our Inquisitive Traveller, my next advice is, That he stay at home; read Europe in the mirror of his own country . . .' Anyway, what are books of travel for?

Needless to say, there was never the slightest likelihood of this sober, not to say sombre, advice being taken. 'The English look on their isle as a prison,' wrote the Abbé Le Blanc in 1745; 'and the first use they make of their love of liberty is to get out of it.' Indeed, their inveterate habit of flitting around Europe had been a favourite subject for satire since the sixteenth century, when the 'Italianate Englishman', with his affected manners, speech and dress, came uproariously upon the stage in the plays of Shakespeare, Ben Jonson and many more. By the eighteenth century, when the habit had become institutionalized by a wealthy aristocracy, mere mockery was not enough; in fact it was out of place. A more constructive style of criticism was needed, something more positive than the rather cross-patch animadversions that such utilitarian critics as Locke and Richard Hurd and Adam Smith could supply. If the practice could not be checked by mockery or outright condemnation, it might be possible to transform it by instruction, to turn it to socially useful purposes. This was attempted as early as 1758 by Dean Tucker in his *Instructions for Travellers*, with its sub-title: *A Plan for improving the Moral and Political Theory of Trade and Taxes by means of Travelling*. The Dean began by enumerating the motives for travel as they were usually stated by the advocates of the Grand Tour: the desire to improve one's taste for the fine arts, to obtain a reputation as a man of 'virtu and elegant taste', and to rub off local prejudices and acquire an enlarged and impartial view of men and things. He then proceeds to enumerate the more foolish motives favoured by the critics: the desire to acquire foreign airs, and to adorn one's 'dear person' with fine clothes and the newest fashions; to visit Italy and Greece 'out of a kind of enthusiastic reverence for Classic Ground' and to pay literary adoration to

'the very Rubbish of an Ancient City'; and to dispel the bore-
dom of 'those who are tired of living at home and can afford
to make themselves as ridiculous everywhere as they please'.
Tucker recommends a preliminary tour of one's own country,
and then a course of solid reading in theology (in order to guard
against the infection of popery), political philosophy, and
political economy. 'The ignorant traveller is of all Beings the
most contemptible.' Lacking a sound instruction, he will not
know what to look out for. The Dean supplies a long list of
questions to which the instructed traveller should try to find
answers. They include everything from comparative manuring
of different soils, the progress of invention, and the securities
afforded for safeguarding civil and political rights and religious
toleration, down to the number of loaded wagons that pass
along the roads and the system of taxation.

Evidently, the *beau idéal* of Dean Tucker would have been
a political economist, a utilitarian, and something of a bore.
Arthur Young, while he was never a bore, was to fulfil most
of his demands. Young's *Travels in France*, on the eve of the
Revolution, answers most of the questions outlined by the
Dean. The Suffolk farmer was the very type of 'the man with
a notebook', and he is only the greatest of a multitude who
travelled for information about existing conditions. But Arthur
Young's travels were not the Grand Tour. Indeed, Dean
Tucker's adjurations, if acted upon, would have turned the
Grand Tour into something quite different. In fact, it never
did turn into anything different. For long enough yet, the
aristocracy, great and small, was to go its more or less splendid
and care-free way. Long into the 1760s, the little Scotch laird,
James Boswell (or 'Baron Boswell', as he chose to be known
in Germany), was jaunting his way to immortality without a
thought for political economy, or indeed any other kind of
economy, while the old laird of Auchinleck, back home in
Scotland, groaned under the financial burden and commanded
him to return. 'This much I can say, that you have spent a
vast deal of money . . . much beyond what the sons of gentlemen near double my estate have spent on such a tour . . . You
have had full opportunity to be satisfied that pageantry, civil
and ecclesiastic, gives no entertainment to thinking men, and

that there is no end nor use of strolling through the world to see sights before unseen, whether of men, beasts, birds or things, and I hope you will return with a proper taste and relish for your own country . . .' The most that Lord Auchinleck could hope for, he said, was that young James would return 'a man of knowledge, of gravity, and modesty, intent on being useful in life. If this be so,' he added, much after the style of John Locke or Adam Smith, 'your travelling will be a little embellishment to the more essential talents . . .' On no account should James linger in Paris on his way home. 'There is nothing to be learned by travelling in France.' Three or four days in Paris would be ample. Lord Auckinleck was writing in August 1765. James Boswell arrived at Dover in the following February, having seduced Rousseau's mistress *en route*. Grand Tour or no Grand Tour, Boswell would always have been Boswell. What a young man got out of the Grand Tour depended finally upon what he brought to it.

It was not until many years after James Boswell was back in Scotland, that Frederick Hervey, 4th Earl of Bristol and Lord Bishop of Derry, drew to the close of a Grand Tour that had lasted half a lifetime. Bowling along the roads of France and Italy, leaving a trail of Hotels Bristol in his wake, he was for many years the best-known traveller and collector in Europe. In 1792, he began to build a splendid repository for his treasures at Ickworth, the old home of the Herveys, in Suffolk. With its pillared portico, its vast rotunda, its curving corridor-rooms flanking the central dome and running out to east and west wings on either side, it was to have been a house to rival Holkham itself. Unfortunately, the French Revolution broke out in 1789, and in 1798 the armies of the Revolution entered Rome. History, as Edward Gibbon discovered when he fled from Lausanne before the self-same intrusion in 1793, was still going on. The French confiscated the Lord Bishop's treasures, and the Lord Bishop himself spent nine months in prison in Milan. He died in Rome in 1803, and Ickworth House, minus his treasures, was to remain a gorgeous and unfinished monument to the Grand Tour *manqué*. Something new had come into the world, as Goethe observed of the battle of Valmy: the first of the 'wars of the people'. The little wars of the eighteenth century, those 'temperate and indecisive contests' of the kings, had scarcely affected the Grand Tour. 'Il Cavaliero Coke' had set out while the War of the Spanish Succession was still unconcluded. Horace Walpole came home from his travels nearly two years after his country had gone to war with Spain, nine months after Frederick the Great invaded Silesia, and all that appears to have worried him was the possibility of his being captured by Catalan pirates on his journey in a felucca from Genoa to Antibes. Laurence Sterne, ordered south for his health in the winter of 1762, was quite easily able to travel through the dominions of the King of France, with whom his Britannic Majesty was still at war. As late as 1790, young Wordsworth and his friend Jones, returning from their tramp to Italy,

> . . . cross'd the Brabant armies on the fret
> For battle in the cause of Liberty.

This happy state of things, when wars were still kingly contests and not yet ideological fights to the death, was fast coming to an end. From 1793 to 1815, with only a brief period of intermission after the Peace of Amiens, the errant English were to be shut up in their island. Grand Tours were confined to soldiers and sailors, travelling under conditions of some squalor and considerable danger.

All the same, it would be misleading to describe the Grand Tour as a victim of the French Revolution. For some time past, travel had been undergoing social change. More and more people of middle-class origin had been making some show of 'tourism'. The very word suggests rather an alternative than a transformation. These people certainly went on tour, but they did it on the cheap, and quite without grandeur. Thomas Patch, a Londoner of obscure parentage who was to become a well-known etcher and engraver at Florence, is said to have hitch-hiked his way to Rome some time before 1750. 'Dr. Viper', or the quarrelsome Philip Thicknesse, turned continental travel into a family picnic. True, his travels were confined to France, but he certainly showed what could be done to adapt tourism to the income of a family man of limited means. Disappointed of a legacy, for which he had waited hopefully for some years, he decided that he could live more cheaply, and educate his children, in France. On his second journey, in 1776, he packed his family into a heavy French cabriolet at Dessein's hotel at Calais, along with pots and pans and musical instruments, his wife's parakeet and his own pet monkey, and set out for Rheims, Dijon, Lyons, and Nîmes and the Mediterranean shore. They took their meals by the roadside picnicking on one occasion under the arches of the Pont du Gard. While the kettle boiled for tea, father played tunes on his guitar, much to the delight of the peasants, who 'danced in a manner not to be seen in England'. Jocko, the monkey, dressed in French jackboots, with his hair *en queue*, rode much of the way postillion upon the carriage-horse, a sight which put 'whole towns in motion . . .' This was certainly not the classical Grand Tour. It was tourism *à la* Swiss Family Robinson, the descent from the sublime to the ridiculous. When the two Cambridge undergraduates, William Wordsworth and Robert Jones, tramped from Calais to Lake Maggiore in the summer vacation of 1790, the age of the hiker was already in sight. All that was needed, now, was the steamship, the railway, and the family car. The Grand Tour was already adapting itself to the century of the Common Man. It may confidently be said to have ceased to be the Grand Tour. The story that began with Thomas Coke ends with Thomas Cook.

CHAPTER 14

The Country House

THE COUNTRY house to which the English gentleman carried the treasures he brought home from his spending spree on the Grand Tour is still regarded as England's greatest contribution to the fine arts. After 1760 and the end of the Seven Years' War, there came a period of rising rents when the incomes of the landed nobility and gentry increased rapidly in proportion to their acres. By the end of the century there were some 400 landed gentlemen enjoying incomes of £10,000 a year from estates of 20,000 acres. These were the men who now set the pace in building and improving their 'seats'. Syon House, Harewood House, Woburn, Bowood, and many others were rebuilt, refurbished, landscaped from 1763 onwards. But it was a universal 'game' in which wealthy gentry and minor nobility could, and did, take part on a slightly less lavish scale. By 1790 wealthy gentry had incomes of £3,000 to £4,000 a year, and there were 700 or 800 families in this happy class. No wonder even the miserly Mrs Norris[1] could advise the foolish but wealthy and highly 'eligible' Mr Rushworth to 'spare no expense. Have everything done in the Best Taste.' By then Humphrey Repton was *le dernier cri* at five guineas a day. 'Smith's place is the admiration of the County, and it was a mere nothing before Repton took it in hand. I think I shall have Repton,' says foolish Mr Rushworth. Jane Austen's irony is not wasted on these 'modern status-symbols', and those who sought them. 'By some improvements you may raise it into a Place—from being a mere gentleman's residence it becomes the residence of a Man of Education, Taste, modern Manners and Good Connections.' Thus Mrs Norris sums up the later Georgian aspirations. It was possible to have plenty of fun on quite

[1] See *Mansfield Park*, by Jane Austen.

modest means. The poet Shenstone, earlier in the century had demonstrated with a great deal of publicity that a single poet of no great means could 'devise' a very pretty 'retreat' at Leasowes, complete with temples, Gothic shepherd's lodge, serpentine paths, and eye-catching views. Dr Johnson thought Leasowes was next to Mr Port's place at Ilam, which was high praise indeed. So the lesser gentry, with steady incomes of £1,000 to £3,000 a year, set to work. 'And so you have a *garden* of your own, and you plant and transplant and are dirty and amused', Thomas Gray wrote to his friend Nicholls in June 1769. 'Are you not ashamed of yourself?' Of course, he knew very well what everyone admired and imitated from George III and Mr Pitt downwards. The lofty Chatham had remarked that Shenstone's 'old oaks and beeches had done everything for him', to which Shenstone retorted that he hoped he had done something for Nature, too. It was irresistible, 'improving' Nature, and their own status, indulging their taste for both 'allegro' and 'penseroso' moods in house and garden. Even the City merchants caught the prevailing mania. The 'Cits' Country Boxes' aped serpentine walks, sunken fences, temples, miniature streams and cascades, for 'Madam's Taste can never Fail'. It was at this time (1781) that an enterprising business-man at Turnham Green set up a board announcing: 'Ready-made Temples sold here', and in 1784 Coade's catalogue included not only a River God, nine feet high, holding an Urn through which a stream might be carried (100 guineas complete), but a 'Psyche fitted with spring tubes for lights' at 5 guineas, Madonna busts at 15s. each, along with 3-guinea busts of Queen Elizabeth, Homer, Marcus Aurelius, Cicero, Edward VI, Vandyck, and Lord Chatham.

The influence of the landowners was all-pervasive, but the men who were so busy beautifying their territories at such vast expense employed wealth not only from land, but also from industries of various kinds and from the riches opened up by the recent expansion of commerce and overseas empire. Coal and iron made many fortunes, like the 'Bridgwater Millions'. Government contracts helped many to build and beautify. The Rt Hon. Thomas Harley, having made a fortune on army clothing contracts in the American War, in 1778 set about rebuilding Berrington Hall, Hereford, where he was M.P.[1] Indian nabobs came home with bulging pockets and exotic architectural notions. West Indian sugar plantations were the mainstay of the Beckfords, father and son, financing Fonthill and its lofty Gothic tower. Boroughmongers of the Bubb Dodington order continued in such types as Sir Gerard Vanneck who, having acquired the rotten borough of Dunwich, called in Sir Robert Taylor to rebuild Heveningham Hall in Suffolk in 1778. Vanneck instructed Taylor to convert the old house into a worthy 'seat', and Taylor's successor, Wyatt, produced elevations similar to a street or terrace in London or Bath, a stuccoed range with keystone capitals of coade-stone outside and Etruscan rooms within, rooms with elegant green walls and white wood, encrusted with cameos and figures in red vases, not to mention a vast array of statuary. It only needed Capability Brown's magic wand to change the dry little Suffolk pond into a serpentine river, and Heveningham stood high above its waters for all the world to admire, a modern monument which amply compensated for the medieval glories of Dunwich vanished beneath the North Sea.

The Vannecks, like many others, took a pride in using the latest prefabricated materials as well as the latest architectural ideas. Coade-stone had been first made in 1769 and was much advertised and widely used. Cast-iron railings and gateways owed much to Darby's new smelting methods. Stucco was all the rage, for, as John Gwynne said in his *London and Westminster Improved* (1766): 'No public edifice ought to be built of brick unless it is afterwards stuccoed, for a mere brick face makes a mean appearance.' The great Brown himself strongly supported this view, objecting to the 'clash' of red brick with his improvement of Nature in the surrounding park. Mathematical or Rebate tiles of white helped to hide the unsightly red. But even these, widely used in the south of England, and greatly admired, did not please the Lord Bishop of Derry when he came to build his house at Ickworth in Suffolk in the 1790s. He wrote sternly to his daughter: 'You beg me on your knees that Ickworth may be built of white stone bricks. What Child! building a house of brick that looks like a sick, pale, jaundiced

---

[1] Henry Holland's estimate of £14,500 for building included two water-closets, with marble bowls and mahogany seats.

red brick!—I shall follow dear old Palladio's rule and cover house, pillars and pilasters with Palladio's stucco!' But in admiring Palladio at that time of day the Lord Bishop was, as in many other ways, a law unto himself.

For taste—that heritage from an expensive education and a prolonged Grand Tour of Europe—was eclectic in the later eighteenth century in all ways but one. Nobody, not even the conservative George III, could any longer abide Palladian architecture. The works of Burlington and Kent were 'out'. Practically everything else, from the ends of the earth and the beginning of time, was 'in'. Sir William Chambers, creator of the garden architecture at Kew, and author of a celebrated *Treatise on Civil Architecture*, had become the acknowledged architectural head of the orthodox, Tory, Court circle. He had been tutor to the youthful George III, and along with his compendious knowledge of Chinese building, he offered an eclectic scholarship based on Italian and French classicism. He disliked the extremes of 'Gothic' taste and 'Athenian Stuart's Attic deformities'. Somerset House in London and the stables he designed for the Duke of Richmond at Goodwood show that he possessed elegant simplicity, fastidious taste, and chaste discipline, to use the favourite language of his time. These were the hallmarks, as everyone knew of George III and his blameless consort, not to mention their swarming nurseries of innocent young princes and princesses. The King extended his patronage and considerable sums of money to the Royal Academy of Arts founded in 1768 by Sir Joshua Reynolds and his friends, and Sir Joshua believed that 'Good Taste is acquired after wide reading, Grand Tours, etc.' And governed by 'reasonableness of outlook'. Therein he showed the influence of the classical writer, Longinus, on the philosophical ideas of the time, best summed up in Burke's essay on the Sublime and the Beautiful. However, although the Academy agreed with George III and Chambers on the need for a new style of simplicity 'improved by art and care' and devoid of neo-Palladian pomposity, it soon gave evidence of finding the Court ideas dull and pompous too. Indeed, its members welcomed the 'High Game' and the new classical excitement purveyed by the Adam brothers.

'Manufacturers of every kind felt the *electric* power of the Adam Revolution,' wrote Sir John Soane later on, and the period from 1763 to the middle 'seventies was to be the great age of combined magnificence and utility instituted by the Adam firm working at Harewood, Bowood, Kedleston, Osterley, and Syon House. The brothers employed a large 'regiment of artificers', which included Angelica Kauffmann, the celebrated lady painter, who decorated the ceilings, while Capability Brown landscaped the gardens. Their synthesis of movement and excitement, fused with the antique style, is best seen at Syon House (1762–70). Here Sir Hugh Smithson, becoming first Earl and then Duke of Northumberland, celebrated his newly acquired dukedom by ordering the Adam firm to convert a medieval and Tudor quadrangle of a former Middlesex convent into a neo-classical palace. 'The Syon Symphony was to have a classic form, romantic overtones (which Robert Adam, always a Romantic at heart, could readily supply), and exquisite ornament.' The apartments were to be the synthesis of magnificence and utility, with the huge dining-room, centre of eating, drinking, and conversation, as the *pièce de résistance.*

The Adam triumph was so complete that the inevitable reaction set in after 1770. This was heralded and helped by Horace Walpole, who persuaded Mrs Montagu, Queen of the Bluestockings, who had one house designed by Adam, to call in 'Athenian Stuart' to refurbish Montagu House in Portman Square. After treatment, Horace found it 'grand, not tawdry, nor larded and embroidered and pomponned with shreds and remnants and *clinquant* like all the Harlequinades of Adam'. To drive home the criticism of Adam, he wrote in 1784, after surveying Henry Holland's beginnings at Carlton House: 'How sick one shall be after this chaste palace, of Mr Adam's ginger-bread and sippets of embroidery.' Like the fickle Athenians of old, the English were now veering in many other directions. The Whigs, under the combined leadership of the Prince of Wales and Charles James Fox, had found a 'Whig' architect in Henry Holland, a son-in-law of Capability Brown. He was a neo-classicist and followed French influences; he was also one of the new tribe of professional builders and architects (his father was a master-builder) and deeply interested in fire-proofing, the use of the white brick from Suffolk, and the revival of 'cob' for agricultural dwellings. His French interests were strengthened by the young Prince of Wales's friendship with Philippe, Duke of Orleans (later 'Egalité-Orleans'), the richest young man in France and an enthusiastic Anglo-maniac. Henry Holland not only remodelled Carlton House for the Prince. He also designed Brooks's Club for the inner circle of Whigs, and worked at Woburn and Althorp for the great Whig Dukes. At Woburn he was called upon by the Duke of Bedford to design a miniature Temple of Liberty, principally to enshrine Nollekens' bust of the great Whig hero, Charles James Fox. But Holland showed variety and versatility in altering much of Woburn Abbey itself, designing a great riding-school and a tennis-court leading to a Chinese Dairy. His *chef-d'œuvre*, however, was undoubtedly his last work at Southill in Bedfordshire, the remodelling of Whitbread House for the great brewer. Samuel Whitbread II, when he succeeded, was not only a brewer millionaire, but a Member of Parliament, and between 1796 and 1800 Henry Holland was given a free hand to remodel Southill, which he did by lovingly filling it with charming loggias, Ionic columns, and his favourite motifs in the Ionic portico style from the Athenian Temple on the Ilissus. He died comparatively young in 1806, and Samuel Whitbread commemorated an ideal partnership of patron and architect by erecting a marble bust inscribed with his own verses on the plinth in praise of 'The labours of Thy Polished Mind'.

Relations were not always as happy as this. Capability Brown, however, generally managed to inspire deep respect, if not affection. His range of 'scenic architecture' possessed all the ingredients required by the *zeitgeist*. His conception of the Sublime and the Beautiful was that of Burke; he was a devotee of the serpentine line of beauty prescribed in Hogarth's *Analysis of Beauty* (1753). By 1764 Lancelot Brown (1715–1783) had shown such capability at Stowe, and elsewhere, that he was appointed Royal Gardener at Hampton Court, and the whole country was frantically seeking his services for the correct setting of architectural gems. The art of living, it was widely held, was now served by Three New Graces: Poetry, Painting and Gardening—and Brown's style was decidedly literary. In a conversation with Hannah More in later life, he compared his landscapes with the winding periods and sentences of Georgian prose and rhetoric. This was not unusual, for the Great Chatham regarded the making of landscape, with its 'eye-catchers' and its follies, as a form of rhetoric. At Bowood Brown planted 100,000 trees as an embodiment of his 'sweet pastorals' and 'elegant elegiacs'. The emphasis was always upon the smoothness of fine turf and the regularity of great clumps of trees, on gentleness and gradual variation of contours, and finally on brightness and clarity, for which noble streams, cascades and fountains and temples were indispensable. Stowe, the seat of Richard Temple, Viscount Cobham, and centre of the Grand Whiggery of the 1750s, became in the 1760s, after Brown had completed the work which Kent had begun, one of the great show-gardens of Europe. It consisted of over 400 acres and a walk-around of more than five miles. Among the many trees and cascades was Gibbs's Temple of Friendship, dedicated to the elder Pitt and the 'Boy Patriots', an eleven-acre lake, and a great Doric arch (dedicated to Princess Amelia) which framed a celebrated prospect of Stowe Castle and the Palladian Bridge. Finally, the 'Grecian Valley' was completed by Brown with serpentine paths adorned by statues.

It was widely believed that beautiful gardens were conducive to beautiful minds, that they induced sweet reveries and noble thoughts. 'By Hagley gardens a villain would be disarmed from executing his dark and bloody purposes; and every passion that corrodes the human breast be lulled into a perfect calm,' wrote Heely in his *The Beauties of Hagley, Envil and Leasowes* (1777); and Melchior Grimm certainly intended no satire when he wrote 'on ne peut sortir d'un jardin anglais sans avoir l'âme aussi affecté qu'en sortant d'une tragédie'. Perhaps the elder Pitt owed some of the sublimity of his mind to the gardens of Stowe and others he admired and planted. From a rather 'dirty' amusement, gardening and a taste for landscape had become the index of the soul. Before long, poor Marianne Dashwood was renouncing any prospective lover who lacked these interests, these qualities of soul. True, Jane Austen thought she was a goose, but to show how far a reasonable eighteenth-century clergyman could go, here are some lines from a 'Sonnet to a Gravel Path' (1797):

> Liberal tho' limited, restrained though free,
> Fearless of dew or dirt or dust I rove—
> And owe these comforts, all derived from thee!
> Take then, Smooth Path, this tribute to my Love,
> Thou emblem pure of legal liberty.

Doubtless it was a serpentine path, but even Brown, accustomed to adulation as he was, would have been surprised at this. We need feel no surprise when it was gravely stated that Thomas Chippendale's designs for his modish Gothic furniture 'had something congenial in them to our old Gothic Constitution'.

By the 1780s both the 'Picturesque' and the 'Gothic' had triumphed. Whether the peace of the 'golden hours' of the Younger Pitt had anything to do with this we do not know, but the coming of the French Revolution and the bloody triumph of extremists gave a great impulse to a sentimental return to our historic and native heritage. The cult of the French taste embodied in the work of Adam and Henry Holland became suspect of atheism and subversion. The great patrons, bored with so much classicism and paganism, turned back to Wren and our Tudor and medieval architecture. Christianity became popular again, and even fashionable. Cathedrals were restored and ecclesiastical architecture was admired. After all, one did not need to be a Wesleyan in order to agree with John Wesley that a lot of the statues and Venuses at Stowe were 'coarse' and 'lewd'. At Stourhead in 1776 he had said that attempting to reconcile statuary with nudity was contrary to Common Sense and Common Decency. In fact, the Puritan streak in the English quickly told them that statues of nymphs and satyrs could arouse far from noble thoughts and might lead to excesses of the kind now visible in the bloodstained streets of Paris. It was up to the English to support both Church and State by living in Gothic houses, or *cottages ornées* set in woods and gardens, rugged rather than smooth and insipid, with plenty of ivy-clad ruins and dark moss-grown woodland paths. Payne Knight's 'The Landscape' (1796) went even further than

Gilpin's essays on 'The Picturesque' (1792) in attacking Brown
and his pupil Repton, for the essence of the Picturesque was
'reverie and enchantment', as this in turn was one of the prime
sources of Moral Virtue. The Gothic Ruin School which had
persisted quietly since the days of Batty Langley and Horace
Walpole was now the height of fashion, and the young Beckford, coming into his father's huge fortune, thoroughly despised
the old Lord Mayor's classical house, and gave orders to Wyatt,
the fashionable architect (who was willing to build Roman,
Greek, or Gothic as the customer might demand) to rebuild
Fonthill 'as an ornamental building which should have the
appearance of a convent, be partly in ruins, and yet contain
some weather-proof apartments'. Wyatt, who had practically
rebuilt the inside of Salisbury Cathedral, was obviously the
man for the job. The millionaire with his mania for medieval
art, who yet despised Horace Walpole's 'Gothic mouse-trap'
at Strawberry Hill, and adored the Italian Primitives, set five
or six hundred men to work all through the freezing winters
in order to give a Georgian body a brand-new suit of Plan-
tagenet clothes. Here was the Romantic temperament at work,
striving for sublime effects, including an octagon tower 276 feet
high. It was neither his, nor his architect's, fault that it fell
down so ignominiously. His vast park was enclosed by twelve-
foot walls eight miles round, not only to keep out vulgar
intruders, but to keep in the wild-life that he so greatly admired.
He did not want to slay the wild deer like William the Conqueror, but to consort with and love them like St Francis in
a medieval paradise. At the same time he wanted to be kept
warm and to have all the mod. cons. The Romantic era had
truly arrived. The *Lyrical Ballads* appeared in 1796, and their
authors owed much to this return to the primitive and the
medieval.

No less striking among the later Georgian achievements,
though after a different fashion, was Ickworth House in Suffolk,
planned jointly by the 4th Earl of Bristol (and Lord Bishop of
Derry) and his architect, Francis Sandys, in 1796. Ickworth
was born of some of the impulses of Romanticism, but principally of the Enlightenment, natural science and geometry.
Another variant of these later Georgian years is the Indian

style of Sezincote in Gloucestershire, built for Sir Charles Cockerell in 1805, with its Moghul carving done by Cotswold craftsmen, and its Indian and Moorish farm buildings, the whole representing 'the Romance of the East'. A period-piece contemporary with Uvedale Price's *Essays on the Picturesque* is the copybook Gothic of Luscombe Castle, near Dawlish in Devon, designed by Charles Hoare (1799–1804), landscaped by Humphrey Repton, the architectural genius supplied by John Nash. Taking them together, Fonthill, Ickworth, Sezincote and Luscombe, the eclecticism in which Georgian architecture came to its last flowering is revealed as the negation of a style, the inauguration of the chaos which was to prevail throughout the nineteenth century. 'A well-educated British gentleman', wrote The Lounger in 1786, 'is of no country whatever, he unites in himself the characteristics of all foreign nations; he talks and dresses in French, and sings Italian; he rivals the Spaniard in indolence, and the German in drinking; his house is Grecian; his offices Gothic; and his furniture Chinese.'

CHAPTER 15

The Curious Incident

NAPOLEON once summed up the causes of the French Revolution in the single word 'Vanity'. He meant that the French made a revolution out of concern for their wounded *amour-propre* or self-esteem. They had suffered defeat in the field of battle and humiliation in the field of diplomacy for long enough, and all because—it was easy to assume—they had had corrupt and ineffective government for even longer. One victory, Fontenoy, Napoleon said, had given the monarchy another forty years' life. Yet all the world knew, as the French knew themselves, that they were the most rational and civilized people in Europe. The Revolution of 1789 might be regarded as a gigantic effort on the part of France to pull herself up by her bootstraps, to put her government—and more especially her administrative mechanism, on a level with letters, the fine arts, and the art of living. At the very least, it was to put France's power and effectiveness in the world on a level with that of her ancient enemy and rival, the nation of shopkeepers beyond the Channel. Supposing they were able to do this, would they not be invincible? Somewhat apprehensively English observers asked themselves the same question when they saw the process beginning. As Daniel Hailes, Secretary to the British Embassy in Paris, put it to the home government when a meeting of the Estates-General was foretold in 1788: 'If France with all the vices of her government has been for so many ages in a situation to act often so brilliant and always so formidable a part in the affairs of Europe, what may be expected from her when those vices shall have been eradicated, and when she shall be in possession of a Constitution . . . similar to that of her neighbour and rival?'

It might seem that in the last years of the War of American

Independence the English were in a somewhat similar position to that of the French in the last years of the *ancien régime*. Never before had they suffered such humiliation on account of incompetent government as during the years when Lord North presided over, and Lord George Germain (Secretary for the Colonies) actually directed operations against the American colonists and their European allies. A bare outline of the events of the next ten years might suggest that Britain was on the verge of final catastrophe. Even before the war was over London suffered the worst outbreak of violence it had ever known—or was ever to know again. Before the Americans had attained recognition of their independence, Ireland had secured home rule. After Lord North resigned, governments came and went with a rapidity to rival the kaleidoscopic rapidity of the first ten years of the reign. The Marquess of Rockingham lasted twelve months, Lord Shelburne for ten, Fox and North in coalition for less than nine. Even when the younger Pitt came in in December 1783, men talked of a 'mince-pie administration', because it seemed unlikely to survive the Christmas season. Then the King fell ill of what seemed like madness, and the greatest pro-consul the Empire had ever known was impeached for misrule in India. Coleridge was not to write his *Fears in Solitude* until 1798, but the poem gave voice to the repentant mood that was already settling upon humane men's minds in the 1780s.

> We have offended, Oh! my countrymen!
> We have offended very grievously
> And been most tyrannous.
>   Therefore, evil days
> Are coming on us, O my countrymen!
> And what if all-avenging Providence,
> Strong and retributive, should make us know
> The meaning of our words, force us to feel
> The desolation and the agony
> Of our fierce doings?

Of course, it was easy to cry 'Woe, woe!' or 'Repent, repent!' and to point to recent misfortunes or miscarriages as signs of Divine disfavour upon a corrupt and sinful people. Yet, in fact, the country as a whole was not the least affrighted, and very far indeed from losing its nerve. The years following upon 'Lord North's War' were years of abounding energy and enterprise, the years of Richard Arkwright, the man who invented the factory-system, if anyone may be said to have invented it; the years when Josiah Wedgwood laid out Etruria, when Jedediah Strutt built the temple of ribbed-hosiery at Belper, when James Watt's steam-engines were being installed in wool and cotton mills up and down the land, when Thomas Coke was turning his Palladian palace by the North Sea into the greatest agricultural show on earth. These were indeed the crucial years of Great Britain's transition to a modern industrial society. In the twenty years between 1780 and 1800 Britain's total industrial production was doubled. It was about to assume a scale unknown in the previous history of the world. Almost exactly thirty years after the disaster supposedly inflicted upon the Empire by the loss of America, Sir Patrick Colquhoun could write that 'an aera has arrived in the affairs of the British Empire . . . discovering resources which have excited the wonder, the astonishment, and perhaps the envy of the civilised world'.

And these years of rapid economic expansion, so often to be contemned by the intellectual Luddites of a later age, were accompanied by a whole spate of movements, mostly of spontaneous generation and only tardily patronized by Parliament, for the furtherance of a greater humanity. An event like the impeachment of Warren Hastings might seem providentially designed for the exposure of imperialism in all its cruelty and greed, but in fact it remains a magnificent tribute to the essential rightness of heart of the people who, in the midst of revolution and war, could carry it through. By thus upholding the moral quality of empire they not only made sure that the empire of the East should never go the way of the empire of the West, but that Empire should some day give place to Commonwealth. Contemporary with this seemingly self-inflicted wound came the first serious endeavours to end the vast cruelty of the traffic in African slaves. The Society for the Abolition of the Slave Trade was founded in 1787, and in the following year the question made its first appearance before Parliament. Although

17. Adam Smith,
the author of
The Wealth of Nations

18. Jeremy Bentham

19. William Pitt
the Younger

20. 'Le jongleur', a
caricature of Pitt
the Younger

the slave trade was not to be abolished by statute for another twenty years, resolutions condemning it received support from Burke and Fox and Pitt some years before the French Revolution broke upon the world with its gospel of liberty, equality, and fraternity. There was on foot the widespread endeavour to make Christianity a religion of social action. The Evangelical revival was to be the crowning glory of eighteenth-century humanitarianism. Its bible was Wilberforce's *Practical Christianity*, which appeared in 1797. Ten years earlier, he had founded his Society for the Suppression of Vice, a sequel to the King's Proclamation against Vice and Immorality. The cause of moral rearmament was given impetus by the earthquake shock experienced at Manchester in 1777, interpreted by many people as a warning of the wrath to come. 'There is no divine visitation which is likely to have so general an influence upon sinners as an earthquake,' John Wesley observed.

The most alarming event of these years, however, was no geological disturbance in the north of England, but a terrifying explosion of violence in London itself. All through the eighteenth century London experienced rioting at fairly frequent intervals, so that Elie Halévy could speak of England, 'the sole European country where the reigning dynasty had been set up as the result of a successful rebellion', as 'the home of insurrection . . . the typical country of rebellion'. Perhaps he should have said London rather than England, for there was a peculiar savagery about the violence of the Londoners as compared with provincial people, a destructive fury which on occasion resembled that of the Paris of the Fronde and of the great Revolution itself. A London mob pouring out of back-streets and cellars on a course of arson and pillage was a terrifying thing. It acquired a name which suggested an estate of the realm: the Mobility. When Edmund Burke spoke of 'the swinish multitude' he was not referring to the political people, though his enemies fastened that libel upon him. He was referring to the hordes of nightmare figures which went on record in the backgrounds of the pictures of William Hogarth. Again and again this phenomenon storms across the page of history: in 1733 to howl down Walpole's Excise Bill; in 1751 to preserve the 'Eleven Days' which government were supposed to be stealing from the people by the reform of the Calendar; in 1753 to maintain the disabilities of the Jews; in 1763 to roar for 'Wilkes and Liberty'; in 1768 for Wilkes and the electors of Middlesex.

In 1780 it was the oldest cry of all: 'No Popery!'. It might have been imagined that this peculiar form of intolerance had declined with the enlightened eighteenth century. Two years before, Parliament had passed a limited and conditional Catholic Relief Bill removing certain disabilities suffered by Roman Catholics in the matter of property rights and religious worship while still leaving them largely excluded from political life and offices of trust. It was a non-party measure which passed through both Houses of Parliament without a division. Yet within a short time various associations were formed for the defence of the Protestant religion, and a neurotic young crackpot of the ancient family of Gordon was adopted as sponsor and spokesman of the movement. Whether or not, as Horace Walpole said of the Gordons, 'they were, and are, all mad', certainly Lord George's conduct during the 'time of terror' which followed was that of an aristocratic lunatic. The peculiarity of the 'curious incident' known as 'The Gordon Riots' lies not at all in the fact that the incident happened but in the fact that it was literally an incident, something that came and went with the short sharp violence of a dog's solitary bark in the silence of the night. It was none the less terrifying for that, and not only to the respectable or well-to-do inhabitants of London. Some modern historians, at a safe historical distance, have liked to imagine that it only scared property-owners, or that vague and convenient entity which they label 'the bourgeoisie'.

The initial assault in the Gordon Riots was upon the chapels attached to the Sardinian and Bavarian Embassies, the most obvious targets for rioters concerned with 'foreigners' (a term which then included Scots and Irish), the despised continental wearers of those badges of slavery and general inferiority to the 'free-born' English, wooden shoes, second only by way of offensiveness to their attachment to a slavish Popish religion. Thereafter the attack spread to the houses of wealthy Roman Catholic citizens, to Blackfriars Bridge and the Bank of England, and finally to the prisons, notably Newgate, which was fired on the night of 6 June amidst scenes of frenzied jubilation.

About 100 houses were burned, pulled down, or otherwise damaged, involving a loss of some £100,000. 'No Popery' mobs were in possession of London streets (City, Strand, Southwark, Shoreditch, Spitalfields, rather than the slum quarters of Holborn or St Giles-in-the-Fields) for a week. The magistrates and the City Corporation remained singularly inactive for several days, in fact until the rioters turned from the property of Roman Catholics to property in general probably for fear of themselves incurring attention. It is on the whole clear that the enmity of the poor was directed at the property of the well-to-do, and even among the Roman Catholics it was seldom that the poorer members of that communion were made to suffer. Property rather than persons bore the brunt, the lives lost being those of rioters throughout. Of these, 285 were killed, 173 wounded. Of 450 prisoners taken, 160 were put on trial and 25 hanged. Even in the matter of property, the rioters exercised discrimination. Targets for destruction had obviously been carefully selected, and where neighbouring property suffered damage it appears to have been through the spread of fire and flame by the wind. There was never anything 'wholesale' about it.

These facts have led to speculation about the existence of a 'central command', or the appointment of something in the nature of section-leaders to keep control. No evidence has been discovered of either, and while there must have been 'lists' of houses to be attacked, none have survived. These and other puzzles have thrown a good deal of suspicion upon the old and easy assumptions about the 'faceless mob', the outpouring slum and cellar population into the streets, the ascription of everything to 'criminal elements', the dismissal offhand of political motivation. Unfortunately, the problem is not much relieved by dropping 'mob' for 'crowd'. A crowd in action, especially if composed considerably of youngsters (and the frequency of youths and boys in the Gordon Riots is well testified from the records of the subsequent trials), is to be distinguished from a mob only by a sympathetic imagination. The most that can be said about the Gordon rioters is that the very small fraction which stood trial were, as might be expected of a random sample gathered from those who failed to escape arrest, a representative cross-section of the working population. Very few had previous convictions, and many could produce testimony to character. The mid-twentieth century is not by any means the only age which has experienced the 'teenager' problem, though it is the first which has been foolish enough to give it a name. 'What signify the irregularities of a mob, more than half composed . . . of boys and women . . .?' James Mill was to ask forty years later in the year of Peterloo. But not Manchester, or Birmingham, Nottingham or Stockport at their worst ever succeeded in frightening the country like the No Popery riots in the capital of the Empire in the age of Lord North. The Prime Minister had his hat torn off as his carriage passed the Horse Guards. It was cut into pieces and sold at a shilling a piece. When his house was attacked on the night of 7 June, Lord North mounted to the roof to see London blazing in seven places. When, a day or two earlier, the House of Commons were discussing Lord George Gordon's petition, the Protestant Champion had gone out to speak to his followers raging outside. He was heard to say, 'Lord North calls you a mob.' Lord North was generally right.

Apart from their reminiscence of an earlier fanaticism, and the evidence they provide of dissociation between governors and governed in eighteenth-century London, the Gordon Riots have only a long-term and traumatic importance in English history. They were confined to London, indeed to the City. They lacked affiliation elsewhere. In that self-same year, there was on foot a widespread movement for 'economical reform' in Yorkshire. Christopher Wyvill's 'Yorkshire Association' had its inception among the M.P.s and freeholders of that extensive county for the purpose of bringing pressure to bear upon Parliament for not only 'economical' but also representational reform. Within a few months the Association movement had spread to some dozen counties, and there was a prospect of a nation-wide link-up with a delegate committee in London, which was interpreted by some as an attempt to overawe Parliament by a representative body on the lines of the rebellious American Congress. But there was never any question of this provincial reformist movement having anything to do with the Gordon Riots. The riots indeed had the effect of causing many people who had supported the Association to withdraw their suffrage out of nervousness about any move that might seem to weaken the hand of established authority. Burke's Bill for Economical Reform was rejected in February 1780, though he was able to carry some of his proposals when he came in as Paymaster in Rockingham's second ministry in 1782. So little connexion was there between parliamentary reform and anti-Catholic agitation that the eccentric but liberally minded Duke of Richmond had the greatest difficulty in making himself heard against the 'No Popery!' uproar outside when he tried to move for 'a more equal representation of the People in Parliament' from his place in the House of Lords on 2 June, the day of Lord George's mighty Procession of Protestants from St George's Fields to Westminster. The Duke was somewhat hard of hearing and for a time imagined that the barracking came from the Noble Lords around him. When at length he understood what was going on outdoors, he expressed his regret, as 'a friend of the people, to see them so improperly assembled and acting in so unwarrantable a manner'. Needless to say, his motion got no further. Neither House could transact much business that day.

The memory of those days and nights, when Lords and Commons travelled home six in a coach for safety, and when the night-sky pulsed with fire like an inferno, was to remain in the background of Englishmen's minds for half a century and more. Ten years later the shadow of the guillotine across the Channel fell upon eyes which still held the images of fire and flame and the roaring mob. The very word 'Mob' was to retain reverberations of terror long into the nineteenth century. It even resounded in the imagination of Jane Austen's young lady who, at the mention of 'expected horrors in London . . . pictured to herself a mob of three thousand men assembling in St George's Fields: the Bank attacked, the Tower threatened, the streets of London flowing with blood'. No-one who could remember the Gordon Riots was likely to underrate the dangers of the French Revolution.

CHAPTER 16

The Age of Pitt

THE FINE flower of eighteenth-century civilization which blossomed in every department of English life in the age of Lord North save the political—the age of Johnson and Gibbon, of Reynolds and Gainsborough, of Goldsmith and Garrick and Fanny Burney—was fast drooping on its stalk. Nor was it to bloom again until the exotic blossoms of the Indian Summer of the Prince Regent, some time after George III had withdrawn to the melancholy solitude of his final years at Windsor. Gibbon finished his history at Lausanne in the summer of 1787 and made for home, intending to spend Christmas at Bath and to present the final volumes to Lord North. When he came home from Switzerland for the last time in 1792, the French revolutionary armies were advancing on Geneva. There was too much history going on for an historian to feel safe. This particular historian was the kind of man that a revolutionary mob likes to hang.[1] When he attended a dinner party in Lincoln's Inn during the Gordon Riots, 'a deep toned and clear voice was heard from the bottom of the table, very calmly and civilly impugning the correctness of the narrative and the propriety of the doctrines of which it had been made the vehicle'.[2] After a suitably brief but solemn contention with the owner of the voice, the historian begged to be excused and went home. The younger generation was knocking at the door, for the voice was that of the younger Pitt.

Gibbon had already outlived his age, a splendid age of elegance and wit and noble generalizations. The age that was dawning was to find his polite deism trivial and his polished

[1] It was Walter Bagehot who first said so.
[2] According to Bland Burgess, the historian had been animadverting upon 'fashionable levities' in the political doctrines of the moment.

periods tedious. 'Gibbon's style is detestable, but his style is not the worst thing about him . . .' This was the voice of a toddler of 1780 who had become the man 'Coleridge'.[1] What did the men of the new age want? They wanted, chiefly, seriousness. For the age of the French Revolution was indeed a serious, not to say solemn, age. It would have liked to hang Gibbon, and Lord North, and a dozen more late Augustans in a row. Johnson could have survived in security, for he was fundamentally serious and properly terrified of death and damnation. His *Rasselas* (1759) has been called 'the last stand of Augustanism, a Palladian façade of reason, before the liberation of the unconscious impulses in man's nature brought about by the Romantic revival'. When James Boswell wanted to reform his character he would write in his *Journal* the fearful admonition: 'Be Johnson.' Thirty years Johnson's junior, he liked to imagine his hero a far less complex and troubled character than we know him to have been. Johnson's lifetime (1709–1784) covered the last thirty-five years of Pope and the first twenty-seven years of Blake, and he contained within himself the dialectic of the century. Gibbon was out of date by 1780, but Johnson, who had looked into the abyss with Dante and Shakespeare and a very few more, was up with the times when he died in 1784. In that year Catherine Earnshaw died, and Heathcliff's demon was at large on the moors. Johnson could have encountered them both without total strangeness, which is as good a test of the transcendentalism of genius as could be imagined. In that year, too, William Pitt the younger, who had become First Lord of the Treasury at the age of twenty-five and had faced for several months a hostile House of Commons at the head of a minority, secured an overwhelming majority at the elections, and set out upon the great Ministry of eighteen years which carried the country, through *sturm und drang*, into the nineteenth century.

Pitt's headship of his age and country over these years is quite a different matter from the presidency of Lord North in the 1770s. 'There is now no Prime Minister,' Johnson had said in 1775, 'there is only an agent for government in the House of Commons. We are governed by the Cabinet, but there is no one head there, as in Sir Robert Walpole's time.' In the Premiership

[1] See Coleridge's *Table Talk*, 15 August 1833.

of William Pitt he would have recognized the revival of a mastery as great as that of Walpole though different in its quality. As for the King, he had found his greatest servant, a man replete with his own Patriot purposes, equipped with the conventional eighteenth-century subordination of a ministerial servant to 'the Royal Master', but with the highly developed will-to-power of his magnificent and tiresome father. Not that Pitt was any more 'given to the King by the people' than any other beneficiary of John Robinson's electioneering skill.[1] Like that of Walpole, Pitt's authority was very much the result of his indispensability to the King, who saw the fearful alternative in the Falstaffian features of Charles James Fox. Like that of his father, to whom he owed the great asset of his name, his authority with the nation was the result of what, in the Earl of Chatham, the City of London had called 'a certain kind of happy contagion of his probity and spirit'. While Mr Pitt held the reins men knew that the country's affairs were in the hands of a good man of business, and this was the age of business *par excellence*. 'One would suppose that man had lived in a bleaching-ground all his life,' one manufacturer said to another after waiting upon the Prime Minister in 1795. And even when he was on holiday the Prime Minister was regularly attended by a little man who handed him a slip of paper at least once a day. The little man was not a bailiff serving a writ for debt, as those might have imagined who knew the appalling confusion of his private finances. Nor was he delivering a *billet-doux*, as many might have imagined who knew not the Prime Minister's bachelor tastes. The slips of paper recorded the price of Consols.

Burke, delivering himself of his purple passage on the perilous position of Marie Antoinette in 1790, marvelled that 'ten thousand swords did not leap from their scabbards to avenge even a look that threatened her with insult'. The age of chivalry was gone, he sighed, the age of sophisters, economists and calculators had arrived. The age, indeed, of *The Wealth of Nations*, and of Jeremy Bentham, who refused to apologize for speaking of morals and legislation in 'a mercenary language'. Swords leaping from scabbards held no attraction for a Prime Minister

---

[1] Secretary to the Treasury. See *Parliamentary Papers of John Robinson 1774–84*, ed. W. T. Laprade.

who cherished peace in the interests of a balanced budget. When in 1791 Burke waited upon the Prime Minister hoping to elicit some enthusiasm for intervention in the French Revolution, he found him 'dead and cold'. The great man had said: 'Depend upon it, Mr Burke, things will go on very much as they are until the Day of Judgment.' [1] And in a manufacturing age, Pitt was a manufactured statesman. As Coleridge said, 'he was cast rather than grew', like one of the cannon made by his great father for the Seven Years' War. To quote Coleridge again, 'he was always full-grown' and never experienced the 'awkward-ness of a growing intellect'. Something of 'revelry and de-bauchery' would have done him good. But 'Mr Pitt's conduct was correct . . . he was a severe student . . .' He was never 'The Younger Pitt' save in the chronological sense, and in order to distinguish him from his father. Much that was achieved by the Enlightened Despots in the later eighteenth century may be properly described as a process of *rétablissement* —the re-establishment of orderly and efficient government after the stresses and strains of the wars which occupied so large a place in the Europe of the *ancien régime*. Pitt's work over the first ten years of his Ministry belongs to the same process. The author of his standard biography in the present century, J. Holland Rose, called his first volume *William Pitt and National Revival*. The work of these years was the recovery of Great Britain from the financial consequences of the American War and the restoration of her place among the European powers. When Pitt came to power the country was friendless and alone, a cipher in the affairs of Europe. The belief was widespread that England's sun had set, dimmed by wealth and luxury and the spirit of corruption. She had, said the Emperor Joseph II, 'gone down to the rank of a second-rate power like Sweden and Denmark'. Chatham's old ally, Frederick the Great, described her as a land ruined by an unfortunate war and unable ever again to become a formidable rival to France. With the coming of Pitt, however, the old warrior expressed his confidence that Chatham's son would restore her 'to the importance she had formerly held in the scale of Europe', and would render her 'as

[1] Burke replied: 'No doubt, sir. But it is the day of no judgment that I am afraid of'.

great and respectable as his father had done'. The young Premier no doubt would have taken the word 'respectable' in the literal sense in which Frederick intended it: meaning not merely worthy of a certain deference for its decency, but worthy to be feared for its strength. The son of Chatham could be trusted to know that in the Europe of the great 'Greats', Frederick and Catherine, the respect of other nations was to be won by strength. Moreover, he would have understood what the greatest of all 'Greats' meant when he attributed the French Revolution to wounded *amour-propre* or the need to make France efficient and feared in the world again. Within less than five years he had ended Great Britain's isolation, gaining for her the alliance of Prussia and the United Provinces in the Triple Alliance of 1788.

The root of his achievement was his pursuit of Great Britain's traditional policy of checking French designs on the independence of the Low Countries. The Stadholder of the United Provinces, William V, Prince of Orange, was, like George III, a grandson of George II. Moreover, he was married to a niece of Frederick the Great. It was, no doubt, too late in the day for dynastic considerations to govern the course of power politics, but there were other and more cogent reasons why Great Britain and Prussia should wish to assist the Stadholder and his lady when they were menaced by the advent of a 'Patriot' party which threatened to turn them out. The conflict between 'Patriot' and 'Orange' factions in the United Provinces presented France with an irresistible temptation to intervene, to fish in troubled waters or (at the risk of mixing metaphors) to play with fire—much as she had done in the affairs of the American colonies. The devious ways in which France sought to dominate the Dutch in the crisis of 1785-7 closely resemble the Hitlerian tactics in the 1930s: the patronizing of 'Free Corps' to 'liberate' the Dutch from Orangist oppression, and the exertion of pressure from an armed camp at Givet on the French side of the frontier. Fortunately the British Ambassador at the Hague was the astute, vigorous, and profoundly anti-French Sir James Harris (later Lord Malmesbury), and the British Foreign Secretary was the no less anti-French Marquess of Carmarthen. Pitt took little part in the business, but his energetic and watchful servants checked the French manœuvres at every point. In 1788 a Prussian land-force and a British fleet moved into action, and the French backed down. French domination of the Low Countries was thwarted once more, and out of the joint action of the allies was born the Triple Alliance. More important perhaps was the fact that the ancient French monarchy had been made to suffer its last deadly humiliation by diplomatic defeat. When, partially in consequence of this humiliation, the French overthrew their monarchy a year or two later, Britain was already in a position to enter upon the role of coalition-maker and paymaster of allies who would fight France with little pause for twenty years.

Pitt had already won an earlier move in the perennial Anglo-French game, a game in which he was not a devoted player, since he would greatly have preferred Anglo-French friendship. But again it was the French who took the initiative which brought about their own defeat, this time in a trade contest. At the Peace of Versailles in 1783, the Anglo-French treaty had contained a clause stipulating that the two countries should negotiate a commercial treaty within two years. Vergennes now took the initiative, pressing for the fulfilment of the obligation. Pitt for a time seemed to drag his feet. He aimed to secure a commercial treaty with Ireland first. An economically United Great Britain would be a superior bargaining force when negotiating with France. In the summer of 1785, the French began to impose higher taxes on certain British goods, and then (much to the wrath of English manufacturers) actually prohibited British textile and hardware products. This pressure process culminated in a favourable Franco-Dutch commercial treaty in the early winter, and Pitt, touched in his most sensitive place, sprang into action. He sent a first-class negotiator, William Eden (later Lord Auckland), as special envoy to Paris. Eden was to give his name to the commercial treaty which ensued, a measure which opened the extensive home markets of France to British cotton-goods and hardware, incidentally helping to create an economic crisis in French industry in the winter which preceded the meeting of the Estates-General. Maximilien Robespierre, Deputy to the Estates-General for the industrial town of Arras, liked to say that Perfidious Albion engineered the economic ruin of France preceding the Revolution by this iniquitous treaty.[1]

It is unnecessary to suppose that Pitt's devotion to free-trade, which seemed to be exemplified in this treaty, derived from his having studied *The Wealth of Nations* at Cambridge, nor is it necessary to deride the notion. Nowadays it is the fashion to deny that the policy of any statesman ever owed anything to books, and historians waste a great deal of time proving that Henry VII learnt nothing from the works of Sir John Fortescue, Thomas Cromwell even less from Machiavelli's *Il Principe*, and George III less than nothing from *The Patriot King*. Pitt's tributes to Adam Smith are well known, and he certainly read *The Wealth of Nations* even if it was not compulsory reading for a Whig statesman concerned to improve his country's commercial prosperity in the 1780s. The Eden Treaty reflects the outlook of an enlightened man of the Age of Reason, which is very much what Pitt was, and his hopes and ideals may best be gathered from his defence of the Treaty in the House of Commons against mercantilist critics like Fox and Burke who supposed it to be playing into the hands of 'our natural enemy'.

> To suppose that any nation could be unalterably the enemy of another was weak and childish. It had neither its foundation in the experience of nations nor in the history of man. It was a libel on the constitution of political societies, and supposed the existence of diabolical malice in the original frame of man.

No doubt, he went on, Providence had endowed France with all the best of the earth's natural productions, and with the very best of weather, but the same Divine favour had endowed Britain with a Constitution which favoured her enterprise and stability, and 'which had gradually raised it to a state of commercial grandeur'. Never did Pitt speak so surely in the tongue of his own century.

When, in Part I of *The Dynasts*,[2] Thomas Hardy showed Pitt

---

[1] Robespierre was sometimes thought in England to have been an Englishman or an Irishman by birth, whose real name was Robert Spier. A Frenchwoman, writing to William Eden's wife, actually referred to him as Bob Spier.

[2] Act 5, Scene v.

riding to Guildhall after Trafalgar to make his famous speech about England saving herself and Europe, he portrayed one man in the cheering crowd who saved his breath by moving his lips without uttering a word. He made this comic character justify his silence on the ground that 'somebody must save something, or the country will be as bankrupt as Mr Pitt is himself, by all account . . .' All through the early years of his Ministry, the years of the French Treaty and the Dutch crisis, Pitt had been nourishing economy. He knew, no one better, that sound public finance was the substantial basis of all else, and his place in the succession of great Prime Ministers is between Walpole and Peel and Gladstone rather than between Chatham and Churchill. Every schoolboy has always been supposed to know that his finest work was the restoration of order and probity to a National Debt of £231,000,000 and an annual income of some £25,000,000, and that depleted by years of fiscal extravagance and by smuggling on the scale of a national industry. In this, and in his meticulous measures to plug the leaks in the collection of customs duties, he bore a close resemblance to his uncle, George Grenville, as he did also in a certain woodenness of demeanour. While he cut duties sufficiently to make smuggling less profitable, simplifying, standardizing, and centralizing by instituting a Consolidated Fund (1789), and greatly improved the system of auditing public accounts, he did not shrink from imposing new taxes on a large range of articles and amenities, including servants and windows. By thus making taxes the life-long bugbear of mankind, he opened himself to the satire of Sydney Smith in his famous article in the *Edinburgh Review*, with the schoolboy whipping his taxed top and the old man dying in the arms of the apothecary who has paid for a licence to put him to death. In 1798, Pitt ensured himself of a baleful immortality, by instituting the Income Tax.[1]

---

[1] Pitt instituted the tax with a promise that it was only 'for the duration', and when the Napoleonic Wars were over the promise was honoured, though the tax was re-instituted in 1842, apparently for all time. Pitt's rate was 2s. in the pound on incomes above £200 p.a., with a sliding scale below that figure. Such was the dread of the inquisitorial nature of the tax, that it was promised that all returns would be destroyed, a promise which it was attempted—ineffectively—to keep. See Hope Jones, *Income Tax in the Napoleonic War*.

As for the National Debt, it had existed since the time of Marlborough's wars, though men continued to think it somewhat shameful for one generation to shift financial burdens to the shoulders of later generations. Mr Gladstone thought it was thwarting God's benign intentions in making war expensive. In tackling the problem of reducing the National Debt Pitt was simply carrying on the endeavours of statesmen all through the century. He set aside £1,000,000 per annum in a Sinking Fund invested at compound interest, and certainly during the few remaining years of peace this had the desirable effect of restoring respect for the financial integrity of government. So did his practice of raising loans by tender instead of personal favouritism. Romilly said of Pitt that he was 'the first minister who consulted the public interest by accepting the lowest terms that were tendered without retaining a farthing in his own hands for distribution among his friends'. He set a personal example by declining a sinecure normally coming to the First Lord of the Treasury when he first took office.[1] The effect of his measures on the public funds was reflected in the little messages he received so regularly from his man of business day by day. The price of Consols stood at 54 in 1783. They stood at 90 in 1791, and at 97 in 1792. In the latter year he was able to announce in his Budget Speech an estimated surplus of £600,000. Ordinary revenue, which had been £12 million in 1785, now stood at £14 million. The National Debt had been reduced by £5½ million in five years. He proposed to allocate two-thirds of his surplus to the same good cause, and to spend the rest on remission or relief of taxes, notably those on female servants, carriages and windows.

It was in this speech of 17 February 1792 that he made his celebrated and oft-derided prophecy about future peace. Unquestionably, he said, 'there never was a time in the history of this country when, from the situation of Europe, we might more reasonably expect fifteen years of peace, than we may at the present moment'. Fifteen years were the period over which, if our present prosperity continued at its present rate, we might expect the Sinking Fund to amount to £4,000,000 per annum, the limit after which, according to the Act of 1786 inaugurating

[1] The Clerkship of the Pells, worth £3,000 a year.

it, the Fund was no longer to accumulate, but the interest of the capital was to be left open for the disposition of Parliament. He was careful to guard against the possibility of 'events . . . which human foresight cannot reach and which may baffle all our conjectures'.

Twelve months later, almost to a day, the French Convention, having annexed Belgium and invaded Holland, declared war on His Britannic Majesty King George III. Pitt, the economist, the reformer and the optimist after the eighteenth-century fashion, the man who was prepared to see the prospect of peace even where the omens were not evidently propitious because he always nursed the unconquerable hope that mankind was set upon the upward track to international amity and prosperity, this hopeful and much-enduring man was now to be transformed into 'the Pilot who weathered the storm'. He was, even in his great work for national finance and commercial progress in the years of peace, the Father of Victory, victory he was not to live to see, the progenitor of Nelson's fleets and Wellington's armies as certainly as his father had been the only begetter of James Wolfe and Robert Clive and Lord Hawke. Pitt made it possible for a reign which had opened with high hopes and sunk to humiliation and loss to close nevertheless in the blaze of glory which justified Victorian Englishmen like W. S. Gilbert in recalling 'Good King George's glorious days' after all. The Patriot King died mad,[1] but men were to remember his reign for the Patriot Pitt, head of a Patriot People.

[1] Medical research has lately denied this, but the distinction between the old King's behaviour in his last years and insanity would be hard for the layman to discern.

CHAPTER 17

George and the Dynasts

2ND SPECTATOR: I wonder King George is let venture down
on this coast, where he might be snapped up in a moment like
a minney by a her'n, so nigh as we be to the field of Boney's
vagaries! . . .
Lard, Lard, if a' were nabbed, it wouldn't make a deal of
difference. We should have nobody to zing to, and play single
stick to, and grin at through horse-collars, that's true. And
nobody to sign our few documents. But we should rub along
some way, goodnow.

The Dynasts, I, 2, iv

KING: I read it as a thing of signal augury, and one which
bodes Heaven's confidence in me and in my line that I should
rule as King in such an age!

The Dynasts, I, 4, i

GEORGE III is a notable figure in the cast of *The Dynasts*.
Thomas Hardy was born twenty years after the King's death,
and grew up among Wessex folk who remembered him in the
summer days when he resided at Weymouth for the sea-bathing
—and in order to be in the front line for the long-threatened
invasion, for in 1805 he behaved with the same Blimpish
bravado he had shown in the summer of 1779. In the event of
an enemy landing, the Queen and the Princesses were to be
removed inland to Worcester, while he himself advanced towards the invader, taking command in Wessex, Kent or Essex,
according to the enemy's movements. Whatever happened,
he would have his eye on him. His bellicosity was sometimes
embarrassing to his west-country subjects, especially when he
went bathing or cruising. The band played 'God Save the King'
when His Majesty entered the water, and a line of frigates were
posted every night across the entrance to Weymouth Bay. On

at least one occasion the audience at the Weymouth theatre waited until 10 o'clock at night for the curtain to rise because the royal family had not returned from a cruise, and there was so much anxiety for their safety. 'He's a very obstinate and comical old gentleman,' as one spectator remarked, 'and by all account a' wouldn't make port when asked to.'

His health appears to have benefited greatly by his seaside holidays[1] whatever the hazards he may, or may not, have been running. This alone must have gratified his subjects, for there had been a time—scarcely more then ten years earlier—when he was sick unto death, incapable of performing his royal functions. The illness had lasted from November 1788 until February 1789. When it recurred with great severity in 1810 it was to involve the country in a Regency for the last ten years of his reign. But for his sudden recovery early in 1789, for which the nation gave thanks unto the Almighty (for the King's doctors scarcely deserved any) with enormous fervour, his subjects would have been deprived, not only of the royal father-figure, but of 'the Pilot who weathered the Storm', in the very hour when the great storm broke. Had the Regency of George, Prince of Wales begun in 1789 instead of twenty years later, it is at least likely that the Regent would have replaced Pitt by Fox at the head of the nation's affairs. For a few weeks Pitt's enemies had rejoiced at the prospect, affording history's classic instance of counting chickens prematurely. 'Any minute now' was the Foxite slogan in the winter of 1788. Pitt's masterly handling of the 'Regency Crisis', and the King's sudden recovery, made it virtually certain that Charles James Fox would spend nearly the whole of the remainder of his political life in opposition.

Ever since Fox had departed from the North Ministry in 1773 he had steadily incurred His Majesty's rancorous distrust, a distrust which developed into inveterate hatred as the young man became the boon companion of the Prince of Wales. In the King's lurid imagination, Charles James Fox came to bear the horrid features of Sir John Falstaff leading the Prince astray into the paths of factious vice. As an alternative to Pitt, Fox became the King's pet nightmare.

[1] See *The Dynasts*, I, Act 2, Scene i.

> Nay, nay, now Mr Pitt,
> I must be firm. And if you love your King
> You'll goad him not so rashly to embrace
> This Fox-and-Grenville faction and its friends.
> Rather than Fox, why, give me civil war!
> Hey, what?

When Thomas Hardy makes the King reply thus to Pitt's request to be allowed to recruit Fox and the 'brilliant intellects of the other side' for a 'coalition of resources' against the triumphant Corsican, he hardly pitches his Majesty's repudiation of the proposal too strongly. It is likely enough that Fox's gifts were always better suited to opposition than to office. The best-loved man in politics for most of his life, he provided the perfect foil to the bleak and enigmatic Pitt. It was not the Pilot who weathered the Storm of the Revolution but the Tribune of liberty who rejoiced at the fall of the Bastille as the greatest and best event in the history of the world, who won the suffrage of the poets in that great age of English poetry. At his death Pitt was likened by Sir Walter Scott to a stately column, a beacon, a trumpet, a sentinel. But when Fox lay dying Wordsworth wrote: 'A Power is passing from the earth . . .' He spoke for the many thousands who were now sad, who had found in him their glory and their stay. The poem was written at Grasmere on a September evening after a stormy day. It opens

> Loud is the vale! the voice is up
> With which she speaks when storms are gone . . .

It utters no conventional lament of public mourning, but speaks from the heart of sorrow in lonely places where the poet listens to the still small voice.

> Loud is the vale;—this inland depth
> In peace is roaring like the Sea;
> Yon star upon the mountain-top
> Is listening quietly.

It is hardly surprising that the Romantic poets never had a good word to say for Mr Pitt, for they had been Jacobins, or at least, Jacobin-sympathizers, in the 'nineties, and Mr Pitt had put the English Jacobins on trial for treason. One of his spies had heard Coleridge and Wordsworth talking of 'Spy-Nozey' (doubtless a fellow eavesdropper) in their conspiratorial conversations among the sandhills of Somerset in 1797,[1] and Coleridge was to liken Pitt's panic-stricken followers to the bulls of Borrowdale who sometimes run mad with the echo of their own bellowing.[2]

The notion that in prosecuting the 'British Jacobins' Pitt was running away from his own shadow was to afflict his memory for several generations with charges of scaremongering, manufacture of alarmist plots, magnification of 'malice domestic' to match 'foreign levy'. A later century which has experienced the perils of what it came to call 'the fifth column' is less confident in its judgment of established authority in its dealings with the international machinations of revolution. Hester Stanhope, the woman nearest to the Prime Minister in the hour of peril, was to leave it on record that her uncle admitted that Tom Paine 'was in the right of it', but still desired to know what was to be expected of the man who bore responsibility for safeguarding the country from the danger of a bloody revolution? What he did in the emergency is perhaps well enough known since his polities earned him the sobriquet of 'that bloody-handed tool of tyranny'. It was, all the same, a good deal less in severity than what was done in the same national emergency by the men against whom he was contending in France, notably the Committee of Public Safety. He secured the suspension of the Habeas Corpus Act; he passed a number of measures collectively known as 'Coercion Acts', or Sedition Bills, the most drastic of which were those directed against Treasonable Practices and Seditious Meetings; and he put the founder of the London Corresponding Society, and near a dozen more of his fellow 'conspirators', on trial for High Treason. Counsel for the prisoners brought Pitt himself into the witness-box, along with a whole succession of other notables, in demonstrating that his humble clients were not alone in seeking to promote parliamentary reform, although they alone—because they were poor men—were liable to a charge of treason for doing so. It was a shrewd move, and the fact that the Prime Minister himself was

[1] See *Biographia Literaria*, Chapter 10.
[2] See 'The Friend', in *The Collected Coleridge*, 4, p. 219.

compelled to admit his own past complicity in reformist politics
was as good a demonstration of the rule of law in England as
could well be imagined. The acquittal which followed was
greeted with national rejoicings.

Pitt had initiated the type of 'alarmist' policy which was to
discredit his successors in the dangerous years following the war.
Liverpool, Sidmouth, and Castlereagh were to be known as
'Apish Jupiters', feeble disciples of the great man, wishful to
handle Pitt's thunderbolts but incapable of doing so. That they
found it necessary to adopt extraordinary measures to preserve
the peace after the great storm of revolution and war had passed
was held disgraceful even by many of their own Tory supporters.
Pitt at least, it must be conceded, was fighting a war on two
fronts. To him, the 'British Jacobins' (however little Jacobinical
their activities) were the domestic aspect of a European, indeed,
a world-wide enemy. For the French Revolution which inspired these men, while it was a political revolution, was a
revolution which acted like, and in many ways assumed the
aspect of, a religious revolution.[1] As the Reformation began by
capturing a large part of Germany and thence proceeded out-
wards to the conquest of other lands, so the French Revolution,
as Burke had the genius to understand even at the time, began
by conquering France and proceeded to the establishment of
its empire over other peoples. America, it has been said, was
merely the first country to be americanized. France, Burke said,
was the first country to be jacobinized. The Revolution, he said,
'exists in every country in Europe; and among all orders of men
in every country, who look up to France as to a common head.
The centre is there. The circumference is the world of Europe
wherever the race of Europe may be settled.'[2] It may be
doubted whether Pitt possessed the prophetic mind which
enabled the great Irishman to grasp this fact in philosophical
terms. For Burke, as Coleridge so truly affirmed, possessed and
had sedulously sharpened 'that eye which sees all things,
actions, and events in relation to the laws that determine their
existence and circumscribe their possibility'. It was this that
made him, unlike Pitt, 'A scientific statesman; and therefore

[1] Alexis de Tocqueville, *L'ancien régime et la Révolution*, 1856, Book I, Ch. 3.
[2] Burke, *Letters on a Regicide Peace*, II.

a seer.' Pitt's interests ran to a political economy rather than to moral philosophy or to poetry. 'Not a sentence of Mr Pitt's has ever been quoted,' Coleridge said, somewhat prematurely perhaps.[1]

The deficiencies which denied him the suffrage of the poets, the unphilosophical nature of his mind, his insusceptibility to ideas, more especially to ideas which did not at once and obviously spring from 'the routine of reasoning' as understood in the eighteenth century, meant that he would never understand what the French were up to. After all, the French Revolution was 'a new event; the old routine of reasoning, the common trade of politics, were to become obsolete. He appeared wholly unprepared for it: half-favouring, half-condemning, ignorant of what he favoured and why he condemned . . .'[2] He was the last man to dissipate his energies in pursuit of an opposing ideology. He preferred a good night's sleep. Only three times in his strenuous career does sleep seem to have eluded him, and one of these was the night when the news of Trafalgar and the death of Nelson arrived at three in the morning. He stayed up after that.

For all Pitt's untroubled slumbers, indeed, perhaps because of them, England was the most redoubtable enemy of the French Revolution (in the words of the French historian Albert Sorel[3]) 'because she was the only country to oppose her with analogous forces: national principles and popular passions'. This counter-ideology, as usual with the English at war, was largely and until very late unconscious. It assumed the familiar English forms of a religion and a political economy, the latter almost as religious as the former in its dogmatism and in the way it was held. The national Christianity, embodied alike in the Established Church and in the Nonconformist sects, was readily associated with patriotism, since it assumed without question that the old enemy, for long a nation of benighted Papists, was now governed by a gang of revolutionary atheists. Our allies at either extremity of Europe, in Spain and Russia,

---

[1] See his *Character of Mr Pitt*, reprinted in my *Political Thought of S. T. Coleridge*, pp. 68–74.

[2] Coleridge's *Character of Mr. Pitt*, loc. cit.

[3] See Sorel's *L'Europe et la Révolution Française*, Vol. 3, i.

were to derive not a little of their ultimately war-winning spirit from the conviction that in resisting the armies of the French Revolution and of Napoleon they were in arms against the legions of the Devil. The British forces by land and sea were perhaps less confidently inspired by Christian crusading zeal, although both Nelson and George III were apt to talk in such terms, as were Edmund Burke and the Romantic poets who appear to have believed themselves to have inherited his mantle. Coleridge detected in Bonaparte 'the marks that have characterized the masters of mischief, the liberticides and mighty hunters of mankind, from Nimrod to Napoleon . . . the character which Milton has so philosophically as well as sublimely embodied in the Satan of his *Paradise Lost*'. When Wordsworth wrote his great tract on the *Convention of Cintra* in 1809, condemning his country's coming to terms with the French after the victory of Vimiero, he attributed Napoleon's successes not to any superiority in his talents, but to his having made the 'desperate leap' of daring to say with his whole heart 'Evil be thou my good . . .!' in his 'Satanic pride and rebellious self-idolatry'.[1] George III, like the Duke of Wellington, rather preferred to treat the great enemy as an upstart, without title to be addressed as Emperor, indeed as one who had forfeited all title to treatment as a gentleman. The common soldier in the Peninsula, however, made a good thing out of the Spaniards' notion that he was a champion of the Blessed Virgin on account of his buttons bearing the image of Britannia.[2] A more appropriate image would have been a profile of Adam Smith, who first called the English a nation of shopkeepers, a proud title with which Napoleon mistakenly thought to hurt their feelings.

That the nation of shopkeepers eventually won the war, was in no small part a consequence of their devotion to their shops, and especially their workshops. The Carron ironworks, established in 1760, gave the navy the 'carronade', that squat, broad-breeched, handy gun which contributed much to the victories of Nelson's fleets, a superiority which Napoleon him-

---

[1] The references of the poets to Napoleon's Satanic character, and the text of Wordsworth's *Convention of Cintra*, may conveniently be found in *Political Tracts of Wordsworth, Coleridge and Shelley*, ed. R. J. White, 1953.

[2] At any rate, the buttons of the Royal Norfolks.

self acknowledged by his prolonged attempts to right the balance in fire-power by securing these models in sufficient quantity for France. Many years were to pass, however, before British arms in British hands could achieve much for the over-throw of Napoleon's domination of Europe. The opening phase of the war on land, when the English contended with the ancient enemy on their old battlegrounds in the Low Countries, squandering men and money in fruitless endeavours under the Duke of York, were prophetic of fifteen years during which, it was said, Great Britain practically expected nothing from her soldiers, and got what she expected. Between 1793 and 1801, sporadic expeditions cost her 1,350 officers and 60,000 men, of whom 18,596 died on service in the first year alone. In the two years 1795–6 more than 40,000 were discharged on account of wounds or infirmity, principally as a consequence of the West Indian campaigns. In 1799 'the noble Duke of York' lost 10,000 men in five engagements, uphill and downhill. This expenditure of men in small parcels on a diversity of battlefields was to con-tinue with expeditions to Buenos Aires and the Dardanelles in 1807, culminating in the ghastly fiasco of 1809 when Holland was assaulted by attacking the Isle of Walcheren in 'combined' operations. The lack of combination was to be enshrined in the famous verse:

> Bold Chatham with his sword undrawn
> Was waiting for Sir Richard Strachan.
> Sir Richard longing to get at 'em
> Stood waiting for the Earl of Chatham.

The elder son of the great war minister was generally referred to in his military career as 'the last Lord Chatham'. Seven thousand lives were lost, and many millions of gold poured into the sea, and the nation was finally regaled with the spectacle of the Foreign Secretary and the Minister of War firing pistols at each other on Putney Heath.[1]

Throughout 'The Years of Endurance', what men called 'Pitt's Gold' financed—to the tune of £1,400,000,000—succes-sive coalitions against France, costly and fissiparous structures

[1] Castlereagh and Canning fought over Castlereagh's imagining that Canning had demanded his exclusion from the Cabinet for incompetency.

which rose and fell over Napoleonic Europe with some of the
grim monotony of the Shades, Sinister and Ironic, which loom
from the Overworld of Hardy's gigantesque epic. Only at sea,
inspired by the splendid genius of Nelson, did British arms command success. Nelson laid down his life at Trafalgar, and within
twelve months both Pitt and Fox had followed him, nor was
it until 1812, when Wellington got the French on the run in
Spain, that the tide of battle on land may be said to have truly
turned against the French. Naval warfare saved England from
invasion, collared some valuable colonies, and ensured that the
nation of shopkeepers would win the long-drawn contest with
Napoleon's 'Continental System' which was designed to close
Europe to her commerce. It was a contest between the elephant
and the whale. The whale needed to get ashore, sooner or later,
and by the time Wellington could lead his forces to the Pyrenees,
the elephant had marched over Austria, Prussia, and a large
part of Russia. He needed to cross the narrow seas in order to
deliver a blow at the heart of his chiefest enemy. Failing that,
he must trample down the rest of the world until the whale
suffocated in her own element. The objective was not to starve
her out, but to compel her to stew in her own juice. Deprived
of her European markets, Napoleon argued, she would perish
of over-production, unemployment, and (as the Emperor imagined) revolution on the part of her own workless multitudes.
Napoleon actually envisaged himself descending upon the desperate islanders to be welcomed as a liberator at the Mansion
House. Instead, he was driven to Moscow in order to stop up
a gap in his blockade, and to go there in boots and blankets
'made in England'. His designs were not perhaps as crazy as
British historians have sometimes been pleased to imagine.
Great Britain was nearer to capitulation in 1812 than at any
time during the war. Her exports were down by 33$\frac{1}{3}$ per cent,
her poor-law expenditure up by some six million. Prices were
87 per cent above pre-war level, wheat standing at 160s. a
quarter. Men were smashing machines wholesale in the Midlands and the north. 'Orders-in-Council' in retaliation against
Napoleon's Berlin Decrees, had produced Great Britain's solitary war with the United States. The King's recurrent illness
had produced in him a condition indistinguishable from lunacy,

and the Prime Minister was assassinated that year by a poor gentleman who imagined that Mr Perceval had ruined his business.

But the whale was ashore at last. Wellington stormed Badajoz in April, defeated Marshal Marmont at Salamanca in July, and entered Madrid in August. Next year he won the battle of the Pyrenees, and in 1814 invaded France. At 'The Battle of the Nations' (fought at Leipzig) Napoleon suffered a crushing defeat by the allies and abdicated. 'The man who was more than a man', even after the blood-letting of the Moscow campaign, had conducted one of his most brilliant campaigns in defence of his capital, and after his brief banishment to the isle of Elba he was yet to return in triumph to meet his final defeat at Waterloo. So that the whale was in at the death, suitably represented at that moment by H.R.H. the Prince Regent, to whom the fallen Emperor addressed himself in an appeal to 'the most powerful, the most constant, and the most generous of my enemies'. Although the Prince Regent was to convince himself that he had fought in person at Waterloo, it was none the less appropriate that the last scene of the surrender was enacted in the cabin of H.M.S. *Bellerophon*, a first-rate man-of-war, Captain Maitland's veteran ship-of-the-line, and bearing the scars of the Nile and Trafalgar.

CHAPTER 18

War and Peace

My argument is that War makes rattling good history; but peace is poor reading.

Spirit Sinister, The Dynasts, I, 2, v

WHEN THE long war came to an end, patriots were inclined to rejoice more over the victory than over the peace. 'How this victory pursues one's imagination!' Benjamin Robert Haydon kept exclaiming in the days that followed the news of Waterloo. 'Great and glorious Wellington!' On the other hand, it was quite astonishing, the Prime Minister wrote, 'how little interest is taken in what is going on at Vienna, except' he was careful to add 'in so far as it is connected with expense'. The bowed and shabby figure of John Bull bearing on his shoulders the crushing burden of the world's armaments in order to uphold the restored monarchy of France was a favourite cartoon of the first years of peace. And what was there in the peace treaties for us, anyway, people asked? Malta and Heligoland; the Cape of Good Hope, Ceylon, Demerara looted from the Dutch; islands in the East and West Indies, like Tobago, St Lucia and Mauritius, captured from the French; a somewhat puzzling 'protectorate' over the Ionian Islands off the coast of Greece ... France was back to her frontiers of 1790, and Boney was on a rock in the Atlantic.

Liberals were inclined to think even this last achievement of 'that hypocritical knot of conspiring tyrants', our allies among the kings of Europe, was somewhat ungenerous to 'the only tyrant among them who was not a hypocrite'.[1] Progressives like Bentham, Hazlitt and Leigh Hunt mourned over Waterloo as

[1] The view of Shelley. See his *Philosophical View of Reform*, 1819. (Included in my volume, *Political Tracts of Wordsworth, Coleridge and Shelley*.)

a victory of reaction over enlightenment. Particularly galling was it that our representatives were sitting down at Vienna with despots to fasten the strait-waistcoat of Legitimacy on a 'liberated' Europe. 'Under our presiding influence, the Monarchs are leagued against every exertion of popular energy,' one good Whig squire wrote in his journals. Radical journalists went further, denouncing Lord Castlereagh as a scoundrel 'intriguing away his country's interests and bartering the prosperity of its inhabitants for blue ribands, stars and personal advantages'. After so many years of collaboration with the European powers, Great Britain could scarcely decline to participate in the Concert of Europe for the peaceful settlement of problems affecting the balance of power and the peace of Europe in the future. In consequence the government was suspected of sharing the sympathies and the principles of that trade union of tyrants, the Holy Alliance, and until George Canning took over the Foreign Office at the death of Lord Castlereagh in 1822, a despotic, indeed a militarist, spirit was imagined to possess the post-war Administration of Lord Liverpool, a suspicion that was hardly lessened when Wellington entered the government in 1818, the year before the 'Massacre of Peterloo'. When in that year the government passed 'The Six Acts', which closely resembled the exceptional measures taken by Pitt for the preservation of order in 1793–4, Lord Brougham voiced the opinion of many: 'I see Wellington distinctly in the measure, and I can hardly doubt that a design is formed of making the Government of this country less free—and permanently so.'

States at war with each other get more alike, more especially if the war is for survival. Warring governments learn from each other the most efficient ways of mobilizing and organizing their manpower and resources, and especially of preventing dissipation of their war-effort by dissension at home. Controls of every kind are multiplied, liberty is curtailed, centralization of authority is encouraged. Men who have been 'inspired amateurs' of government and administration either become, or give place to, professionals. The State takes on a greater or lesser degree of totalitarianism. This process was especially noticeable in the age of the so-called Enlightened Despots of the eighteenth century, as it has been in the democracies of the twentieth. It might have been expected to become no less noticeable during the life-and-death struggle of the Napoleonic Wars. Little investigation of the extent to which this happened has hitherto been undertaken save in the most general terms, nor is it proposed to undertake it here. What must be said, however, is that the British governments which conducted the war with Napoleon were compelled for survival's sake to regiment their own dissenters and to draw considerably tighter the reins of central government. Pitt's anti-Jacobin measures were an integral part of his foreign policy, an essential part of the war-effort. He was concerned to deny that Great Britain was at war with the French Revolution. He resisted the urge to go to war until the last possible moment and then took his stand upon sound commercial considerations, the defence of English trade against the French opening of the Scheldt in disregard of treaties. He went on to maintain that it was not 'a war against opinions', let alone a crusade. It was a war against an armed doctrine, against 'liberty by compulsion', France having decided (as Pitt expressed it) that 'all Europe was to learn the principles of liberty from the mouth of the French cannon'.

As for the concentration of authority, from the beginning Pitt's Ministry had assumed a tightly knit character, which the exigencies of war served only to increase. Taking office at the King's behest at the head of a minority in the House of Commons he had, like Walpole, created for himself a suffrage drawn from sources alternative to the royal favour. This was not on the whole difficult, since the King knew that the only viable alternative to Pitt was the hated Charles James Fox. After his long and arduous endeavours to maintain his 'independence', the King had proceeded gently but certainly out of the frying-pan into the fire. In entrusting his affairs to Pitt, he had found a servant who—with all the respect and loyalty in the world— was to be his master. He maintained Pitt in power against the raging of the Fox–North legions of the House of Commons for many weeks until, in March 1784, he secured an overwhelming majority at the polls. It was as corrupt an election as any of the century, and to speak of Pitt's having been returned by the tumultuous approval of 'the people' would be absurd. He was given his great majority, as every man invested with the King's favour was certain to be, by electoral management from the Treasury. On Pitt's side also was the unpopularity of the Fox–North coalition, the approval of the City of London, and the widespread confidence that the nation's affairs were safe in the hands of a young man of a little less than twenty-five so long as he bore the splendid name of 'Mr Pitt'. He said, much in the style of Chatham, 'I place much dependence on my new colleagues; I place still more dependence on myself.'

In its early years his Administration was perhaps an even more 'curious show' (as Burke might have said) than the celebrated Tessellated Pavement of his father's manufacture in 1766. An assemblage of William Pitt's friends and relations (a number of them culled from the 'old boy network' of his Cambridge days), king's friends, useful wielders of influence, amiable noblemen, and hangovers from previous administrations, it is remembered by the epithets levelled at it by contemporaries: 'A lutestring Administration' (Charles Townshend), 'A boyish prank . . . a set of children playing at ministers', 'The mince-pie Administration' (the general opinion that it would be ended by Christmas). Lord Rosebery's phrase, delivered in 1891, was: 'a procession of ornamental phantoms'. It was to last, with many chops and changes, for eighteen momentous years.

For the first time since Walpole the Chief Minister was the centre of authority, and departmentalism was destroyed. The Cabinet became homogeneous and disciplined, an essential condition in time of revolution and war. It was made perfectly plain that a new era had dawned when Pitt secured the dismissal of the Lord Chancellor, Thurlow, for indiscipline in 1792. By that time there was a strong inner Cabinet consisting of the triumvirate of Pitt, Grenville and Dundas. It is more than a little doubtful whether it would have been legitimate to speak of either the Prime Minister, or the Cabinet, in any modern sense of those terms, at any earlier date. Now it was plain where authority lay. There were to be, and there still are, wheels within wheels, inner and outer circles. Not every Premier after Pitt was to be a strong man, or even credible. 'Hardly any fact in history is so incredible' Walter Bagehot was to write in 1856, 'as that forty and a few years ago England was ruled by Mr Perceval.' But Mr Pitt ruled with all the authority, and none of the perversity of his great father. Between them, father and son made a vast amount of the modern history of England.

Like their kinsmen the Grenvilles, the Pitts were not born to the purple. They were men of business, meaning not trade or commerce, but the 'business' of civil government. When the elder Pitt acquired Burton Pynsent in Somerset, he rejoiced for the first time in his life to be a 'landed gentleman', taking immense delight in planting trees and laying out his lands. His younger son inherited his father's tastes as an arborealogist and indulged them happily when he acquired Holwood (near Bromley) in 1785. 'We are all turning country gentlemen very fast,' he wrote to Wilberforce. Both men, however, are better remembered as favourite sons of the City of London, and both identified themselves with the fortunes of the great commercial community which was to dominate Europe, and the world, throughout the nineteenth century, the father as the builder of Empire, the son as its saviour and promoter. The men who carried the great war to its victorious conclusion, and preserved the ensuing peace, were Tory country gentlemen of the great party founded in the days of the French Revolution and Napoleon by the younger Pitt, and inspired by their master's liberal free-trade principles. It is not true that Pitt, in Disraeli's words, 'created a plebeian aristocracy' in order to carry through a free-trade policy. He did not make peers of 'second-rate squires and fat graziers', nor did he catch them 'in the alleys of Lombard Street' or clutch them 'from the counting houses of Cornhill'. In the whole of his career he only recommended for a peerage one banker, and only one who had even an indirect connexion with trade.[1] He recommended men whom his contemporaries in an age of warfare delighted to honour, distinguished soldiers and admirals and diplomatists. Nor would George III, who was most jealous of the honour of the peerage, have consented to anything else. And when Lord Liverpool spoke of England's debt to Watt, Boulton and Arkwright—'as

[1] Robert Smith, who became Lord Carrington, and Lord Berwick of Attingham, grandson of a draper of Shrewsbury. See A. S. Turberville, *The House of Lords in the Age of Reform, 1784–1837*, Ch. III.

useful to their country in their generations, as any of the
Legislators of old'—he was only speaking as any country
gentleman in an increasingly industrial society would have
spoken. Thanks largely to the training they had received under
Pitt, the men of Lord Liverpool's government understood the
interests of a thriving business community. They were, one and
all, like their master, pupils of Adam Smith.

When the war came to an end, however, neither William
Pitt nor Adam Smith were adequate mentors for statesmen
confronted with the social problems of a people emerging from
a long and arduous war during which they had undergone an
industrial revolution. Not that a pupil of Adam Smith was likely
to fall into the heresy of believing that social or economic
problems were susceptible to solution, or even alleviation, at
the hands of statesmen and governments anyway. To speak of
a 'backlog of political and social reform which had piled up
during the war-years when such problems had inevitably been
postponed' is strictly meaningless. If the statute-book seems
remarkably blank as far as social and political reform is concerned over the years of Regency England, that is no cause for
surprise to anyone who has grasped the nature of the orthodox
political economy of the age. When he introduced the 'Waterloo
Corn Law' in 1815 in order artificially to maintain agricultural
prices in the post-war slump, Lord Liverpool felt called upon
to apologize for such unorthodox legislative interference. 'The
general principle, supposing all nations, or at least the most
considerable nations, to act upon it', his Lordship said, 'was
that in these cases the Legislature ought not to interfere, but
should leave everything to find its own level.' Which was,
as Coleridge observed, 'the paraphrase, or ironical definition
of a storm'. Such a definition suits Regency England very well.
The war, Coleridge wrote (looking back in 1817), had 'brought
about a national unanimity unexampled in our history since the
reign of Elizabeth'. It was a unanimity grounded upon moral
feelings. Party warfare had been stilled, for both parties had
found themselves in the wrong, the one having mistaken the
moral character of the revolution, the other having miscal-
culated both its moral and its physical resources. It had been
possible to regard machine-breaking as industrial sabotage of

the war-effort, and for farmers to make high profits out of the enclosure of commons and the ploughing up of marginally profitable land at a time of high corn prices in the name of patriotism. Many a reputation for patriotism was also made by subscribing to the cost of the war in the form of response to Mr Pitt's appeàl in 1798 for voluntary gifts of money, an appeal which raised two million within the year, the King having led off with £20,000, although there was a bitter outcry against the Income Tax of 2s. in the pound which was imposed in 1799. The removal of the common focus with the slackening of the war-effort in 1815, when the Income Tax was repealed, brought into force once more all the manifold centrifugal forces at large in an industrial society. As Harriet Martineau expressed it when she wrote her *History of the Thirty Years Peace* in 1847: 'The foundations of the State were loosened; there was no cohesion in the materials of which the State was built up.'

This was the fantasy of a lady whose politics and political economy were founded on what Coleridge called (*à propos* of Newton) 'an ultimate particle'. When the poet met Miss Martineau he said: 'You appear to consider that society is an aggregate of individuals.' Miss Martineau agreed without difficulty that she did. To consider society to be anything else she would have thought childish for, like most other people of her time and country, she had neither interest in nor knowledge of the forces of social cohesion. To Miss Martineau individuals composing society are attracted or repelled like the dancing particles of an atomic system. An atom is an atom, neither more nor less, and society is the flux of individuals in any one moment of existence, holding together or falling apart, coming together or dissolving, in simple accordance with their more or less enlightened self-interest. Between 1832 and 1834 Harriet Martineau published nine volumes of 'Illustrations of Political Economy' couched in the form of *Tales for the People*, for the promulgation of this blithe and improving faith. 'The people want this work,' she said, 'and they shall have it.' She had put her gifts as a romancer at the service of the theory of rent and the principles of *laissez-faire* as taught by Ricardo and Malthus and Adam Smith, combining human interest and economic doctrine so cunningly that she made a substantial income while promoting social peace, making the labouring classes patient and the capitalists secure.[1]

Miss Martineau's labours for the promotion of social peace by the spread of political economy were undertaken when the dangerous post-war years were over. The most perilous years were 1816–19. People were talking of a *bellum servile*. 'The country is mined beneath our feet.' If the military were withdrawn from London 'Four and twenty hours would not elapse before the tricoloured flag would be planted upon Carlton House', the poet-laureate wrote to the Prime Minister from the Lake District. Southey imagined that he could smell sedition 'even among these mountains'. Miss Martineau herself recalled those days as the time when ladies barricaded windows with ironing boards 'in preparation for seiges from thousands of rebels whose footfall was long listened for in vain through the darkness of the night'. Parliament set up Secret Committees of both Houses to look into the extent and nature of the danger, committees which, after examining the information supplied by magistrates and informers, never failed to report the existence of plans for a nation-wide insurrection.

Sporadic outbreaks did occur; in 1812 the machine-breakers in the northern and Midland counties, by their ubiquity, their secrecy, their loyalty to one another, maintained a reign of terror which was only held in check by horse-patrols of regular troops which for a time turned large areas into an armed camp. The Ely and Littleport bread-riots of 1816 resulted in the execution of five ringleaders, and in the same year large crowds of unemployed colliers and ironworkers staged an orderly hunger-march from South Wales, dragging wagons of coal. There were short sharp outbreaks at Spa Fields in London in December, and some rhetoric about capturing the Tower. In the following March another hunger-march set out, this time from Manchester, some six hundred weavers bearing petitions to the Prince Regent begging measures for the remedy of the wretched plight of the cotton-trade. Each man carried a blanket for shelter *en route*, thus earning the name of 'Blanketeers'. Only one man got to London, hundreds being rounded up as they crossed the Dove from Staffordshire into Derbyshire,

[1] See Theodora Bosanquet, *Harriet Martineau*, p. 48.

presenting the magistrates with the double problem of where to house them and what to charge them with. The Duke of Northumberland likened them to the revolutionary Marseillais marching to Paris in 1792. There was something more truly sinister about the attempt of Jeremiah Brandreth, the pauper desperado, to march a couple of hundred Derbyshire labourers to Nottingham on a rainy night in June of that summer, because they talked about themselves as participants in a General Rising that was expected to take place simultaneously that night all over the three Kingdoms. Perhaps their leader believed it, though he talked to his followers even more volubly about the rum and roast-beef awaiting them in Nottingham. The objective was a Provisional Government, which they appear to have thought had something to do with provisions. For their part in this farcical affair, three leaders were executed for high treason in the autumn, and many more deported to Botany Bay. The most memorable and execrable event of these stricken years, however, was the riding down of a peaceful demonstration in St Peter's Fields, Manchester, in August 1819, with the loss of eleven lives and the wounding of many hundreds, a tragic and clumsy piece of mismanagement by magistrates and yeomanry which was at once christened the 'Peterloo massacre'. The abortive plan of Arthur Thistlewood and the Cato Street conspirators in the following February to massacre the Cabinet *in toto* was intended to wreak vengeance for Peterloo. By that time George III was dead and the Prince Regent had assumed his title of George IV.

There is no evidence whatever that these sporadic events belonged to anything in the nature of a general design, or that there was anywhere at any time even the shadow of a central command exercising co-ordinative direction or guidance. Nevertheless government would have been failing in its most elementary duty had it not taken precautions, looked into suspected conspiracy, even by the employment of spies, and dealt firmly with open disturbances. It came in for justifiable criticism when, as in the Derbyshire uprising, it was suspected that a secret agent had gone beyond merely detective activities and acted as an *agent provocateur*. It was at this point that the notion got abroad again, as it had been abroad in the years of

Pitt's repression in the 1790s, that the government was pursuing an unscrupulous alarmist policy, deliberately conjuring up the spectre of revolution in order to justify wholesale measures of repression. 'Probably no English Government has ever been quite so near, in spirit and licence, to the atmosphere that we used to associate with the Tsar's government of Russia ...' wrote J. L. and Barbara Hammond in 1919.[1] The Tsar himself, however, when he visited this country in 1814, expressed a different opinion. Alexander told the Home Secretary, Lord Sidmouth, that Russia's superior humanity in these matters consisted in her use of agents to prevent crime, while the English let men commit crimes and then punished them severely.[2] No visiting Russians or anyone else ever discovered anything faintly resembling a 'revolutionary consciousness' let alone a 'working-class culture' among the people of Regency England.

There was a widespread and somewhat novel conviction that hunger, low wages, unemployment, indeed most of the economic distresses from which Englishmen suffered, had something to do with politics. Instead of submitting to such distresses as akin to bad weather, or consequent upon the laws of Nature or the disfavour of Divine Providence, men were increasingly wishful to know whether they were not within the power of men to remedy by political endeavour; indeed, whether, after all, that was not what politics should be about? This notion, which has become a commonplace among men of a later time, was still only faintly dawning. The dawn was encouraged by the intellectual triumph of the eighteenth century which philosophers called 'the Enlightenment', with its hopeful faith that mankind could control its environment by taking thought. In France that faith had come to fruition in the Revolution, and in the career of Napoleon Bonaparte who believed, as H. A. L. Fisher once put it, that everything could be improved from a tea kettle upwards. Jeremy Bentham in England encouraged his followers to believe the same. Many remained sceptical. 'Man cannot create abundance where Providence has inflicted scarcity,' Lord Sidmouth went on insisting. 'The alleviation of the difficulties is not to be looked for from the

[1] See *The Skilled Labourer*, p. 371.
[2] Edward Pellew, *Life of Henry Addington, Viscount Sidmouth*, Vol. 3, p. 120.

intervention of the Government and Parliament.'[1] Nor would Adam Smith approve of such intervention. Mr Pitt himself had been heard to say that a few days' rain might produce consequences for which even he could see no adequate remedy, 'an admission of England's wisest statesman' Lord Sidmouth's nephew commented, which 'shows how little real control mankind have over the sources of their prosperity, and how entirely dependent they are, even for the means of subsistence, on the mercy and protection of Divine Providence'.[2] The Prime Minister himself was fond of quoting Dr Johnson's lines:

> How small, of all the ills that men endure,
> The part which Kings or States can cause or cure.

The people ought to be taught, he was insisting at the time of Peterloo, that the 'evils inseparable from the state of things should not be charged on any government'. He was confident that inquiry would reveal 'that by far the greater part of the miseries of which human nature complained were at all times and in all countries beyond the control of human legislation'.[3] Few things are more pathetic than the puzzled indignation of the governors of Regency England when men, and especially working men, began to disbelieve it. Their horror at such a departure from the orthodox political economy[4] was almost equal to their horror at the prospect of a revolution.

Here, in the last years of the reign of George III, was born what might best be described as 'social politics'. At the time men spoke of the politics of bread and cheese, or of politics at last becoming 'a knife-and-fork question'. The change had begun to show itself from the day in January 1792, when the shoemaker, Thomas Hardy, and a few friends founded the London Corresponding Society. When in the following August this society issued an Address to the Inhabitants of Great Britain on the subject of Parliamentary Reform, it opened with the words, 'Let no man imagine himself unconcerned in the

[1] Edward Pellew, *Life of Henry Addington, Viscount Sidmouth*, Vol. 3, pp. 85, 90, 145.
[2] Ibid., Vol. I, p. 270.
[3] Hansard, *Parliamentary Debates*, Old Series, XLI, 497.
[4] W. R. Brock, *Lord Liverpool and Liberal Toryism*.

proposed reform.' For a truly representative Parliament would (among other things) bring 'the necessaries of life more within the reach of the poor'. It would take care that youth were better educated, prisons less crowded, old age better provided for . . . Such politics appealed especially to men engaged in industry. Asked what was the object of the Sheffield Society's meeting, a witness in the trials of 1794 replied: 'To enlighten the people, to show the people the reason, the ground, of all their complaints and sufferings . . .', more especially why a man who worked thirteen hours a day the week through was not able to maintain his family, 'that is what I understood of it . . .' Of course many men, in hard times, resorted to direct action, strikes, machine-breaking, agitation for Minimum Wage Bills, trade union activity despite the Combination Laws. To secure a vote for Parliament, and to turn Parliament into a legislative agency for economic and social reform, seemed a long way round. It might be better in the long run. . . . But in the long run we are all dead. It was a hard fight to get the working men of the new industrial England to become patient parliamentary politicians, requiring all the skill and propaganda of men like Cartwright and Cobbett, Sir Francis Burdett and the Westminster Radicals. Yet it was largely in consequence of the labours of such men, and many more whose very names are forgotten, that parliamentary democracy became something closer to a reality in a later century.

CHAPTER 19

Politics and Morals

THE OLD KING's reign came, to all intents and purposes, to an end in 1810, although he was to live for another ten years. In 1811, by virtue of the Regency Bill, the Prince of Wales took his place at the head of the unique amalgam of squalor and bravura known as 'Regency England'. The people grieved for the poor old King shut away at Windsor Castle, old and blind and wandering in his wits. But it turned out, as the Wessex countryman had predicted when there was a danger of his being 'nabbed' by Napoleon, that 'it wouldn't make a deal of difference . . . we should rub along some way, goodnow.' In fact, the country did very well. Despite economic depression and social unrest, the Regency was in many respects the most brilliant period of the King's nominal reign.

If an age may be judged by its literature, the Regency is to be matched only by the reign of Queen Anne or the closing years of Queen Elizabeth. Wordsworth (*The Excursion*, 1814) and Coleridge (*Christabel* and *Kubla Khan*, 1816) were still active, Byron was at his peak (*Childe Harold*, 1812–18), Keats and Shelley were at their splendid beginnings. Cary published his great translation of the *Divine Comedy* in 1814. The essayists, Hazlitt, Leigh Hunt and Lamb, were making 'occasional literature' everlasting. The *Waverley* Novels began in 1814, and nearly all Jane Austen came out between 1811 and 1818. It was the flowering time of the great reviews, the *Edinburgh*, the *Quarterly*, the *Examiner*, the *Westminster*. Prophets and pundits abounded, all on fire with blue-prints to put the country right and/or to build the New Jerusalem. Blake and Bentham, Robert Owen and Cobbett and Major Cartwright, they all had their visions and their specifics in these years. It was as if a dam, built up during the long years of the war for survival, had now burst. 'The anomalous occasions and stupendous events of the contest had aroused us like the blast of a trumpet from the clouds,' wrote Coleridge; 'and as many as were capable of thinking were aroused to thought.' Being lately awakened from a trance, the *Black Dwarf* said, many in their hurry to dress put their garments on wrong. The stress of thought is the striking phenomenon of these years. Its quality varied from the merest common sense to the sheerest lunacy. To the historian it abounds in social criticism, often utopian, sometimes apocalyptic.

Coleridge himself was undoubtedly the greatest social critic of the age, though his work was little understood, and even less influential, for another generation or more. Like Bentham, with whom J. S. Mill was to bracket him as one of 'the two great seminal minds of England in their age', he was a teacher of the teachers of the future. His name, Mill predicted, was 'one of the few English names of our time which are likely to be oftener pronounced, and to become symbolical of more important things, in proportion as the inward workings of the age manifest themselves more and more in outward facts'. He was, indeed, to act like intellectual or spiritual yeast. Only a small minority read his prose works at the time they were written, and only a minority of a minority can have read the *Lay Sermons* in which he set forth his thoughts on the causes of the present distresses and discontents. His influence in his own day, like that of Bentham again, was rather through discipleship than the printed word. It was in the month of April 1816 that the poet found asylum in the house of Dr James Gillman at the Grove, on Highgate Hill, and thither for the rest of his life the disciples wended. 'Coleridge sat on the brow of Highgate Hill, in these years,' wrote one of them, Thomas Carlyle, 'looking down on London and its smoke-tumult, like a sage escaped from the inanity of life's battle; attracting towards him the thoughts of innumerable brave souls still engaged there . . .' In that self-same year, 1816, and in the year following, he composed the two *Lay Sermons*, addressed to the Higher and Middle Classes. He spoke of composing a third, addressed to the labouring classes. It was never written, nor perhaps did it need to be, for all that he had to offer his age and country was contained in the other two. He did, however, address himself to specifically political agencies on two occasions: in 1818 when he wrote two Addresses in support of the elder Peel's Factory Bill, and in 1817 when he sent a letter to Lord Liverpool on the vital and urgent necessity of rescuing speculative philosophy from false principles of reasoning if Church and State were to be saved from ruin; 'at least', Lord Liverpool endorsed the letter, 'I believe this is Mr Coleridge's meaning, but I cannot well understand him'. This will be readily understood by anyone who reads the letter,[1] but it says much for the Prime Minister that in the crisis-year of 1817 he tried.

The pained surprise of the old poet when, on his meeting with Miss Martineau at Highgate, he discovered that this popular teacher of the people took it for granted 'that society is an aggregate of individuals', no more and no less, indicates at once where he differed from the common run of opinion in his day. He wished to suggest that organized human society was in some absurd way (Miss Martineau would have said) different from the mere sum of its parts, that it was subject to natural laws 'in virtue of its aggregate character and organisation'. When he wrote his letter to Lord Liverpool he gave this suggestion its most positive, assertive form. 'It is high time, My Lord,' he said, 'that the subjects of Christian Governments should be taught that neither historically nor morally, in fact or by right, have men made the state; but that the State, and that alone, makes them men . . . that the flux of individuals in any one moment of existence is there for the sake of the State, far more than the State for them, though both positions are true proportionally . . .' In case this should appear to be the High State doctrine of Hegel and the German Transcendentalists, and Coleridge should appear to belong to the intellectual ancestry of dictatorship, totalitarianism or the wickedness of a later century, it should be said here that he was stressing the neglected side of the truth. What he liked to call 'the mechanico-corpuscular philosophy', or the philosophy of an ultimate particle, with all its consequences for political thought in notions of the State as a collection of demiurgic atoms held together by some temporary compact, had been in the ascendant since the Restoration and John Locke

[1] Which may be found in my *Political Thought of S. T. Coleridge*, pp. 209–16.

(always the villain of the piece for Coleridge). To counter such intellectual treasons to the Platonic tradition, to the English mind of Bacon, Shakespeare, Milton, Sidney, only the over-balance of its intellectual opposite could avail. It is not really surprising that Miss Martineau and the political economists and the Benthamites gave him up as a professor of opium-induced transcendental nonsense or, as Carlyle preferred it—'bottled moonshine'. Miss Martineau was to prophesy that if Coleridge were remembered at all it would be neither as a poet, nor as a philosopher, but as a warning. His philosophical utterances, she convinced herself, were produced by the same kind of action as Mr Babbage's calculating machine,[1] only 'the latter issues from sound premises, while few will venture to say that the other has any reliable basis at all'.

Coleridge was not alone in his glory as the Romantic poet turned social critic or political philosopher, though he was certainly the greatest of them. The political importance of the Romantic Movement in Europe, and especially in Germany, has been long understood, although controversy still continues on the question whether it made for liberalism or reaction. Its significance in England was for long obscured by native pride in the homespun Locke and Bentham, whose teachings chimed so well with the energies and interests of a manufacturing and mechanistic society. What had a poet to teach the politician and the economist anyway? Two brief quotations may be apposite: 'Berkeley indeed asserts . . . that without an habitual interest in these subjects, a man may be a dexterous intriguer, but never can be a statesman,' these subjects being God, the human mind and the *summum bonum*. And again: 'What solemn humbug this modern political economy is!' for its entire tendency is 'to denationalize, and to make the love of our country into a foolish superstition. It would dig up the charcoal foundations of the temple of Ephesus to burn as fuel for a steam-engine.' No primary work by a Romantic poet is included among the texts for the History of Political Thought in the University of Cam-bridge, even in 1968.

[1] Charles Babbage (1792–1871) was promoting his invention for calcu-lating by machinery at this time. His 'small engine model' was being much talked of in the years 1820–2.

At the time, in the years of the Regency, English people were more concerned with the Mammon of Unrighteousness and Moral Rearmament. Mammon was well represented by the Prince Regent himself, and by the wondrous achievements of his extravagance. 'Le gaspillage des Princes' has often been another name for the fine arts in building, town planning and public display. The Prince Regent was the first prince of cultivated taste to preside over this country since Charles I. He was responsible for the splendour of John Nash's London, some of which has survived two world wars and a great deal of 'commercial development'. The English country house had hitherto been England's finest contribution to the fine arts, but now she was to match her rural beauties with a style instead of a scramble in urban living. Of course, Regency architecture was frequently otiose, sometimes ponderous, and generally open to the charge of concealing gimcrack structure behind its stucco, though it must be said that Nash was a great stickler for domestic amenities, good ventilation, good plumbing, and 'all modern comforts'. His critics were pert enough with their sobriquet of 'The Age of Stucco', predicting dire disclosures when the handsome faces developed cracks and began to flake off. 'Some of the plaister streets are really magnificent,' wrote Maria Edgeworth. 'But there is ever some voice which cries Must fall! Must fall! Must fall! Must scale off!—Soon, soon, soon.' Morally, of course, the whole show (for a show it was) was infected with the domestic depravity of the Modern Babylon which it is always easy to imagine going on behind classical façades. For elegance notoriously covers a multitude of sins. The Age of the Elephantine was perhaps more appropriate for a dispensation presided over by the Prince Regent. The frowning façades, towering columns, cavernous porticoes have a flamboyant, overpowering and somewhat shameless air, as if they were intended for the haunts of a populous, overdressed, boastfully successful society. The Prince certainly intended to put Napoleon's Paris in the shade, for England was now top nation, and he had convinced himself that he had taken a leading part in making her so.

The English never really loved it. Even now visitors may be seen wandering half-heartedly around the Regent's Park (looking for the Zoo, generally) and giving little sniffs of embarrassment as they pass rapidly through York Gate and along Cumberland Terrace. Ostentation always gives them twinges in the purse. The Duke of Wellington represents them best, even though, like so many typical Englishmen, his blood had been strained through the filter of the Irish Ascendancy. The Duke was fond of contrasting himself with Napoleon in that he always wished to avoid fighting a *great* battle. It was the same with his economy of words, his neat and simple dress, his preference for small women and Arab horses. He would have celebrated Waterloo, if at all, with *Eine Kleine Nachtmusik* not the *Eroica* Symphony. And George III, under whom he lived for half a century, was himself 'mere English' (perhaps because he had been saying so all his life). And when the Regency was over it all came back, if indeed it had ever been away: domestic virtue, moralistic religion, plain living (though not high thinking), and 'The Good Old King' lived again in his granddaughter.[1] That is the best of George III, with all his shortcomings, and perhaps because of them. He provides a paradigm of the English with all their duller virtues and vices—and with poetry left out.

It soon became clear that the wickedness of the Regency was only an expensive top-dressing on a society fast developing the moral earnestness of the Victorians. Not all the notorious wickedness of that glittering society could detain the English for more than a fleeting moment from pursuing their predestined course towards the virtuous shores of the Victorian Age. For one thing, the moralistic revival of the early years of the King's reign had never ceased to count its victories. Evangelical religion pitched its tents on Clapham Common in 1807 when a number of well-to-do families in the neighbourhood, notably the households of Henry Thornton and Zachary Macaulay, champions of the anti-slavery movement, forgathered round the Rev. John Venn, Rector of Clapham. The Saints, as the members of the so-called Clapham Sect were called, were, in a sense, the Methodist wing of the Church of England. They were not only pious but wealthy, and in politics they were sound Tories.

---

[1] Victoria was born before the old King died, starting in life as a Regency girl, something of which Prince Albert was to cure her.

They were, as Sydney Smith once said, enthusiasts for the suppression of vice in everyone with less than £500 a year. They were also great tractarians, not in the Oxford sense, but as sponsors of the Religious Tract Society which was founded in the same year and proceeded to pour out a torrent of sententious 'improving' literature—the kind of trash that Thackeray was to satirize, all about the spiritual adventures of pious washerwomen, mealy-mouthed milkmaids, or sanctimonious shepherds. Nothing is more incongruous than these revoltingly religiose parcels of prose in that age so famous otherwise for the firm, masculine writing of such men as Hazlitt and Cobbett. Indeed it was Cobbett who trounced the evangelical pietism of Wilberforce, Hannah More, Sarah Trimmer, and the Saints of Clapham. These 'canting hypocrites' simply wanted to 'teach the poor to starve without making a noise'. Their purpose was 'keeping the poor from cutting the throats of the rich'. Parson's sermon, once a week or fortnight, used to be quite sufficient for the religion and morals of the village. 'Now we had a busy creature or two in every village dancing about with "Tracts" for the benefit of the souls of the labourers and their families.' And among the blessings of life in the United States, he was to write home, he ranked high the fact that there was no Wilberforce. 'Think of that—No WILBERFORCE!!!'

Cobbett was unjust to the Evangelicals, though as a man of taste and healthy appetites, he can hardly be blamed. Yet the fact is that they taught by example, in a society that was often brutal and (especially at its upper levels) selfishly dissolute, the health that may come of personal responsibility, of disciplined living, of social seriousness. If they too often mistook respectability for a sign of grace, and poverty as a penalty incurred by sin and heedless ways of life, they lived up to the most celebrated work of William Wilberforce, *Practical Christianity* (1797). Their greatest achievement was the abolition of the slave trade (in 1807). Theirs was a vital religion, moral rearmament after the century of Walpole and Warburton, Wilkes and Boswell and Parson Trulliber. The Evangelical mood was represented in the government of Regency England by that element which Coleridge called 'such simpleton saints as the Sidmouth Sect', and by the Prime Minister's concern for the building of 214 new churches at the cost of a million pounds under the Church Building Act of 1818, as strongholds against dissent, infidelity and democracy in London.

Reviving native moralism received an immense impetus to further achievements by the outbreak of the French Revolution, when the horrors which afflicted our neighbours across the Channel were readily put down to the prevalence of moral laxity. The French Revolution, Tom Moore said in his Memoirs of Sheridan, produced reserve of manner and restraint in our upper classes, unpropitious to both wit and humour. Soon it was remarked that the carriages of the nobility and gentry were parked in greatly increased numbers outside the parish church on Sunday mornings, and by the end of the century it was reported that family prayers and the saying of grace before meat were once more becoming habitual in the best regulated families. 'Take back your bonny Mrs Behn', said Mrs Keith when she returned the works of Aphra Behn, 'properly wrapped up', to her great-nephew, Walter Scott, who had supplied them to her at her own request; 'and, if you will take my advice, put her in the fire . . .' Mrs Keith found it 'a very odd thing that I, an old woman of eighty and upwards, sitting alone, feel myself ashamed to read a book which, sixty years ago, I have heard read aloud for the amusement of large circles, consisting of the first and most creditable society in London.' This, Sir Walter thought, was owing to 'the gradual improvement of the national taste and delicacy'. It was doubtless to assist this improvement that Thomas Bowdler produced his *Family Shakespeare* in 1802, a famous edition pruned of the Bard's frequent improprieties, which went through six editions in one year of the Regency. To 'bowdlerize' was soon to become a familiar English verb.

What the French Revolution encouraged by way of moralistic reaction was completed by the French Wars and the culminating victory of Great Britain. Even while the war was still in progress—in 1809—the *Edinburgh Review* was assuring its readers that everyone 'who ever has had an opportunity of comparing the people of England with those of the Continent, must have remarked that, with a sense of honour equally acute, the former possess far more rigid notions of morality and justice'. Mr

Podsnap was already heaving into sight. By 1803 it had already become perfectly clear to a reviewer in the same journal that all European governments were destined gradually to approximate to the freedom and mildness of the government of England. The same type of sentiment was expressed in the form of an appeal for humility towards Divine Province by Coleridge in his second *Lay Sermon* on the present distresses and discontents, in 1817. An Englishman, he thought, should readily perceive 'how large a part of his innocence he owes to his birth, breeding and residence in Great Britain'. For in 'this privileged island' moral prudence was taught habitually, while the interdependence of all classes was promoted by moderation in the superior ranks and emulation in the subordinate and by the 'arterial and nerve-like network of property'. Such were the forces of social cohesion in a society where men were vividly aware of 'the naturalness of doing as others do', and where 'every deviation from outward integrity' was felt as a calculable loss to the offending individual himself from its mere effects . . . Madame de Stael attributed the high suicide-rate in England to 'l'extrême importance que l'on y attache à l'opinion publique: dès la réputation d'un homme est altérée, la vie lui devient insupportable'.[1]

[1] *Réflexions sur le suicide*, 1812. Madame de Stael was not impressed by the usual explanation: the climate. 'Je n'en puis juger, car le ciel de la liberté m'a toujours paru le plus pur de tous . . .'

CHAPTER 20

A New Society

'Dear, dear, they just look as if they had a balance at their bankers.'

David Wilkie, identifying the English among the crowds in the Louvre, 1814

'He was a respectable man. He kept a gig.'

A witness at the trial of John Thurtell for the murder of William Weare, 1822

WHEN George III died in January 1820 he left behind him an England greatly changed since his accession sixty years before. It was more than twice as populous and vastly more wealthy. When he became King he had little more than six million subjects. When he died, he had more than thirteen million. How great had been the increase in wealth cannot be computed at all accurately, but when in 1814 Sir Patrick Colquhoun published his *Treatise on the Wealth, Power and Resources of the British Empire in every quarter of the World*, he could confidently assert that 'An aera has arrived in the affairs of the British Empire, discovering resources which have excited the wonder, the astonishment, and perhaps the envy of the civilized world.' The central decades of the King's reign (1780–1800) had witnessed what is now seen to have been 'the take-off into sustained economic growth', the period in which 'the economy and the society of which it is a part transform themselves in such ways that economic growth is subsequently more or less automatic'. The fundamental characteristic of this period is 'quick emergence of a political, social, and institutional framework which exploits the impulses to expansion . . . and gives to growth an on-going character'.[1] These crucial

---

[1] See *The Stages of Economic Growth* by W. W. Rostow, 1960.

decades marked the transition of the British economy from a lower to a higher phase of production, the creation of the framework of the modern industrial system. Production figures provide only the bare bones of the story. Between 1750 and 1802 coal output increased from 5 to 10 million tons per annum, between 1788 and 1806 the output of pig-iron was quadrupled, and between 1781 and 1800 the import of raw cotton quadrupled. Total industrial production had been doubled during the last twenty years of the eighteenth century, a rate of acceleration which was to continue at a speed better represented by a multiple than by a fraction. All this was producing a 'more-than-industrial revolution'. It marked a social transformation which gave birth to modern English society. 'Most of what we recognize around us as contemporary, as most characteristic of the mid-twentieth century, not merely in the achievements of science and technology, but in social and political organization, is the direct, logistic development of forces set in motion in the Britain of George III.'

When the old King died the horizon was shadowy not only with chimneystacks but with chimney-pot hats, the insignia of the 'shopkeeper-democracy' which is sometimes mistakenly imagined to have been inaugurated by the Great Reform Bill of 1832, a measure which in fact merely admitted a small section of the middle classes to a small share of the political influence of the aristocracy. These people are remembered rather vaguely as the 'Ten-pound householders', the class which Coleridge at the time called 'the least patriotic and the least conservative of any'. Certainly in the last years of George III things were going their way. Two years after George IV came to the throne, the Liverpool Administration was joined by William Huskisson as President of the Board of Trade, and Mr Huskisson was to be the first Cabinet Minister run over by a railway-train.[1] Speed had hitherto been limited to the legs of a horse, and even when man invented the steam-locomotive and the petrol-engine he went on talking about horse-power, just as he continued to measure light in terms of candle-power long after the lights of London were supplied by the London

[1] On the day of the opening of the Liverpool and Manchester Railway in 1830.

Gas Company, which was established on the Regent's Canal at the end of the Napoleonic Wars. Men long continued to wrap their necks in vast quantities of linen after the style of Beau Brummell and the Prince Regent, but those whose avocations took them even remotely into proximity with machinery left off wearing ruffles. Mr Pitt had encouraged them to wear their own hair when he introduced a tax on hair-powder[1] (for economy in the use of flour) in 1795, although many young men remained fond of wearing their hair loose on their shoulders, not to show that they were poets or 'beat' but to express their opposition to Mr Pitt and his war. 'Trowsers' and turn-down collars came into fashion with the meteoric fame of Lord Byron and *Childe Harold* (1812–18).

The social *mores* that were beginning to prevail in the new society were certainly those of the middle class, that favourite *causa causans* (jointly with 'the Industrial Revolution') of almost everything in the history of modern England. Nor, providing the term is used as a pantechnicon or a portmanteau, is the term altogether misplaced. Francis Jeffrey, editor of the *Edinburgh Review*, confidently addressing himself to his public in 1812, spoke of 'that great proportion of our readers which must necessarily belong to the middling or humbler classes of the community', some 200,000 persons capable of reading for both amusement and instruction. Describing his public as 'almost all those who are below the sphere of what is called fashionable or public life, and who do not aim at distinctions or notoriety beyond the circle of their equals in fortune and situation', his definition evidently took more account of status than of class in the economic sense. Culture, virtue, industry—these are the *Review's* yardstick for social approbation. The aristocracy came in for criticism for its idleness and lack of moral fibre, the country gentry for ignorance and general backwardness, the mercantile people—merchants, brokers, loan-jobbers—for hardness of heart, lack of patriotism, a certain readiness to suffer vicariously for the wretchedness of the poor. True happiness,

---

[1] Those wishing to wear wigs had to take out a licence costing a guinea. Their names were posted on the church-door, thus incurring the name of guinea-pigs, perhaps a tit-for-tat for Burke's reference to 'the swinish multitude'.

for the gentlemen of the *Edinburgh*, was attainable only by those in the middle rank of society who were above fear of want and who had sufficient motive for the exertion of their faculties, 'the sound and disinterested part of the community—those who have to pay the taxes', neither the aristocrat nor the bourgeois, nor again the people who never raised their eyes and noses above the ledger or the shop-counter; for, the *Edinburgh* protested, 'we are not absolutely a nation of shopkeepers' although 'we are much afraid that more than nine-tenths of the middling and better sort of people among ourselves belong to this reprobated class of traders and dealers, and have much the same manners with their brethren in America'.

The celebrated 'middle rank' of England was growing very pleased with itself. It was the middle rank 'which gives to science, to art, and to legislation itself, their most distinguished ornaments, the chief source of all that has exalted and refined human nature . . .' This exordium was delivered in the last year of the old King's reign by one who knew himself to be not the least distinguished of those ornaments, James Mill, of the East India House, and the favourite disciple of Jeremy Bentham. Clever son of a Scottish shoemaker, he had come to England, as Bentham put it, 'in the train of Sir John Stuart', of whom his father was a tenant. He knew something of patronage by the aristocracy from painful personal experience, and he had never forgiven them. Nor was he ever to do so. Instead, he transferred his allegiance to Bentham, who was the son of an attorney and grandson of a City pawnbroker. It is perhaps hardly surprising that he came to hold such favourable views about the 'intelligent and virtuous rank' which had supplanted Sir James Stuart as patron of James Mill, although he was to base his preference on what he imagined to be irrefutable arguments from psychology and moral philosophy.

The opinions of that class of the people who are below the middle rank [he came to avow], are formed, and their minds are directed, by that intelligent and virtuous rank who come most immediately in contact with them, who are in the constant habit of intimate communication with them, to whom they fly for advice and assistance in all their numerous difficulties, upon whom they feel an immediate and daily dependence, in health and in sickness, in infancy and old age; to whom their children look up as models for their imitation, whose opinions they hear daily repeated, and account it their honour to adopt.

If one did not know that he was speaking of the 'middle rank' one would be most likely to assume that he was speaking of the aristocracy, or at the very least the gentry, the pillars of society whom Lord Liverpool generally called 'the gentlemen of the parish' and on whom he continued to believe, even in the year of Peterloo (the self-same year when James Mill wrote his *Essay on Government*), the peace and order of society to depend.

Nothing is more striking in this period of social change than the contrast which here presents itself. After Peterloo, the Prime Minister sent the thanks of the Prince Regent to the magistrates and the military of Manchester for their 'prompt, decisive and efficient measures for the preservation of the public tranquillity', under the impression that he was supporting 'the gentlemen of the parish' who, he liked to imagine, 'would have influence enough to check those with whom they are so intimately connected'. James Mill was no less confident that such control would always be better exerted by the influence of the middle rank. What mattered the occasional irregularities of a mob, composed mostly of women and boys, disturbing the peace of some manufacturing town for a few hours? 'The occasional turbulence of a manufacturing district, peculiarly unhappy from a great deficiency of a middle rank,'[1] where there were few 'virtuous families of the middle rank' to break the force of a collision between rich manufacturers and poor workmen, could be no justification for doubting that the great majority of the people would always be guided by that rank. This happy faith of a philosophical Radical was no more and no less misplaced than that of a Tory Prime Minister.

The proximity of a more utilitarian, not to say humdrum, kind of society was to involve the destruction of much that was beautiful in an older England as well as much that was brutal. 'Next after a fox-hunt, the finest sight in England is a stagecoach just ready to start,' Cobbett wrote in 1818. Mr Gray,

[1] A not altogether absurd description of the situation in Manchester in 1819. Mill never makes any direct reference to Peterloo, however.

writing in his *Microcosm* (1803), called it 'a very animated and enlivening spectacle . . . There is something in this coach so impressive and attractive, that as it drives along the road, or through a town, it draws every eye towards it, and the sound of it immediately fills the windows. In many villages the children still take off their hats and shout when it passes.' Its day was short. When Dickens immortalized the coaching-age in *Pickwick* (1837) the railway-age had already begun, and the stage-coach was on its way to commemoration in tap-room prints and table-mats and Christmas cards, the epitome of all that is now supposed to be 'Regency', summing up what Chesterton called the 'rank, rowdy, jolly tradition of men falling off coaches before the sons of Science and the Great Exhibition began to travel primly on rails—or in grooves'. And, of course, the great coaching-lines would die before many years had passed, those populous, picturesque unhygienic caravanserai whence came the Wellers, Jingles, Fat Boys and Job Trotters. Instead there was to be the omnibus and the suburban villa. By 1823, Mr James Ruskin, the sherry-merchant, was already travelling daily between Herne Hill and the City in a horse-drawn omnibus with his chimney-pot hat stowed under the seat. The age of the commuter, the neutered tom-cat, the stiff upper-lip had arrived. There had been something radically untamed about Regency England. True, the Laws of Cricket had been established since 1774, but bruisers still battered each other with bare fists in twenty-two-round contests, gentlemen (including the Prime Minister, the Secretary at War and the Foreign Secretary) fought duels[1] in parks and on commons at daybreak, and nobody went to school if he could help it. It was a quality which D. H. Lawrence imagined to have survived into his own childhood among the Midland colliers, last inheritors of the Old England of Shakespeare and Robin Hood. 'There was a sense of latent wildness and unbrokenness, a weird

---

[1] Pitt fought Tierney, leader of the opposition, on Wimbledon Common in 1798. Castlereagh met Canning on Putney Heath in 1809, by which time opinion was changing on such things, Coleridge calling it 'wringing the dregs from the last drops of Degradation'. However, the Duke of Wellington, always a keeper-up of old customs, fought Lord Winchelsea at Battersea in 1829. The Duke was sixty. He received a letter from Jeremy Bentham beginning 'Ill-advised Man!'

sense of the thrill and adventure in the black Midland nights . . .'
The men were the rough wild lads he went to school with, but
they were wild no longer. The board-school, the Sunday school,
and the women with their 'nice little homes' had made them
tame, got them under.

This was one of the achievements of the much-lauded educational endeavour of the early nineteenth century; the taming
of a peasant people for the factory and the mine. The new
industrial society schooled its workers as a horse-breeder schools
horses. The people of George Borrow were to be turned into
the people of *Hard Times*, the people of *Pickwick* (1837) into the
people of *Our Mutual Friend* (1865). Humphry House in his
study of *The Dickens World* (1941) showed how Dickens's characters changed between these two dates: 'the physique, features
and complexions of the characters have changed . . . almost as
much as their clothes . . . we feel that people use knives and
forks in a different style . . . the people, places and things
become "modern" . . . There is an emotional as well as a
practical "consciousness of living in a world of change", an
apprehension of what the changes meant in detail every day,
the new quality of life they brought.' It was not simply a
question of a new landscape but of a change in 'the scope and
tempo of individual living'. House cites a Home Office description of a wanted man (the Younger Watson, wanted for his
part in connexion with the Spa Fields riot of 1817) which
portrays a character who obviously belonged to the world that
was passing away, a character akin to the Dickens people of
Oliver Twist (1838) and *Nicholas Nickleby* (1839) and quite alien
to the world of (say) *Dombey and Son* (1848). While it is, as he
says, dangerous to be too exact, it is clear that these people
belong to different worlds. As for the precise location of the
dividing line, he would draw it at the coming of the railways
between 1830 and 1848. But the changed life-mode was breaking from the bud before the end of George III's reign, and one
of its principal agencies was the educational procedures involved in the transformation of the peasants into factory-hands.

The machine waits for no man, least of all for the man on
the tramp. The foot-loose Englishman was useless to the mill-
owner, for he was the very stuff on which absenteeism flourishes.

The work-discipline of a machine-age does not 'come natural' to men, for it bears no relation to nature. It must be taught. 'We are the most *lazy-diligent* nation in the world,' wrote Daniel Defoe, long before the new dispensation. 'There is nothing more frequent than for an Englishman to work till he has his pockets full of money, and then go and be idle or perhaps drunk till 'tis all gone . . .' Wages, even high wages, alone were not a sufficient incentive to regularity. Workmen had to be taught to value wages, to lust after a fatter wage-packet. Where necessities are simple and luxuries hardly less so (as with the old-time colliers) a man is not going to trouble himself to work for more money than will get him what he immediately wants. To get him to work not only regularly, but more efficiently it is necessary somehow to multiply and complicate his 'wants', a process that can generally be left to his womenfolk and the advertiser. The initial problem, however, is to get him to work at all, and according to the rhythm required for the profitable use of expensive plant. It is hardly surprising that manufacturers patronized schools where their workers could be disciplined in the desirable industrial virtues of sobriety, regularity, thrift, and indeed general respectability. To apply a certain proportion of profits to the provision of schooling was an investment. If the schooling could be confined to Sundays, all the better.

For a long time it was so confined. Robert Raikes founded the Sunday school movement at Gloucester in 1780. Five years later the Society for the Establishment and Support of Sunday Schools was founded by William Fox, who was unsurprisingly a businessman. By the end of George III's reign there were half a million scholars attending Sunday schools. Industrial towns were especially flourishing centres. The hours of attendance were very like factory hours: 8 a.m. until the time of Divine Service, and 2 p.m. until 6 or 7. The buildings were very like factories, too. 'Sunday Schools, many of them, have been made subservient to the dispositions and will of the manufacturers in reconciling the children to this excessive labour,' one working-class witness said in evidence before a committee in 1832. Nor was it long before the day-school was imitating the Sunday school, for Joseph Lancaster opened his free day-school

at Southwark in 1798. He had 5,000 pupils by 1804. The handling of such large numbers by one master was accomplished by
means of an invention which was thought 'worthy to stand . . .
parallel and rival to the most useful modern inventions in the
mechanical departments'. This was the celebrated, or notorious,
monitorial method, based on the maxim that 'what a boy can
learn, a boy can teach'. The master imparted the lesson to the
older, or brighter, pupils who in turn imparted it to various
groups of the younger or less bright. The master was indeed
simply the overseer in an instructional mill. It was calculated
that a thousand children could be 'educated' in this way at
an annual cost of £300, or less than 7s. 6d. per head. 'Turning
out a product' it was called, or 'the division of labour applied
to intellectual purposes'. As Sir Thomas Bernard truly said,
'the principle in schools and manufactories is the same'. Coleridge was prepared to refer to it as 'this incomparable machine,
this vast moral steam-engine . . . an especial gift of Providence
to the human race . . .' As for the King, he summoned Lancaster to his presence at Weymouth in 1805, turning his head
so that the poor young man never recovered from an excess
of pride and presumption, although the King had chiefly said
that it was his wish that every child in his dominions should
be taught to read the Bible. As may be imagined of an age
when, as Carlyle was to say, no-one could proceed with a piece
of spiritual work but he must 'first call a public meeting, appoint
committees, issue prospectuses, eat a public dinner . . .' two
Societies were instantly set up to promote the great invention
which had so cheaply and completely solved the education
problem. The Royal Lancastrian Society, under the King's
patronage, was the predecessor of the National Society for
promoting the Education of the Poor in the Principles of the
Established Church. Its rival was the undenominational British
and Foreign Schools Society. As if to exemplify the first
principle of the contemporary political economy that competition is the mother of industrial expansion, the two Societies
stimulated the founding of schools, at the same time creating
'the religious difficulty' which delayed the effective entry of
the State into the field of elementary education for many years.
Another long-term effect was to postpone any serious concern

for the training of teachers. Peacock was to mock at the Steam Intellect Society, but a century which worships computers can scarcely join him in his mirth. Nor perhaps is it wise to dismiss the monitorial method as an invention of a generation of Gradgrinds. After all, it has long been in use at Eton, that prehistoric prototype of the comprehensive school.

'Thus we have machines for education . . .', wrote Thomas Carlyle, 'a secure, universal, straightforward business, to be conducted in the gross, by proper mechanism, with such intellect as comes to hand.' Yet Carlyle was no intellectual Luddite. 'What wonderful accessions have thus been made, and are still making to the physical power of mankind; how much better fed, clothed, lodged, and, in all outward aspects, accommodated men are now, or might be, by a given quantity of labour . . .' He lived his first twenty-five years in the reign of King George III, coming to London in 1824, and retiring again north of the Border five years later in order to contemplate it, like Teufelsdrökh in his watch-tower brooding over Weissnichtwo. Thus, when he wrote his penetrating, and too-little-known essay, *Signs of the Times* for the *Edinburgh Review* in 1829, he was the outsider who has been inside, a position which lends a twofold authority to his social analysis and to his piercing vision, as of the child who noticed that the Emperor was wearing no clothes. 'Men are grown mechanical in head and heart, as well as in hand . . . Not the external and physical alone is now managed by machinery, but the internal and spiritual also.' Nowhere, he thought, was the 'almost exclusive faith we have in Mechanism more visible than in the Politics of this time'. True, civil government must include much that is mechanical, much of its work can best be done by mechanism, and to talk of 'the Machines of Society' was a proper enough metaphor. But a mechanical age was taking an over-mighty interest in 'mere political arrangements'. The problem of the nineteenth century, for Carlyle, was not a political problem, but a social even a religious, problem. 'Government can do much, but it can in no wise do all . . . Its duties and its faults are not those of a father but of an active parish-constable.' The industrial problem was not to be solved by politicians, ballot-boxes, or statutes, but 'by those who stand practically in the middle of it'.

Two years later, on the eve of the Great Reform Bill, Carlyle wrote another essay for the *Edinburgh* entitled *Characteristics*. It is a sermon on the text: 'The healthy know not of their health, but only the sick.' It announces the entry of our society into the Age of Self-consciousness. This, the preacher would say, 'is specially the Era when all manner of Inquiries into what was once the unfelt, involuntary sphere of man's existence, find their place and, as it were, occupy the whole domain of thought . . . The beginning of Inquiry is disease: all Science, if we consider well . . . must have originated in the feeling of something being wrong . . .' And thus, in the matter of government, the period of the 'Invaluable Constitution' has to be followed by a Reform Bill. But this new prophet, wielding a rod that the Victorians were to love to kiss, had already[1] concluded: 'To reform a world, to reform a nation, no wise man will undertake; and all but foolish men know, that the only solid, though a far slower reformation, is what each begins and perfects on *himself*.'

[1] In the closing words of *Signs of the Times*.

Whigs versus Whigs

GEORGE III had six successive ministries during the first ten years of his reign. They were all Whig ministries, if they must be given a party name, though it would be better not to use such names at any time before the French Revolution. The Tories having suffered disruption, largely by their association with the name of Jacobitism, the Whigs had the field to themselves. There were enough varieties of Whig to cater for everyone who mattered in politics.

The varieties of Whig were:

1. The Big Whigs or the Revolution Whigs, the Whigs of the Great Tradition of 1688; what they called 'the good old cause'. Their line descended to Walpole, to Hardwicke, and to the brothers Thomas and Henry Pelham. With the reign of George III they were led by the Duke of Newcastle (Thomas Pelham); then by the Marquess of Rockingham. Their principles were expounded by Burke, and they found their great Whig figure on the eve of the French Revolution in Charles James Fox.

2. The Bedford Whigs, followers of John Russell, 4th Duke of Bedford, who believed in much the same things as the Big Whigs, and were mainly interested in securing office for the Bedfords—generally known as 'The Bloomsbury Gang'.

3. Grenvillites, or followers of George Grenville, the brother of Lord Temple, the great Whig magnate of Stowe. Grenville was first and foremost a lawyer, and a highly respected figure in the House of Commons. Though an old family, the Grenvilles had come to the fore by reason of their abilities. They represented a new kind of 'professional' Whig. George Grenville's sister, Hester Grenville, married William Pitt who belonged to the same type.

4. The Chathamites, followers of William Pitt, and by his teaching and example unwilling to be party men. Pitt was their party and their gospels. Some of the first men of the age belonged to this following; notably forward-looking men like Lord Shelburne and young aristocrats like Augustus Fitzroy, Duke of Grafton, both of whom were to become Prime Minister, though neither of them succeeded in the office.

5. 'The King's Friends'—an unfortunate name for a group because it suggested that those who stood aside were the King's enemies, as Burke pointed out. These men were never a party, let alone a sinister cabal serving the King's supposed aims at despotism. They were men who thought it no disgrace to receive favours from the King rather than from a clan-chief in the smash-and-grab of faction. They were never anything more than isolated individuals, sometimes men of old families who had remained loyal to the Crown in the troubled period of the later Stuarts—e.g. Lord North, and the Marquis of Bath. They came in for much abuse from Burke and the author of the *Letters of Junius*; but the King's Friends are no longer imagined to have been a great operative force, secret or otherwise, working for the restoration of the royal authority.

N.B. There is a useful discussion of the Whig sections of this period in H. W. C. Davis, *The Age of Grey and Peel*.

Booklist

SUGGESTIONS FOR further reading, chapter by chapter. These suggestions do not in any sense constitute a bibliography of the subject or of the book. They are intended to supply further reading, and many standard works are taken for granted.

Chapter 1: *Good King George*
There is as yet no satisfactory study of George III. Only Sir Lewis Namier's essay on his personality in *Principalities and Powers* is worth careful study, along with the more personal sections of Richard Pares's *King George III and the Politicians* (1954), notably Ch. III. This is the best book on the political aspects of the reign. Otherwise the article which was written for the *British Medical Journal* (1966 (i)) on the King's 'madness' by Dr Ida Macalpine and Dr Richard Hunter is alone indispensable.

Chapter 2: *The King's Dominion*
There is a wealth of historical literature on England in the mid-18th century, of which the following may be recommended not necessarily as the best but as the most useful for the student and the general reader:
W. H. B. Court, *A Concise Economic History of Britain, from 1750 to recent times* (1954); T. S. Ashton, *The Industrial Revolution, 1760–1830* (1948); Paul Mantoux, *The Industrial Revolution in the 18th Century* (1928); J. D. Chambers & G. E. Mingay, *The Agrarian Revolution, 1780–1880* (1966); M. Dorothy George, *London Life in the 18th Century* (1925); Harold Perkin, *The Origins of Modern English Society (1780–1880)*.

Chapter 3: *Politics*
Steven Watson, *The Reign of George III* (Oxford History of

England), 1960; Namier, *Structure of Politics at the Accession of George III* (1929: rev. ed., 1957), and *England in the Age of the American Revolution* (1930); also his pamphlet, *Monarchy and the Party System*; J. W. Goodwin, *European Nobility in the 18th Century* (1953); G. E. Mingay, *English Landed Society in the 18th Century* (1963).

Chapter 4: *New Reign—New World*
Namier, *Structure of Politics*, as above; and Romney Sedgwick, *Letters of George III to Lord Bute* (1939).

Chapter 5: *George and Dragon*
As Chapter 4.

Chapter 6: *Wilkes and Liberty!*
G. F. E. Rudé, *Wilkes and Liberty* (1962); Raymond Postgate, *That Devil Wilkes* (1939); Peter Quennell, *Four Portraits* (1945); Lucy Sutherland, 'The City of London in 18th Century Politics', in the collection of *Essays presented to Sir Lewis Namier*, edited by R. Pares & A. J. P. Taylor (1956).

Chapter 7: *George Grenville and the Americans*
John C. Miller, *The Origins of the American Revolution* (1945); G. H. Guttridge, *English Whiggism and the American Revolution* (1942); C. R. Ritcheson, *British Politics and the American Revolution* (1954); Sir Ernest Barker, *Traditions of Civility* (1948), Ch. VIII; Burke, *Speeches on American Affairs*.

Chapter 8: *The Stainless Friends*
J. Brook, *The Chatham Administration, 1766–1788* (1956); T. W. Copeland, *Edmund Burke: Six Essays* (1950); Burke, *Short Account of a late short Administration* (1766); John Morley, *Burke* (1879); L. S. Sutherland, 'Edmund Burke and the 1st Rockingham Ministry' (*English Historical Review*, Jan. 1932, pp. 46–72).

Chapter 9: *The Tessellated Pavement*
Brook, as in Ch. 8, above: L. B. Namier & J. Brook, *Charles Townshend* (1964); Lucy Sutherland, *The East India Company in 18th Century Politics* (1952).

Chapter 10: *The Birth of Radicalism*
I. R. Christie, *Wilkes, Wyvill and Reform* (1962); G. S. Veitch, *The Genesis of Parliamentary Reform* (1913, and recently reprinted); H. Butterfield, *George III, Lord North and the People, 1779–1780* (1949); M. G. Jones, *The Charity School Movement*; Simon Maccoby, *English Radicalism* (1935), Vol. I; R. J. White, *Radicalism and its Results* (Aids for Teachers pamphlet, published by the Historical Association, 1965).

Chapter 11: *The Age of Lord North*
There is no satisfactory study of North, though N. W. B. Pemberton wrote a popular biography in 1938. There is a full study of the last part of his Administration by I. R. Christie, called *The End of North's Ministry* (1958); for the conduct of the war in his time, see A. C. Valentine's biography of *Lord George Germain* (1962). For further treatment of some of the topics of this chapter, see G. M. Young's *Gibbon* (1932); Walter Bagehot's *Biographical Studies* (1881) (for Adam Smith); Jeremy Bentham's *Fragment on Government*, ed. Wilfrid Harrison (1948); and C. W. Everett, *The Education of Jeremy Bentham* (1931). Boswell's *Life of Johnson* is full of matter relevant to this chapter.

Chapter 12: *The Discovery of England*
The best brief guide to the subject is Esther Moir's *The Discovery of England* (1964). Of contemporary writing, see the father of Thomas De Quincey, *A Short Tour in the Midland Counties*, etc., published in 1774 under the author's abbreviation, 'By T—— Q——'; *The Torrington Diaries*, by the Hon. John Byng (1781–1794); Tobias Smollett's picaresque novel, *Humphry Clinker*, professes to be a tour of England and Scotland in 1760, and affords a striking panorama. A great deal of the visual aspect of England at that time may be found in F. D. Klingender's *Art and the Industrial Revolution* (1947). For Joseph Wright ('Wright of Derby') see W. Bemrose's *Life* (1885) and the guide to the Exhibition of Wright's work at the Tate Gallery (Arts Council publication, 1958). Much valuable material may be derived from Robert E. Schofield's *The Lunar Society of Birmingham* (Oxford, 1963) and some useful ideas from J. G. Crowther, *The Social Relations of Science* (1941). The late Hesketh Pearson

wrote a typical 'Life' of Dr Darwin, once available in Penguin Books. Donald Read's book, *The English Provinces*, is mostly concerned with the last hundred and fifty years.

Chapter 13: *The Discovery of Europe, or the Grand Tour*
Constantia Maxwell, *The English Traveller in France, 1698–1815*; A. M. W. Stirling, *Coke of Norfolk and his Friends*; Chs. 2, 5, 6; R. W. Ketton-Cremer, *Horace Walpole*, Ch. 4; J. T. Smith, *Nollekens and his Times*, Ch. 1; Adam Smith, *The Wealth of Nations*, Book 5, Ch. 1, Part III, Art. 2; *Boswell on the Grand Tour*, ed. Pottle, 2 vols.; T. Nugent, *The Grand Tour*, 4 vols., London, 1749; Josiah Tucker, *Instructions for Travellers*, London, 1757; Richard Hurd, *Dialogues on the uses of Foreign Travel, etc.*, London, 1764; *The Listener*, 31 Dec. 1959, 7 and 14 Jan. 1960 (reprint of four talks under the heading 'The Grand Tour', by J. H. Plumb & N. McKendrick).

Chapter 14: *The Country House*
Christopher Hussey, *English Country Houses*, Vol. 2, 1760–1800 (Country Life, 1955); Edward Malins, *English Landscape and Literature* (1966); John Fleming, *Robert Adam and his Circle* (1962); Dorothy Stroud, *Capability Brown* (1950); and *Henry Holland* (1966); Kenneth Clark, *The Gothic Revival* (1928); Adeline Hartcup, *Angelica* (1900); E. F. Carritt, *Calendar of British Taste, 1600–1800* (1949); Barbara Jones, *Follies and Grottoes* (1953); John Gloag, *English Furniture* (1934).

Chapter 15: *The Curious Incident*
J. P. de Castro, *The Gordon Riots* (1926); G. F. E. Rudé, 'The Gordon Riots' (a paper contributed to the *Transactions of the Royal Historical Society*, 5th Series, vi (1956), pp. 93–114); Dickens, *Barnaby Rudge*.

Chapter 16: *The Age of Pitt*
J. Holland Rose, *William Pitt and the National Revival* (1911), and the same author's *William Pitt and the Great War* (1911); Alfred Cobban, *Ambassadors and Secret Agents* (1954).

Chapter 17: *George III and the Dynasts*
J. W. Derry, *The Regency Crisis and the Whigs, 1788–1789* (1963);
Edmund Burke, *Letters on a Regicide Peace* (1796).

Chapter 18: *War and Peace*
R. J. White, *Waterloo to Peterloo* (1957); E. Halévy, *History of
the English People in 1815: The Liberal Awakening* (1913 & 1933);
Dorothy George, *England in Transition* (1931); John Summerson,
Georgian London (1945); W. R. Brock, *Lord Liverpool and Liberal
Toryism* (1939); F. O. Darvall, *Public Order and Popular Disturb-
ance in Regency England* (1934).

Chapter 19: *Politics and Morals*
R. J. White, *Life in Regency England* (1963); Theodora Bosanquet, *Harriet Martineau* (1927); Coleridge, *Lay Sermons* (included in *Political Tracts of Wordsworth, Coleridge and Shelley*, ed.
R. J. White, 1953). There are bibliographical references at the
foot of each chapter of *Life in Regency England*.

Chapter 20: *A New Society*
Harold Perkin, *Origins of Modern English Society* (Routledge &
Kegan Paul, 1968); John Clive, *Scotch Reviewers* (1957); James
Mill, *An Essay on Government*, ed. E. Barker (1937); Humphry
House, *The Dickens World* (1941): J. W. Adamson, *English
Education, 1789–1902* (1930); Thomas Carlyle, *Scottish and other
Miscellanies* (Everyman volume 702, 'Characteristics', 1831, and
'Signs of the Times', 1829). Features of the 'new society' as seen
in Regency times are discussed and documented in *Life in
Regency England*, by R. J. White (1963).

Index